World Music Pedagogy, Volume II

World Music Pedagogy, Volume II: Elementary Music Education delves into the theory and practices of World Music Pedagogy with children in grades 1–6 (ages 6–12). It specifically addresses how World Music Pedagogy applies to the characteristic learning needs of elementary school children: this stage of a child's development—when minds are opening up to broader perspectives on the world—presents opportunities to develop meaningful multicultural understanding alongside musical knowledge and skills that can last a lifetime.

This book is not simply a collection of case studies but rather one that offers theory and practical ideas for teaching world music to children. Classroom scenarios, along with teaching and learning experiences, are presented within the frame of World Music Pedagogy. Ethnomusicological issues of authenticity, representation, and context are addressed and illustrated, supporting the ultimate goal of helping children better understand their world through music.

Listening Episode music examples can be accessed on the eResource site from the Routledge catalog page.

J. Christopher Roberts is Lecturer and Coordinator of Music Teacher Preparation at the University of Washington.

Amy C. Beegle is Associate Professor of Music Education at the College-Conservatory of Music at the University of Cincinnati.

Routledge World Music Pedagogy Series

Series Editor: Patricia Shehan Campbell, University of Washington

The **Routledge World Music Pedagogy Series** encompasses principal cross-disciplinary issues in music, education, and culture in six volumes, detailing theoretical and practical aspects of World Music Pedagogy in ways that contribute to the diversification of repertoire and instructional approaches. With the growth of cultural diversity in schools and communities and the rise of an enveloping global network, there is both confusion and a clamoring by teachers for music that speaks to the multiple heritages of their students, as well as to the spectrum of expressive practices in the world that constitute the human need to sing, play, dance, and engage in the rhythms and inflections of poetry, drama, and ritual.

Volume I: Early Childhood Education
Sarah H. Watts

Volume II: Elementary Music Education
J. Christopher Roberts and Amy C. Beegle

Volume III: Secondary School Innovations
Karen Howard and Jamey Kelley

Volume IV: Instrumental Music Education
Mark Montemayor, William J. Coppola, and Christopher Mena

Volume V: Choral Music Education
Sarah J. Bartolome

Volume VI: School-Community Intersections
Patricia Shehan Campbell and Chee-Hoo Lum

World Music Pedagogy

Elementary Music Education

Volume II

J. Christopher Roberts
University of Washington

Amy C. Beegle
University of Cincinnati

NEW YORK AND LONDON

First published 2018
by Routledge
711 Third Avenue, New York, NY 10017

and by Routledge
2 Park Square, Milton Park, Abingdon, Oxon, OX14 4RN

Routledge is an imprint of the Taylor & Francis Group, an informa business

Library of Congress Cataloging-in-Publication Data
Names: Roberts, J. Christopher, author. | Beegle, Amy C., author.
Title: World music pedagogy.
Description: New York ; London : Routledge, 2018- | Includes bibliographical references and index. |
Identifiers: LCCN 2017050640 (print) | LCCN 2017054487 (ebook) | ISBN 9781315167589 () | ISBN 9781138052727 | ISBN 9781138052727q(v.2 : hardback) | ISBN 9781138052796q(v.2 : pbk.)
Subjects: LCSH: Music—Instruction and study.
Classification: LCC MT1 (ebook) | LCC MT1. W92 2018 (print) | DDC 780.71—dc23
LC record available at https://lccn.loc.gov/2017050640

ISBN: 978-1-138-05272-7 (hbk)
ISBN: 978-1-138-05279-6 (pbk)
ISBN: 978-1-315-16758-9 (ebk)

Typeset in Times New Roman
by Apex CoVantage, LLC

Visit the eResource: www.routledge.com/9781138052796

Contents

Series Foreword

Turning and turning in the widening gyre
The falcon cannot hear the falconer;
Things fall apart; the centre cannot hold;
Mere anarchy is loosed upon the world . . .
(from "The Second Coming," W. B. Yeats)

There is a foreboding tone to the stanza above, which at first may seem out of sync with a book on the pedagogy of world music. After all, music education is an intact phenomenon, arguably innocent and pure, that envelops teachers and their students in the acts of singing, playing, and dancing, and this field is decidedly not about falcons. Instead, music education conjures up long-standing images of spirited high school bands, choirs, orchestras, of young adolescents at work in guitar and keyboard classes, of fourth grade xylophone and recorder players, of first grade rhythm bands, and of toddlers accompanied by parents playing small drums and shakers. At a time of demographic diversity, with a wide spectrum of students of various shapes, sizes and hues laid wide open, music education can press further, as the field has the potential to hold court in a child's holistic development as a core avenue for the discovery of human cultural heritage and the celebration of multiple identities based upon race, ethnicity, gender, religion, and socioeconomic circumstance.

Yet there is a correspondence of the stanza, and the disquiet that Yeats communicates, with this book and with the book series, *World Music Pedagogy in School and Community Practice*. I refer the reader to the start of the third line, and also to the title of a novel by Nigerian author Chinua Achebe. A landmark in the world's great literature, *Things Fall*

Apart has been very much in mind through the conception of this project, its design and development by a team of authors, and its thematic weave in these tempestuous times. Achebe's writing of cultural misunderstanding, of the arrogance and insensitivity of Western colonizers in village Africa, of competing cultural systems, is relevant.

We raise questions relative to music teaching and learning: Do things fall apart, or prove ineffective, when they do not reflect demographic change, do not respond to cultural variation, and do not reasonably reform to meet the needs of a new era? Can music education remain relevant and useful through the full-scale continuation of conventional practices, or is there something prophetic in the statement that things fall apart, particularly in music education, if there are insufficient efforts to revise and adapt to societal evolution? There is hard-core documentation of sparkling success stories in generations of efforts to musically educate children. Yet there is also evidence of frayed, flailing and failing programs that are the result of restrictive music selections and exclusive pedagogical decisions that leave out students, remain unlinked to local communities, and ignore a panorama of global expressions. There is the sinking feeling that music education programs exclusively rooted in Western art styles are insensitive and unethical for 21st century schools and students, and that choices of featured music are statements on people we choose to include and exclude from our world.

Consider many school programs for their long-standing means of musically educating students within a Western framework, featuring Western school-based music, following Western literate traditions of notation, Western teacher-directed modes of learning, and Western fixed rather than flexible and spontaneously inventive musicking potentials. All good for particular times and places, and yet arguably unethical in the exclusion of music and music-makers in the world. Certainly, all practices deserve regular review, upgrades, even overhauls. Today's broad population mix of students from everywhere in the world press on diversifying the curriculum, and the discoveries of "new" music-culture potentials are noteworthy and necessary in making for a more inclusive music education.

So, the Nigerian author selected the Irish poet's phrase as meaningful to his seminal work, much as we might reflect upon its meaning so to muster a response to the societal disruption and contestation across the land, and in the world. The practice of musically educating children, youth, and adults may not at first appear to be the full solution to the challenges of local schools and societies, nor essential to meeting mandates in cultural and multicultural understanding. But music is as powerful as it is pan-human, musicking is musical involvement in what is humanly necessary, and the musical education of children and youth benefit their thoughts, feelings, and behaviors. When things fall apart, or seem to be on the brink of breaking up, of serving fewer students and to a lesser degree than they might be served, we look to ways in which the music of many cultures and communities can serve to grow the musicianship of our students as well as their understanding of heritage and humanity, of people and places. Thus, from cynicism springs hope, and from darkness comes light, as this book and book series rises up as a reasoned response to making music relevant and multiply useful in the lives of learners in schools and communities.

THE SERIES

Each of the six volumes in the **World Music Pedagogy Series** provides a sweep of teaching/ learning encounters that lead to the development of skills, understandings, and values that are inherent within a diversity of the world's musical cultures. Written for professionally active teachers as well as students in undergraduate and certification programs on their way to becoming teachers, these volumes encompass the application of the World Music Pedagogy (WMP) process from infancy and toddlerhood through late adolescence and into the community.

The books are unified by conceptualizations and format, and of course by the Series aim of providing theoretical frameworks for and practical pedagogical experiences in teaching the world's musical cultures. Individual WMP volumes are organized by music education context (or class type) and age/grade level.

For every volume in the World Music Pedagogy Series, there are common elements that are intended to communicate with coherence the means by which learners can become more broadly musical and culturally sensitive to people close by and across the world. All volumes include seven chapters that proceed from an introduction of the particular music education context (and type), to the play-out of the five dimensions, to the reflective closing of how World Music Pedagogy contributes to meeting various musical and cultural goals, including those of social justice through music as well as issues of diversity, equity, and inclusion.

There are scatterings of music notations across each volume, mostly meant to assist the teacher who is preparing the orally-based lessons rather than to suggest their use with students. Many of the chapters launch from vignettes, real-life scenarios of teachers and students at work in the WMP process, while chapters frequently close on interviews with practicing music educators and teaching musicians who are devoting their efforts to effecting meaningful experiences for students in the world's musical cultures. Authors of several of the volumes provide commentaries on published works for school music ensembles, noting what is available of notated scores of selected world music works, whether transcribed or arranged, and how they can be useful alongside the adventures in learning by listening.

LISTENING LINKS FOR THE SERIES

Of central significance are the listening links for recordings that are featured in teaching-learning episodes. These episodes are lesson-like sequences that run from 3 minutes to 30 minutes, depending upon the interest and inclination of the teacher, which pay tribute to occasions for brief or extended listening experiences that may be repeated over a number of class sessions. The listening links are noted in the episode descriptions as well as at each chapter's end, and users can connect directly to the recordings (audio as well as video recordings) through the Routledge eResource site for each of the Series' volumes, linked to the catalog page of each volume on www.routledge.com/Routledge-World-Music-Pedagogy-Series/book-series/WMP.

All volumes recommend approximately 20 listening links, and Chapters 2-6 in each volume provide illustrations of the ways in which these listening selections can develop into experiences in the five WMP dimensions. From the larger set of recommended listening tracks, three selections continue to appear across the chapters as keystone selections which are intended to show the complete pathways of how these three recordings can be featured through the five dimensions. These learning pathways are noted in full in Appendix I, so that the user can see in one fell swoop the flow of teaching-learning from Attentive Listening to Engaged Listening, Enactive Listening, Creating World Music, and Integrating World Music. A second Appendix (II) provides recommended resources for further reading, listening, viewing, and development of the ways of World Music Pedagogy.

***

As a collective of authors, and joined by many of our colleagues in the professional work of music teachers and teaching musicians, we reject the hateful ideologies that blatantly surface in society. We are vigilant of the destructive choices that can be made in the business of schooling young people, and which may result from racism, bigotry, and prejudice. Hate has no place in society or its schools, and we assert that music is a route to peace, love and understanding. We reject social exclusion, anti-Semitism, white supremacy, and homophobia (and other insensitive, unfeeling or unbalanced perspectives). We oppose the ignorance or intentional avoidance of the potentials for diversity, equity and inclusion in curricular practice. We support civility and "the culture of kindness," and hold a deep and abiding respect of people across the broad spectrum of our society. We are seeking to develop curricular threads that allow school music to be a place where all are welcome, celebrated, and safe, where every student is heard, and where cultural sensitivity can lead to love.

ACKNOWLEDGEMENTS

This collective of authors is grateful to those who have paved the way to teaching music with diversity, equity, and inclusion in mind. I am personally indebted to the work of my graduate school mentors, William M. Anderson, Terry Lee Kuhn, and Terry M. Miller, and to Halim El-Dabh and Virginia H. Mead, all who committed themselves to the study of music as a world-wide phenomenon, and who paved the way for me and many others to perform, study, and teach music with multicultural, intercultural, and global aims very much in mind. I am eternally grateful to Barbara Reeder Lundquist for her *joie de vivre* in the act of teaching music and in life itself. This work bears the mark of treasured University of Washington colleagues, then and now, who have helped to lessen the distance between the fields of ethnomusicology and music education, especially Steven J. Morrison, Shannon Dudley and Christina Sunardi, Many thanks to the fine authors of the books in this Series: Sarah J. Bartolome, Amy Beegle, William J. Coppola, Karen Howard, Jamey Kelley, Chee Hoo Lum, Chris Mena, Mark Montemayor, J. Christopher Roberts, and Sarah J. Watts. They are "the collective" who shaped the course of the Series, and who toiled to fit the principles of World Music Pedagogy into their various specialized realms of music education. We are grateful to Constance Ditzel, music editor at Routledge, who caught the idea of the Series and enthusiastically encouraged us to write these volumes, and to her colleague, Peter Sheehy, who carried it through to its conclusion.

As in any of these exciting though arduous writing projects, I reserve my unending gratitude for my husband, Charlie, who leaves me "speechless in Seattle" in his support of my efforts. Once again, he gave me the time it takes to imagine a project, to write, read, edit, and write some more. It could not have been done without the time and space that he spared me, busying himself with theories behind "the adsorption of deuterated molecular benzene" while I helped to shape, with the author-team, these ideas on World Music Pedagogy.

Patricia Shehan Campbell
December 2017

Acknowledgements

The authors would like to thank Marla Butke, Michael Hawrylycz, Karen Howard, Carol Scott Kassner, and Patricia Shehan Campbell for editorial feedback and formatting assistance. Appreciation is also extended to the teachers who so kindly gave their time and shared stories, photographs, and figures for this volume: Jeremy David, Julie Froude, Tim Fuchtman, BethAnn Hepburn, Stephanie Magnusson, Darcy Morrissey, and Aik Khai Pung. We would also like to thank our families for their patience and support during the writing process.

Episodes

Listening Episode music examples can be accessed on the eResource site from the Routledge catalog page.

1

Teaching and Learning in Context

A loud bell resounds throughout the urban elementary school building as 200 children of many different ethnicities in grades 1 through 6 (ages six through twelve) stream onto two separate playgrounds for a much-needed recess break on a sunny spring day. The six- through ten-year-olds run and skip to the monkey bars and swing sets on the "little kids" playground, eager to play on their favorite equipment. Two girls begin to swing a long jump rope for two other girls who jump in while rhythmically chanting, "Cinderella, dressed in yellah, went upstairs to kiss a fellah . . . ." Several other girls watch and wait for their turn to jump. Some of the girls and boys are playing a chasing game, while a group of girls appears to be competing to see who can do the most cartwheels in a row.

Most of the older children on the "big kids" playground (reserved for grades 4 through 6) are playing in small groups of about six to ten children, kicking and throwing balls or playing touch football. Some of the children are standing around the perimeter of the playground talking and giggling with each other, and a few children are sitting or standing alone, watching others play. A teacher on recess duty approaches a child who is watching a music video on his cell phone . . . perhaps he has forgotten the "no cell phone" rule. The teacher confiscates the device, to be returned at the end of the school day. Another group of boys and girls are paired up, motivated by the challenge of perfecting the pattern of bumping fists, fronts and backs of hands to the beat of a new hand-clapping game that they learned during music class, "Choco-choco-la-la, choco-choco-te-te, choco-la, choco-te, choco-la-te!"

The bell sounds again, and one class of third grade children line up outside the music room. Two of the girls at the front of the line begin singing an Afro-Peruvian song that they had been listening to and practicing for the past two weeks in music class, and when Ms. Trembly opens the door, a blonde boy eagerly asks, "Can we play the cajóns and the donkey jaws again today with the recording of the Afro-Peruvian band?" Ms. Trembly smiles and says, "Si, señor!" as the children file into the room and sit on the floor in rows facing the interactive whiteboard, ready to participate in another lesson inspired by World Music Pedagogy.

Diving into World Music Pedagogy

In elementary school, children enter into most musical experiences with enthusiasm and energy, ready to "dive in" to instruction that involves listening, singing, and moving activities with a wide variety of music. Elementary school music education has the potential to change and expand children's musical values if teachers use age-appropriate methods to introduce a wide variety of music to children. From the onset of their education, across the primary grades, and through their intermediate-level studies (that may run to grade 5 or 6 in American schools), the world of music is open and available to children as teachers present and facilitate it. One way of opening children's ears and minds to an amazing multiplicity of musical practices and products is through World Music Pedagogy (WMP), in which active repeated listening in conjunction with participatory music making engage children in coming to know the sounds, transmission processes, and performance practices of music from around the world.

Children today find themselves in an educational atmosphere in which technology is bringing distant lands closer, student populations are growing more diverse, and 21st-century skills such as global awareness, multicultural literacy, and social justice literacy are often emphasized. This is an exciting time for educators to develop more culturally sensitive teaching methods and to bring more culturally diverse content and knowledge into their classrooms. The elementary school years are a time of great physical and cognitive development during which children start formal schooling, discover a sense of identity, explore their social roles, and develop preferences and orientations that they will carry into adolescence. These years are among the most impressionable periods in a child's life for building multicultural awareness, understanding, and empathy for cultural others. Elementary school music educators are in a unique position to encourage children's cultural awareness through active engagement in listening, singing, playing instruments, creating, reading, and writing musical genres and practices from groups of people who live locally, as well as those who live on the other side of the planet.

The purpose of this volume is to address the ways that the five dimensions of World Music Pedagogy can serve as a framework for building children's understanding of the beauty and benefits of diversity by opening their ears and minds to the sounds, functions, processes, and practices of various musical cultures within the context of elementary (primary) schools in the United States and other countries where multicultural, intercultural, and diversity-oriented education is valued. World Music Pedagogy is unique among other methods for teaching music of the world's many cultures, in that a strong focus is placed on listening, as well as on determining how musicians of particular cultures teach and learn music. This chapter includes definitions of terms to be used throughout the text, provides a bit of historical context for multicultural and world music education in American public education, offers a rationale for implementing World Music Pedagogy in elementary school music classrooms, addresses developmental characteristics of children ages six through twelve, suggests ways to choose world music for elementary-aged children, and provides some ideas and resources that can help teachers get started with World Music Pedagogy in elementary music classrooms.

"World music" in the context of World Music Pedagogy refers to both the sonic qualities and sociocultural contexts of various musical processes and products from cultures both near and far from children's homes and schools. It is not the catchall phrase used by music marketers to categorize all recordings that do not fit into the usual record store classification system. World Music pedagogues view the Western classical tradition as one of many rich musical cultures that should not necessarily be prioritized above other musical practices. A music teacher who uses World Music Pedagogy wants to open children's ears, bodies, and minds to listen to and interact with many varied musical styles and cultural expressions, from Afro-pop to Aboriginal Australian music, from European to Japanese court music, from Appalachian to Sri Lankan folk music, from Javanese shadow puppet theater to South Indian *kathak* dance, and so much more! Teachers of elementary school-aged children know that active music making opens many doors for young musicians who can be inspired by or want to perform the music that they have been listening to. Therefore, just as important as close listening to the sonic qualities of each musical culture (often through recordings) is the *process* by which the music is taught and learned, in a way that respects both traditional transmission practices and the needs of the children being taught in a contemporary elementary school setting.

The Dimensions of World Music Pedagogy

Elementary school music teachers who implement World Music Pedagogy in their classrooms utilize many resources, such as sound recordings, videos, maps, and world music instruments. They also invite "culture-bearers" (musicians who were raised in the culture in which the music and/or dance originated and/or is currently practiced) to share their music and stories. Through the five dimensions of World Music Pedagogy, children are encouraged to repeatedly listen to recorded or live music in order to experience and explore varied musical cultures. These dimensions (also called "phases") are Attentive Listening, Engaged Listening, Enactive Listening, Creating World Music, and Integrating World Music (Campbell, 2004). It is common for teachers to implement strategies from more than one of these dimensions in a single lesson.

The first dimension of World Music Pedagogy is Attentive Listening, in which children listen to a brief musical selection (often from an unfamiliar culture), attending to particular sonic qualities and patterns of the music in order to begin an examination of the ways that musicians make music in various geographical, societal, historical, and/or cultural contexts. Elementary school music teachers who use World Music Pedagogy carefully select music and structure activities that will catch the ears of children and provide a basis for further study. Even when musical selections are too challenging and complex for elementary-aged children to perform, the students can listen attentively, answering carefully posed questions from teachers and following visual aids such as listening maps or various types of music notation.

Engaged Listening, the second dimension of World Music Pedagogy, occurs when the listener is asked to participate in the music in some way while the musical selection is playing. Children might clap or play a rhythmic pattern on body percussion, sing or play part of a melody, move to demonstrate the form while listening to a piece performed by a culture-bearer or sounded via audio or video recording. Engaged Listening can be almost any type of musical participation while the musical listening sample is sounding, and in an elementary classroom situation, teachers plan "participatory musicking" activities so that children can tap, hum, sing, play, or move along with the music at a volume that makes it possible for everyone to hear the selection.

The third dimension of World Music Pedagogy, Enactive Listening, is similar to Engaged Listening in that it involves participatory musicking but at a much deeper level. Planning for Enactive Listening requires the teacher to choose a musical recording that matches the children's skill level so that they can perform all or most of the selection with and without the musical selection sounding, attempting to replicate it as closely as possible. Once children have practiced Enactive Listening, they may choose to perform the music for an audience.

Attentive, Engaged, and Enactive Listening will often motivate school children to want to invent their own music, and Creating World Music—making their own music that is inspired by the sounds and/or musical practices of a particular culture—is the fourth dimension of World Music Pedagogy. Children ages six through twelve can be encouraged to extend, improvise, arrange, and/or compose music that reflects the sounds and structures of the musical culture under study at developmentally appropriate levels. Elementary school music teachers must thoughtfully consider which musical practices best lend themselves to children's understanding at a level that will allow them to synthesize their knowledge into new music.

The fifth dimension of World Music Pedagogy is Integrating World Music, in which the listening selection is contextualized in order for children to develop greater cultural awareness. There are many avenues through which teachers can open doors to cultural understandings for elementary-aged children through music. Stories, maps, language, food, musical instruments, costumes, and currency from various cultures can be utilized to connect musical learning with children's experiences with people outside of school and also with other subjects within school, such as visual arts, drama, technology, physical education, language arts, social studies, math, and science. Visits from culture-bearers or guest artists can also enhance World Music Pedagogy integration experiences, but teachers should not shy away from World Music Pedagogy if they do not have access to such visitors from far-away locales because there are many other resources available, which will be discussed in this volume.

Together, these five WMP dimensions create a rich experience in which children can come to better understand musical practices of people who may be different from them. As their ears and eyes are open to new sounds and cultural values, children may learn acceptance and awareness of "others" that can last into their adult lives.

Organizing World Music Pedagogy Experiences for Elementary School Children

Teachers who use World Music Pedagogy know that in-depth experiences are usually more valuable than those that simply skim the surface of a particular musical culture. Therefore, World Music Pedagogy plans will almost always take place across multiple lessons, and units of study might even last for an entire semester or school year within an elementary school music curriculum. Such lessons or units could be comprised of the comparison of a particular musical element or instrumental family across cultures, an in-depth study of a particular musical culture, or an in-depth study of a particular cultural issue, theme, or musical function across cultures. For example, third graders might compare the percussion ensemble traditions of various African and Latin American cultural groups, sixth graders might listen intently and delve into the culture and performance practices of xylophone music of the Shona people of Zimbabwe, and first graders might study the ways that lullabies are performed by Navajo, Pashtu, and Aboriginal parents and caretakers.

There are many different ways to apply the dimensions of World Music Pedagogy in a curriculum for primary and intermediate level children. For example, a teacher may select several musical pieces from a particular culture for a series of Attentive and Engaged Listening experiences that integrate with the cultural knowledge they are studying in their social studies curriculum, and choose not to utilize the Enactive or Creative dimensions of WMP. Another example is that a teacher may choose to use all five WMP dimensions with one piece over a series of lessons, first asking students to attentively listen to particular aspects of the piece, encouraging them to participate in Engaged Listening experiences with the same piece during a subsequent lesson, providing activities that allow children to listen enactively in the next lesson, then challenging children to improvise new musical ideas while preparing a performance of the piece over the next few lessons, all the while integrating cultural information and experiences into each lesson.

World Music Pedagogy in Context

Elementary Music and Multicultural Education

World Music Pedagogy has close ties to multicultural education, and scholar-educators such as James Banks and Geneva Gay have informed the thinking of theorists and practitioners of multicultural music education. James Banks's (2013) four levels of multicultural curriculum reform can be observed in an increasing number of elementary music classrooms today. A *contributions* approach to curriculum reform occurs when the curriculum remains unchanged but the content is occasionally varied. In an elementary music class, if a teacher selected one song played on a North Indian *bansuri* flute for fourth grade students to play on the recorder, this would be viewed as an intervention at the contributions level if it was the only piece and there was little or no attention paid to the cultural context. In the *additive* approach to curriculum reform, the diverse content is more extensive than in the contributions approach, but the curriculum is still viewed from the perspective of the dominant culture. If the fourth grade teacher planned a series of lessons that incorporated pieces from different flute traditions of the world, but still addressed the differences in timbre or the significance of the music compared to Western recorder repertoire, that would be an example of the *additive* approach. The *transformation* approach to curriculum reform occurs when a topic is viewed from the perspective of diverse ethnic and cultural groups. An example of the transformation approach would be if fourth graders learned to play penny whistles and/or Native American flutes instead of recorders, and ideally would include visits from Irish and/or Native American culture-bearers performing on their penny whistles and/or Native American flutes. They would also discuss their role in the culture, with conscious attention paid to helping the children replicate the specific inflections of the different flute genres. A *social action* approach occurs when students take action to achieve change about a social issue. Social action curriculum reform would occur if fourth graders, after completing a unit on various flute cultures, decided to make panpipes that they could distribute to Peruvian children who did not have access to their native instrument.

Along these same lines, the theory known most often as Culturally Responsive Teaching (also known as Culturally Responsive Pedagogy) encourages pedagogy in which students' cultural experiences outside of school are recognized in many facets of school curriculum to increase academic achievement. According to Geneva Gay (2010), preparing for Culturally Responsive Teaching (CRT) includes five main elements. These might be applied to elementary music classrooms in the following ways: (1) *developing a knowledge base* regarding cultural diversity, in which an elementary school music teacher in Albuquerque, New Mexico, who is working with Navajo students would take time to speak with Navajo parents and read as much as possible about the Navajo culture, (2) *constructing culturally relevant criteria* in which a primary school music teacher in Sydney, Australia, who is working with a large Vietnamese population would teach the children to sing Vietnamese lullabies and folk songs, (3) *expressing cultural caring* and *creating a learning community* in which a music teacher at an elementary school in St. Paul, Minnesota, would greet his Hmong children in their native language each time they come to music class and encourage them to share their cultural experiences and stories with the rest of the class, (4) *understanding cross-cultural communications*, in which a music teacher in Honolulu who teaches many native Hawaiian children would include many small group collaborative music activities because native Hawaiian culture tends to be collaborative and group-oriented, and (5) *developing cultural congruity in classroom instruction*, in which a European American elementary music teacher with many African American students might adjust some of her classroom management routines after speaking with African American parents about their home disciplinary practices. CRT in music teaching is not just about selecting music from diverse cultures, but specifically responding to the cultural strengths, characteristics, perspectives, and needs of students in the context of each classroom in all aspects of the teaching and learning process.

Although teachers who use the dimensions of World Music Pedagogy in their elementary school music classrooms might also practice Culturally Responsive Teaching, WMP differs from CRT in that WMP is typically less focused on bringing students' own cultural experiences and learning styles into all teaching and learning activities through all of the five elements as outlined by Geneva Gay. WMP is more aimed at the pedagogy of how musical expressions and cultures from around the world are taught and learned, as informed by both ethnomusicology and music education. Of course, teachers who use WMP might use their knowledge of their students' cultural identities to inform music selection for WMP lessons, and like any good teacher, they should express cultural caring and create a learning community, but WMP is most specifically about the sounds and cultural origins of the music, and CRT is more focused on the culturally defined communication and learning styles of individual children.

Elementary Music Publications and Professional Development

One method of tracking the historical development of multicultural music with elementary-aged children in schools is through an examination of the main series textbooks and accompanying music recordings that have been widely utilized in North American general music classrooms, published by MacMillan McGraw-Hill and Silver Burdett. Originally, the musical materials in these publications were almost exclusively

Eurocentric. Following the Tanglewood Symposium, more culturally diverse music began to creep into the series textbooks in the 1970s, although the accompanying recordings were often performed by European American singers and players. Even as the content grew more multicultural, the musical material was not always vetted by ethnomusicologists or cultural insiders, so there were cases in which authors provided very little or inaccurate information about the origin of some songs and pieces.

This began to change in the 1980s when World Music Press and others published music teaching materials with recordings made by culture-bearers and the series text recordings also improved in terms of more accurate cultural representation. Ethnomusicologists and music education scholars worked closely together to publish teaching resources for elementary school music teachers that included recordings and information about a variety of musical expressions of the world. Throughout the late 1990s and early 2000s, a greater variety of the world's music cultures became yet even more available to music teachers, as the internet provided easy access to videos created by musicians around the world.

During the last decade of the 20th century, elementary music specialists began to see an increase of presentations by culture-bearers from a variety of world music cultures at music education workshops and conferences, such as those offered by the Music Educators National Conference and the American Orff-Schulwerk Association. The publication of the *Global Music Series: Experiencing Music, Expressing Culture* in 2004 and the launch of summer courses dedicated to WMP provided elementary school music teachers with further resources for curriculum and teaching/learning through World Music Pedagogy, which "concerns itself with how music is taught/transmitted and received/learned within cultures, and how best the processes that are included in significant ways within these cultures can be preserved or at least partially retained in classrooms and rehearsal halls" (Campbell, 2004, p. 26). Participants in teacher education programs in World Music Pedagogy have an opportunity to gather in community to learn from culture-bearers and examine and create lesson plans that use the plethora of world music resources available via the internet, with particular attention to the Smithsonian Folkways Recordings website.

Listening and sharing cultural information is at the forefront of World Music Pedagogy as the main means through which students gain a better understanding of the way that diverse human groups make meaning through music. This book offers a resource for delving into the theory and practice of World Music Pedagogy with children in grades 1 through 6 (ages six through twelve years).

Development of Children Ages Six through Twelve

Children's Intellectual Development

Increased cultural awareness begins with children's perceptions of cultural objects and practices through listening, seeing, touching, tasting, and smelling. This sensory information is processed by children differently as their brains develop. Children ages six through nine (first through third grades) are gradually improving their impulse control and attention spans, so they are increasingly able to listen to music for longer periods of time as they mature. They like to challenge themselves intellectually and physically, so the Engaged, Enactive, and very basic Creative components of World Music Pedagogy are especially well suited for children in early elementary school.

Between the ages of nine and twelve (grades 4 through 6), children can think more quickly and efficiently and they get better at solving problems. Their spatial working memory expands, which is important for the oral/aural transmission that is so often utilized in the performance aspects of WMP. Scientific reasoning and the ability for metacognition develops and tastes and skills become better defined. Teachers who use WMP often encourage children to reflect upon their own musical values and compare them to those of others who may be different from them, and children from grade 3 onward are especially well suited to this intellectual challenge.

Children's Social-Emotional Development

Teachers who utilize WMP often have goals of helping children become more self-aware as well as helping them become more aware of the perspectives of others. Social-emotional development refers to children's social experiences and the ways that they manage emotions and establish relationships with others, including adults and peers, and also the development of their own self-identity. During the elementary school years, children develop skills for interacting with teachers and classmates at school, and they also learn to express their needs appropriately in social situations. Children are also experiencing and interacting within the realms of parents and family life, community interactions (religious institutions, sports/leisure activities, etc.), and the consumer world in which toys, books/magazines, technology equipment, etc. are marketed with children at the forefront.

Children's Musical Development

Musically, the elementary school years are marked by increasing physical dexterity and skill. Children of elementary school age enjoy and learn through active physical involvement, and many components of World Music Pedagogy encourage listening and active physical involvement at once. Although children develop at different rates and have various abilities and skills based on individual previous musical experiences both in and out of school, music teachers in many locations have designed music curricula based upon specific expectations of children's musical skill and knowledge that are developmentally differentiated across the grade levels.

A few musical developmental characteristics are described here to offer a beginning awareness of what children might be able to do in music classes related to World Music Pedagogy during the early elementary (ages six through eight years), middle elementary (ages eight through ten years), and upper elementary (ages ten through twelve years), with an awareness that not all children are the same and will progress at different paces. More details regarding musical development of children can be found in Campbell and Scott-Kassner (2018).

EARLY ELEMENTARY (AGES SIX THROUGH EIGHT)

Children ages six through eight (in grades 1 and 2) are quite curious, so it is a perfect time to encourage them to inquire about music of various cultural groups and to explore playing instruments from around the world. They may have difficulty staying in the correct key, and they may need help differentiating between singing and speaking voices. In terms of movement, their hand-eye coordination and skipping and snapping skills are developing, and their large motor skills are more developed than small motor skills. Simple singing games and movement activities from around the world are usually enjoyable to early elementary-aged children. With practice, by age seven or eight, children should be able to maintain a steady beat with an external source, making it possible to engage in tapping, playing an instrument, or moving the beat while listening to a Zimbabwean children's singing game or a Oaxacan *marimba* piece. They can also respond to gradual changes in pulse and dynamics, so these concepts can be drawn to children's attention while listening to a *taiko* drumming piece or an Afghani lullaby.

MIDDLE ELEMENTARY (AGES EIGHT THROUGH TEN)

During the middle elementary years (second through fourth grades), children develop the ability to sing songs from various world music cultures with easy harmonies (melody over a vocal ostinato or sustained pitch). By the time they are ten years old, they should be able to perform rounds, descants, and countermelodies after a great deal of practice singing in unison first. Their sense of tonality and meter is emerging, and they can respond quickly to musical changes during Attentive Listening lessons. When developing WMP lessons, teachers should keep in mind that children in this age group are growing the ability to perceive more complex patterns and sequences, so by the time they are ten years old, they can be challenged to listen for melodic steps and skips, scales and modes, including Indian *ragas* and Arabic *maqams*. In terms of movement, small motor skills and hand-eye coordination are developing so that by age eight or nine they can play recorder, Native American flutes, and keyboard instruments. They may also enjoy learning folk dances from various cultures. At this age, children can play simple melodic ostinati on xylophones, and nine-year-olds can learn simple Mexican *marimba* ensemble parts or easy parts to Nigerian xylophone pieces. As children approach the upper elementary ages, they have increased control of breathing that may lend itself well to playing wind and brass instruments, and they might enjoy playing conch shells or trying the *didgeridoo*!

UPPER ELEMENTARY (AGES 10 THROUGH 12)

Children in the upper elementary (fourth through sixth grades) usually enjoy a good challenge or competition, so they may enjoy singing three-part songs or songs in four-part canon, playing and/or creating challenging *marimba* or drumming pieces, creatively solving musical problems or puzzles, or playing challenging musical games from around the world. They may experience their first vocal change during these years. This is a good age to begin to play guitar or other stringed instruments, Trinidadian steel pans, or Balinese *gamelan* instruments. In the area of movement, they can perform rhythmic canons (moving to music that was previously sounded while listening to the next sequence), and they can respond to two distinctive features of music through simultaneous movement (i.e. clapping rhythm while stepping the pulse). This may be a good age range at which to teach a bit of *gumboot* dancing from South Africa, some African American step dance moves, clogging, or Irish step dance. Children in upper elementary grades may balk at listening to unfamiliar music, especially if they have not become accustomed to doing so in their earlier elementary school years. Therefore, it can be helpful to plan ahead for ways to help students connect unfamiliar music to familiar music and/or be ready to "sell" the music to the pre-adolescents, by starting with familiar musical examples and clearly communicating the advantages of listening to the unfamiliar music.

Children's Music Education

Music Outside of School

Because World Music Pedagogy is a child-centered approach, it is important for teachers to learn as much as possible about children's musical lives in their homes and communities. Children whose families have financial means and artistic motivations often study piano and/or band or orchestra instruments outside of school in private studios. A small percentage of children whose families have access to resources might also have the opportunity to participate in ethnic or world music or dance classes outside of school, such as Ghanaian drumming, Irish step dance, Appalachian dulcimer, African American step dance, *Mexican mariachi*, or a plethora of other possibilities. Immigrant children might practice the musical cultures of their parents and grandparents at home. Some children may receive formal or informal music training through

Figure 1.1 Child playing Appalachian mountain dulcimer

Photo courtesy of BethAnn Hepburn

religious institutions such as churches or Hebrew schools. Wise music teachers find ways to connect to these "outside" musical experiences by inviting children, parents, or culture-bearers to visit the music classroom in order to introduce all of the children in the class to various musical traditions of their surrounding communities.

Music in School

School music curricula for elementary schools vary according to school location, teacher training, etc., but national and state standards are often used to frame general learning expectations for students in elementary schools. In 2011, the College Board published a report called *International Arts Education Standards: A survey of the arts education standards and practices of fifteen countries and regions*, which showed that the national standards for all of the examined countries included primary goals of (a) generating and solving problems, (b) expressing and realizing [music], and (c) responding and appreciating [music]. This report also noted that almost all of the countries' arts standards "promoted exposure to the arts of other cultures and emphasize the importance of cultural context in responding to arts examples." World Music Pedagogy is an excellent approach for addressing standards that relate to cultural context and cross-cultural understanding.

21st Century Skills and Global Society

During the latter decades of the 20th century, a growing educational movement placed greater focus on preparing young people to better function in a rapidly changing technological and more global society. Reports by academics, business leaders, educators, and governmental agencies used the term "21st Century Skills" to label an extensive collection of skills, knowledge, work habits, and character traits thought to be important for succeeding in contemporary collegiate programs and workplaces. Among others, 21st century skills include global awareness, multicultural literacy, humanitarianism, civic, ethical, and social justice literacy, oral and written communication, public speaking, and listening, all of which can be addressed through World Music Pedagogy.

The Partnership for 21st Century Skills is an advocacy organization that promotes the "Four C's of 21st Century Education" which include *Critical thinking*, *Communication*, *Collaboration*, and *Creativity*. *Critical thinking* includes taking multiple perspectives into consideration and re-evaluating a viewpoint or position in light of new information. In the elementary school, music teachers can utilize World Music Pedagogy to encourage children to use critical thinking related to music that they listen to from other parts of the world, by challenging students to pose a lot of questions about the context of the music they are listening to and asking them to articulate their own points of view as they learn more about the functions, transmission, and performance practices of a particular musical tradition. *Creativity* is demonstrated as children improvise a new melody to a Trinidadian steel pan piece, compose their own music in the style of a Nigerian xylophone piece, or write a new song in American folk-song style. *Communication* and *collaboration* among music students is often necessary for Engaged and Enactive (performance) aspects of World Music Pedagogy, as children are encouraged to participate in music making together as a class, or even in larger groups at all-school sing-alongs, dances, or performances.

Music Education Approaches

Most American elementary school music teachers use active music making methods in which children are expected to sing, play instruments (which might include recorder, small percussion, xylophones, ukulele, and/or keyboard), create, read/write, move with, and listen to music. The two most prominent active approaches to teaching music in United States' public schools are the Orff Schulwerk approach and the Kodály concept.

ORFF SCHULWERK

Children's imaginations take center stage in this approach to music education. Music, movement, speech, and drama are integrated, and children learn to create their own music. The Schulwerk teacher serves as a facilitator of children's music learning through playful and engaging activities that include musical imitation, exploration, improvisation, and composition. Children in an "Orff-based" music class participate in rhythmic speech chanting, singing, moving, playing instruments, and listening to music, so they build music and movement vocabulary that can be utilized to create their own music and dance. The unity of music and movement within the Schulwerk philosophy has some similarities with the conceptualization of music and dance as one that occurs in many African cultures.

The central forum for dissemination of the teaching philosophy and processes of the Orff Schulwerk approach is the Orff Institute, located at the Mozarteum Academy for Music and Drama in Salzburg, Austria. The *Guidelines of the Orff Institute* (2011) note that the Schulwerk is "sustained by a humanist world philosophy, and an educational concept marked by anthropological conditions which recognizes the capacity in all human beings to communicate and express themselves

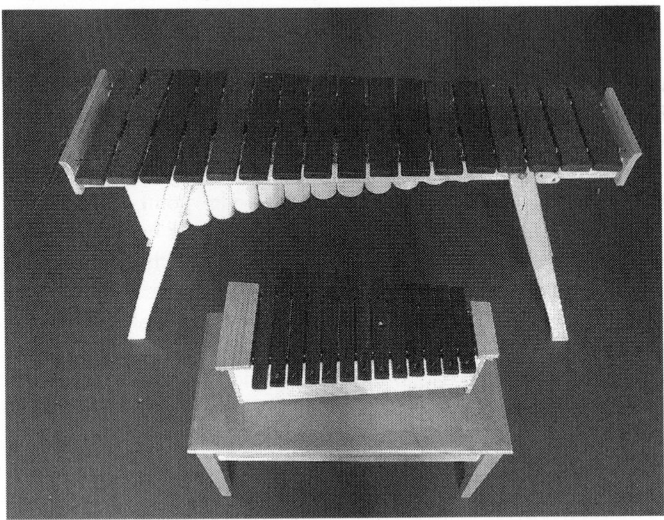

Figure 1.2 Comparison of marimba (top) to a Orff xylophone (bottom)

through speech, movement and music" (p. 91). This humanist world philosophy lends itself well to the incorporation of a variety of musical materials for use in the "Schulwerk classroom." The original musical materials of the Schulwerk were written by Carl Orff and Gunild Keetman in five volumes of *Music for Children*, beginning with pentatonic and progressively adding more complex melodic and harmonic structures in each volume. These volumes include pieces based on German nursery rhymes as well as basic rhythmic and melodic structures of European music traditions, scored specifically for body percussion, speech, percussion, recorder, drone instruments, and voice. These elemental pieces are intended as starting points to encourage improvisation and composition and are not usually performed exactly as written. The volumes do not include pedagogical instruction, so teachers learn what is commonly known as the "Orff process" through teacher education courses.

Many elementary music teachers find that the philosophy and oral/aural teaching and learning processes of the Schulwerk lend themselves well to incorporating musical cultures of the world into their classroom curricula. For example, "Orff instruments" (barred xylophones, metallophones, and glockenspiels) can be utilized to approximate Nigerian xylophone music, Balinese *gamelan* music, or Mexican *marimba* music. As improvisation and composition are central to the Orff Schulwerk approach, students are sometimes encouraged to create their own music in the style of a particular cultural tradition.

THE KODÁLY APPROACH

This approach to teaching music is based on the work of Hungarian composer, philosopher, and educator Zoltán Kodály, who lived from 1882 to 1967. As a college-aged music student in Budapest, Kodály became interested in folk music, and along with his contemporary Bela Bartok, began collecting music throughout Hungary. During this time, he came to believe that the musical skills of the population were lacking, and he developed strong beliefs concerning the importance of music education. Kodály wrote,

> It is much more important who the singing master at Kisvárda is than who the director of the Opera House is, because a poor director will fail. . . . But a bad teacher may kill off the love of music for thirty years from thirty classes of pupils.
> (1964, p. 124)

Kodály-inspired teaching is more of a philosophy than a method. Its main tenets include that music is the right of every human being, not just the musically gifted; music should exist at the core of the curriculum; students deserve only the "best music"; the voice is the best teaching tool because it is "free and accessible to all"; music education should be a participatory, experience-based endeavor, one that is highly sequential; and music educators should be the best possible musicians and the best possible educators.

On its surface, some ideas of Kodály-inspired music education seem unsuited to issues of studying the musical cultures of the world. To Kodály, "best music" meant that music education should begin with folk music of the mother tongue, gradually leading to Western classical art music. Additionally, Kodály emphasized the importance of conventional music literacy, with a sound before symbol approach to learning to read and write, believing that it was essential to creating lifelong music makers.

However, Kodály is perhaps better understood in the context of the historical period in which he lived. In many ways, he was a rebel. While today folk music is central to many school curricula, at the turn of the 19th century, those who sat beside Kodály in the Academy believed that folk music was inferior. In this way, Kodály gave voice to the common man and woman and their experiences, and he greatly diversified the musical content in the curricula of the time. Further, Hungary in the early 1900s (and indeed through the 20th century) was subject to the push and pull of its stronger neighbors, constantly worrying about protecting its borders. Its population was relatively homogeneous, far different from the populations of many countries around the world in the 21st century. Were he alive today, many believe that Kodály's view of "best music" would include the wide variety of musical traditions that can be found within each country as well as throughout the world.

OTHER ACTIVE TEACHING APPROACHES

Carl Orff's philosophy of movement was influenced by the methods of Emile Jacques Dalcroze, a Swiss composer and music teacher who believed that turning one's body into a finely tuned instrument through moving rhythmically and playing challenging ear-training games would set a strong foundation for musicianship. As the Dalcroze approach requires students to listen actively in order to gain musical awareness through moving their bodies, World Music Pedagogues can utilize eurhythmics exercises as part of Engaged Listening exercises. Some examples include singing *solfège* patterns while listening to a Polish piano piece by Frederick Chopin, listening and responding through expressive movement to the rising and falling motion of a recording of a *shakuhachi* (Japanese bamboo flute) melody, or improvising rhythmic patterns during or after listening to percussionists perform using *rumba, bolero, serto*, or other drumming styles. The Dalcroze approach is practiced throughout the world, with teaching centers found predominantly in Europe. The United States, Canada, China, Taiwan, Thailand, Russia, Israel, Mexico, Argentina, and Australia also contain a small number of teaching centers.

Edwin Gordon (1927–2015) was an American music teacher of children and a well-known professor and researcher in the areas of music aptitude and audiation. Gordon's Music Learning Theory (MLT) is a comprehensive method for music teachers of many areas, including band, orchestra, jazz, choir, early childhood, and elementary music. The main goal of the method is to *audiate* (think in music with understanding), similar to the way that people think in language with understanding. Edwin Gordon categorized eight types of audiation, including three that might directly apply to World Music Pedagogy: listening to familiar and unfamiliar music, recalling familiar music from memory, and creating and improvising unfamiliar music.

World Music Pedagogy in Elementary Schools

Implementing World Music Pedagogy with elementary-aged children involves preparation on the teacher's part, both in terms of musical knowledge and practical matters. How do teachers select music for Attentive, Engaged, and Enactive Listening lessons with children? What materials and instruments are needed to bring music from various world cultures into music classrooms and stimulate children's curiosity, participation, performance, creative expression, and cultural understanding of music's many meanings? How do teachers arrange learning activities into meaningful curricula?

Choosing a Musical Culture

The first step in creating lessons using the approach of World Music Pedagogy is to identify the musical culture to explore. Elementary music teachers may have a variety of reasons for choosing to create a unit of music on the Andean panpipes rather than the Zimbabwean-style *marimba*. Teachers may select a culture based on (a) their own knowledge, (b) students' skills, (c) a desire to integrate with the children's general class or with current events, or (d) a Culturally Responsive curriculum design that recognizes the cultures of children in the class and/or those of marginalized people.

When music teachers have pre-existing knowledge and affinity for a musical culture, a unit of WMP can use that knowledge as a starting point. Teachers should still search for recordings of culture-bearers making the music to provide as deep an experience as possible for the students, but the pre-existing knowledge may allow a teacher to begin lesson planning with a basic understanding of the musical genre, which can aid in planning. Teachers might also have a desire to learn more about an unfamiliar culture. If a teacher has long been intrigued by the sounds of West African drumming but never learned anything about it, it can be a perfect reason to explore the Ewe drumming traditions of Ghana and create a unit for students.

At times, a musical culture may be selected because it complements the existing music curriculum or fits well with the children's skill development. If third graders are learning to play the recorder, that unit on Irish tin whistle music may be an effective way to employ previously known skills; if fifth graders have developed impressive skill on xylophones, that unit on *marimba* music of Zimbabwe may lead to increased development and connection.

A musical culture also may be selected because it complements the curriculum in other subjects that the children are studying. If fourth graders are exploring indigenous Canadian cultures with their social studies teacher, it can be a perfect time to teach a unit on the social dance music of one of the First Nations; if first graders in the United States are studying their neighbor to the south with their classroom teacher, a music unit on music of Mexican *son*, *mariachi*, or *ranchera* styles can help make connections between the subjects.

At times, current events can lead a teacher to decide to create a curriculum based on a particular musical culture. An earthquake in Chile that makes the morning papers can lead a teacher to explore the *cueca* music from that South American country for second grade students; upcoming Olympic games that take place in China can lead to a unit on Peking opera; a terrorist event in which a Gallic Frenchman attacks a Muslim mosque peopled mostly by immigrants from Algeria can lead to a unit on either Algerian or French music—or even both.

World Music Pedagogy is primarily intended to be used as a way to bring unfamiliar musical genres to children in class. However, if the class includes a small subset of students from a particular part of the world, teachers may choose to create a unit of music based on their heritage. In Minneapolis, for example, a school in which 5% of the students were born in Somalia may inspire a teacher to create a unit on the music of Somalia. The students and families from that country will see their culture represented in the curriculum, and other students will gain knowledge about their classmates. This can also be effective when a new student from another culture enters a school.

One benefit of World Music Pedagogy is the ability to work towards social justice. When cultures are marginalized or stereotyped, teaching the music of those people can allow children to move beyond the common conceptions perpetuated by the media and the broader society and lead to a more nuanced understanding of their lives. For example, the Roma people of Eastern Europe (traditionally called "Gypsies," a term that is not preferred by many Roma themselves) have long experienced discrimination due to stereotypical ideas about them, and they have a long and rich musical culture that can lead to a strong unit of WMP.

Selecting Music

Even if music teachers do not have extensive experience with a musical culture, they can find culturally representative music selections by utilizing videos and sound recordings. Such recordings might be found through publications or reputable sources on the internet that include a great deal of cultural and contextual information, confirming that the music is an accurate representation of a particular culture (i.e. performances by people of the culture in the original language and/or facts regarding where and how the music was taught, learned, and recorded). Even more valuable resources might be found by consulting school staff members, other teachers, and/or community members who are from different cultural backgrounds. Such culture-bearers might be willing to share their own musical heritage with the music teacher and/or with the children. A "Recommended Resources" list can be found in Appendix 2 of this volume.

"AUTHENTICITY" OF MUSICAL MATERIAL

Elementary music teachers may feel a bit hesitant about incorporating some musical cultures into their curricula if they are unsure about whether the music will be viewed as "inauthentic" by people who may know the music well. There are varying views regarding authenticity within the field of multicultural music education, and the advice from experts has changed over time as they have grappled with the meaning of authenticity in a world in which increased globalization and cross-cultural sharing has produced more fluid boundaries between musical cultures and has spurred more questions about "ownership" of particular musical products and practices. The prevalent perspective today is that all music is moving and changing, and therefore, it is difficult to pin down a precise "authentic" version of a musical product, and that teachers and students should feel free to listen to and explore new music cultures in music classrooms. Of course, it is important to be as well informed as possible and to educate students about the history and cultural context of sonic experiences.

Although even well-intentioned teachers cannot emulate all of the qualities of an original musical piece or practice, they can learn as much as they can about the music's sociocultural, communicative, and personal meaning and try to capture and communicate as much of this meaning as possible when introducing a new musical culture to children. Teachers can also share with the children the ways that they learned the music.

The goal in World Music Pedagogy is not for a musical recording to be emulated exactly, but for teachers and children to strive for the most respectful and meaningful representation that is possible for the time and pace in which it is being taught and learned. In addition to authenticity, *appropriation*, or using music without permission, is another consideration—some music is not appropriate for the classroom, such as sacred music of native cultural groups and musical practices that are the provinces of particular people or groups.

When examining recordings and videos for classroom use, accurate representation of a culture is greater if the musical material meets most of the following criteria:

- Performers are native to the culture
- The music was created and/or arranged by someone native to the culture
- Instruments are native to the culture
- Text is performed in the original language
- Cultural and contextual information is provided (source, year, performers, location, etc.)
- If intended for Enactive Listening, performance, or creative production by children, the music is not intended for sacred use only.

YouTube can be tempting because of the sheer volume of videos available, but care must be taken to seek as much information as possible to verify accurate representation with a culture-bearer and/or a respected scholarly source. Aiming to maintain the music's original language, instrumentation, media, tunings, harmonization, and arrangements is also important when striving to maintain authenticity. However, if the realities of the classroom situation (i.e. lack of instruments or the skill level of the children) require changes to be made, this is fine, as long as children are made aware of the original context and meaning as much as possible, and every effort is made to replicate the sounds of the recording as closely as possible. It is also important for teachers to remain open to the perspectives that the children bring to interpreting the meaning of the music, as the teacher and students come to know it in a different context. Recognizing and celebrating diversity is one of the benefits of World Music Pedagogy.

"AUTHENTICITY" OF TRANSMISSION

An important dimension of World Music Pedagogy is consideration of the way that the music is taught and learned in its original context. If the music is simplified too much or if didactic adjustments are made unnecessarily, the experience of learning the music may not be as rich for the children. For example, if a Ghanaian drum rhythm is usually learned aurally and the teacher notates the rhythmic pattern and asks the children to read it instead of imitating it, the communal and dynamic nature of the teaching and learning process will be neglected, and the children might also miss some of the musical nuances that can only be imitated by watching the movements of the lead drummer.

It stands to reason that live music is preferable to recorded music when children are learning to listen to or perform unfamiliar music. Although it may not always be practical, it is beneficial to bring at least one culture-bearer into the classroom to perform for the children, and possibly also involve them in Engaged, Enactive, and/or Creative experiences with the music being shared. The human-to-human connection can be especially powerful in classroom situations. When a first grade child meets an Indian-American community member named Shahid who has been invited in to play the *sitar* (stringed instrument) for her class, she has the opportunity to directly experience the musician as a person, the music in real time, and the instrument up close through the senses of touch and smell in addition to seeing and hearing. When a fifth grade child can ask questions of a classmate's mother who is teaching the students to play the *bodhrán* (an Irish hand drum) during music class, he will likely have a much richer experience than he would have by simply watching a video recording.

MUSIC THAT CHILDREN LIKE

At times, when music teachers incorporate music of various cultures into their curriculum, they choose repertoire that represents the cultures of the children in their classroom. At other times, music is selected because it will provide the children with a sonic experience that is different from that with which they are familiar. During this age, children's developing independence of thought means that they identify music that they like—and also that they dislike. A well-selected music example can draw children's attention, eliciting their engagement as they move towards a deeper understanding of the music. A poorly selected musical example, on the other hand, can lead some children to feel detached from the lesson, and, in the extreme case, become disrespectful towards the music and culture, directly impacting the educational experience of all children in the class. Teachers should be mindful of specific musical characteristics that have been found to elicit enthusiasm on the part of children.

Children typically prefer music with faster tempi and a beat that stays steady and strong. In the popular music that characterizes listening experiences in other parts of their lives, rarely is it slow (the occasional pop ballad excepted), and never does it have a beat that fluctuates. Selecting repertoire that has a consistent beat and faster tempi will help engage children.

In addition to music that is up-tempo, children prefer music that has a stable tonality. The music that surrounds them in their daily life is almost always consonant, and when the music ventures too far into a tonality that strays from their experience, children in the middle and upper elementary grades can shut down mentally. Like all generalizations, there can be exceptions; for example, Balinese *gamelan* ensembles typically rely on unfamiliar scale systems that do not correlate with the 13-note chromatic scale of the West. In addition, two instruments within the ensemble will often be tuned so that parallel tones are slightly different, providing a shimmering sonic effect that lies at the core of its aesthetic sensibility. In this case, children often find it hauntingly beautiful, probably due to the unique instrumental effect.

With popular music, children and youth prefer music in which the voice is central to the performance. However, with preference for music of the world's cultures, the opposite has been found to be true—children and youth favor instrumental music over vocal works. The sounds that accompany novel instruments can cause children in grades 1 through 6 to sit up and take notice, wondering, "How in the world is that sound even MADE?" Their naturally inquisitive minds are piqued by most experiences with new instrumental music.

Vocal music stands at the center of many musical traditions, it is the most common musical activity in many elementary music classrooms, and children tend to like vocal timbres that are similar to what they hear in their daily lives. When teachers select vocal music from diverse musical traditions, the particular language and vocal timbre can be of consequence. For example, some cultures from the Middle East value a male sound that is high-pitched and nasal, and Bulgarian women's choral music has a unique vocal quality and special vocal effects. Much in the way that opera singing can cause children to laugh, such vocal styles may be different enough that children may have a difficult time moving beyond the initial shock at the sound to be able to engage with the piece. While many instrumental timbres initially sound odd to children, there is something about unusual vocal timbres that makes some children uncomfortable. Each chapter in this book will detail further musical characteristics that can lead to successful experiences with each dimension of WMP.

Materials and Instruments

In order to implement World Music Pedagogy in the elementary music classroom, teachers should have access to the best sound system possible for their budget, including good speakers. In addition to typical instruments found in elementary music classrooms (xylophones, metallophones, hand drums, various small unpitched percussion instruments, guitars, ukuleles, and recorders), teachers may also want to invest in some instruments from various cultures. These include, but of course are not limited to, small percussion instruments such as *agogô* (Yoruba), *afoxé* (Brazil), rainstick (Mexico), pitched instruments such as the *mbira* (Southern and Central Africa), and/or a stone *marimba* and drums such as *bongos* (Cuba), *djembe* (Mandinka), *taiko* (Japan), steel pan (Trinidad & Tobago), or *cajón* (Peru). For a more comprehensive listing of world music instruments, see *Musical Instruments of the World: An Illustrated Encyclopedia* (Midgley, 1976).

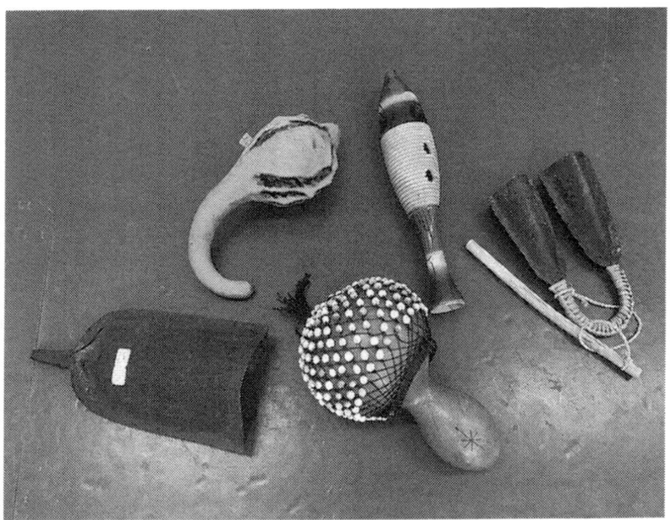

Figure 1.3 Small percussion instruments

Elementary music specialists who don't have instruments such as these could research local community resources to see what might be available to borrow and/ or adapt instruments that are already in the classroom to provide children with instrument-playing experiences. Teachers without access to classroom instruments might select recordings from the world's many body percussion traditions, such as American juba dance (hambone) or Spanish *flamenco* (*palmas*) to serve as models for Engaged or Enactive Listening experiences. Those whose classrooms are equipped with frame drums may select music from the many regions of the world in which frame drumming is common, including South America (Brazilian *ginga tamborim* or *pandiero*), Europe (the Irish *bodhrán*), the Middle East (*daf* or *dayereh*) and North Africa (*bendir*). Children who have access to larger drums such as *tubanos* might be able to engage in performing and creating music from African cultures that use *djembes* or Latin American cultures that use *congas*.

One of the benefits of World Music Pedagogy is that it provides children with a broader perspective of the world of music. Traditionally, children learned in school that there are four families of instruments: strings, woodwinds, brass, and percussion, but of course, there are many more ways of classifying instruments! For example, the Hornbostel-Sachs System that is used by many ethnomusicologists classifies instruments by the way that sound is produced: idiophones (body of instrument vibrates), membranophones (membrane vibrates), chordophones (strings vibrate), aerophones (air vibrates), and electronophones (sound is produced by electronic instruments that are amplified).

Length of WMP Learning Experiences

Lessons that incorporate World Music Pedagogy can manifest themselves in a variety of different lesson structures, from simple to complex. Depending on the teaching

Figure 1.4 *Djembe* and *conga* drums

context, the music curriculum, and the teacher's interest and time, different approaches can be taken at different times. Teachers might create a unit of study in which they choose (a) one musical selection from a musical genre for in-depth study, (b) multiple selections from the same genre, (c) selections from different genres from one geographic location, or (d) selections from various musical cultures that represent a musical construct or skill.

The simplest approach to World Music Pedagogy is to simply choose one piece of music from a particular culture and teach it through the five dimensions of WMP. If the teacher attends a festival in the local city and observes Brazilian *choro* music, it may lead him to find one song that can be easily integrated into an already packed curriculum. Although the children only learn one piece, best practice suggests that the learning experiences be spread over at least two or three class periods.

To allow children the ability to more fully understand a particular musical culture, the teacher can choose multiple pieces that are from the same genre. When the teacher uses recordings to teach three Maori stick games from New Zealand, the students can compare and contrast the experiences to develop a fuller understanding of the genre.

Other units can consist of exploring the music of a country or region broadly, and teachers can create a series of lessons that address different genres of the area. Fifth graders can learn a multi-part choral piece, a folk dance, and a singing game from Lithuania, all of which can lead to a more extensive grasp of the role of music in the culture. In a separate but related approach, third graders learning about France can be led through a unit that highlights the diversity of that country. In addition to teaching a classic French chanson, the teacher can incorporate a drumming piece from Ivory Coast, a former French colony, and a song from the Roma, the people traditionally called gypsies who traveled from place to place and currently face a high degree discrimination in France and elsewhere.

A unit can also be comprised of a number of pieces from different countries that connect to the musical curriculum. For a group of fourth graders embarking upon the exciting prospect of learning the recorder, they can also use the dimensions of World Music Pedagogy to learn about—and play the music of—*siku* panpipes from Peru, the *shakuhachi* end-blown flute from Japan, and the flutes of the Chippewa people of North America. The extent of culture-specific knowledge is necessarily reduced in these units, but they can effectively use world music to integrate across the music curriculum.

Structure of This Volume

Chapters 2 through 6 illustrate pedagogical action relative to musical diversity in typical classroom and rehearsal settings in elementary school. Each chapter focuses on different dimensions of World Music Pedagogy, although in practice, teachers usually utilize more than one of these dimensions (Attentive Listening, Engaged Listening, Enactive Listening, Creating, and Integrating activities) in one lesson or unit of study. Each of these chapters will answer questions that teachers might pose regarding each of the WMP dimensions. Introductory vignettes and closing "Teacher Feature" sections frame each chapter with narratives, questions, and answers from the "real world" of teaching various music cultures in public elementary schools. The vignettes at the beginning of each chapter offer a peek into elementary school settings, in which the teacher is using techniques specific to World Music Pedagogy. The "Teacher Feature" that ends each chapter provides perspectives from elementary school music teachers who have explored various means of bringing the musics of the world to their students.

Multiple illustrations of teaching and learning experiences through "Episodes" with recommended recordings will serve to address these questions in ways that are immediately applicable to teaching practice. Three of these musical examples will return in Chapters 2, 3, 4, and 6 as "Learning Pathways" episodes (consolidated in Appendix 1) to demonstrate how WMP dimensions might be used together over time. Each of these three recordings for the "Learning Pathways" was selected for salient sonic and cultural characteristics that children age six through twelve may be drawn to, as well as the possibility for elementary-aged children to be able to perform at least part of the selections on instruments that might be available in many elementary school music rooms. All of the recordings for the "Learning Pathways," and most of the musical examples from the other three or four stand-alone episodes in each chapter, can be found on the Smithsonian Folkways Recordings website, and many of these exact authentic recordings can also be accessed via YouTube. The recording for "Learning Pathway #1" is a singing game called *Maburu We (Oh, a Shoe, a Shoe)*, performed by young children of the Bakgaladi culture group in Botswana, Africa. This song was selected because children from around the world can relate to singing games, and because the song and the accompanying body percussion are simple enough for elementary school-aged children to perform. The recording for "Learning Pathway #2" is *El Carnaval de mi Tierra*, a song from El Salvador, that was chosen for its upbeat style and celebratory nature, as well as performance possibilities for middle and upper elementary school children. The recording for "Learning Pathway #3" is a 1:35-minute clip taken from the recording *Suwa Onbashira Kiyari-Taiko* from Japan. This selection was chosen due to the prominent and repetitive percussion instrument patterns that can be played by children as well as the theatrical drumming style of *taiko* that children enjoy watching and performing. Each of these recordings have interesting cultural stories and possibilities for teaching about various functions of music, as well as issues of immigration resulting from war and marginalization of native groups following colonization. Although these may seem like "heavy" topics for elementary-aged children, they are often exposed to these concepts through news media and other sources outside of school, so there is no reason for teachers at the elementary school level to avoid addressing these issues using age-appropriate language, metaphors, and examples that children can understand.

Chapter 2 addresses the second dimension of World Music Pedagogy, attending to questions such as, What is Attentive Listening? How do children attend to music in their everyday lives? How do teachers select music for Attentive Listening? What questioning techniques can be utilized in formative and summative assessments of children's Attentive Listening experiences? How can teachers design Attentive Listening lessons in order to maximize student engagement? The chapter also calls attention to ways that teachers might help children make meaningful connections to musical cultures in elementary music classrooms through acknowledgement of their own perspectives and musical values.

In Chapter 3, readers will find a rationale and methods for encouraging children to participate in music making as part of World Music Pedagogy through the participatory musicking dimensions of Engaged and Enactive Listening. Chapter 3 also provides discussion of the ways that authentic transmission processes from various cultures can inform pedagogy with children in Western classrooms and the participatory responses that children of different ages and stages, including those in early elementary (ages six through eight), middle elementary (ages eight through ten), and upper elementary (ages ten through twelve), might have as WMP is implemented.

Chapter 4 provides a description of some methods through which to share/display the games, songs, dances, and instrumental work discussed in the second and third chapters, as well as a description of how each of the WMP dimensions might apply within the context of a performance. Issues include selecting repertoire, designing concerts for large numbers of students, performance venues, and aesthetic and ethical compromises that must be made in order to move musical products to new performance contexts in school assemblies for children, at evening or Saturday school functions (PTA meetings, arts festivals), and in community settings.

Chapter 5 offers a rationale for teaching and learning improvisation and composition in schools, then focuses on means for implementing children's improvisation and composition in the World Music Pedagogy classroom. Listening examples that can inspire and inform improvisation and composition are included. Questions that are addressed include: How is improvisation and composition utilized in various musical cultures' practices/traditions? How can teachers engage students in improvisation and composition activities that are related to the musical processes and products of music practices/traditions from different cultures? How do teachers and students make decisions related to tradition, authenticity, and context?

Chapter 6 broadens the view by examining the ways in which music can be a gateway to understanding culture through WMP. This chapter will provide theories and examples of means for connecting children's learning of music with their experiences in other subjects, which may include the arts, technology, physical education, language arts, social studies, math, and science. Ethnomusicological concepts such as authenticity, representation, and context are addressed in depth in this chapter.

Chapter 7 summarizes some of the main points of the volume and includes suggestions for ensuring WMP's impact, validating and shaping identity through music, with attention to how music is cultural knowledge and how musicking is a means to awareness and understanding that is ethnocultural and intercultural.

How to Read This Volume

The dimensions of World Music Pedagogy are presented sequentially here, but it is essential to emphasize that when presenting lessons for elementary school students that are inspired by World Music Pedagogy, the lesson should not necessarily follow an order of Attentive Listening—Engaged Listening—Enactive Listening—Creating World Music—Integrating World Music. The nature of the individual pieces of music and the development of the group of children in specific classes will inform the ways in which the teacher designs the lessons.

Similarly, there is no one way to read the chapters in this book. Some suggestions:

- World Music Pedagogy begins with the musical sound, and as such, it is suggested that Chapter 2 (Attentive Listening for Cultural Awakenings) and Chapter 3 (Participatory Musicking, which includes both Engaged and Enactive Listening) be read first. From there, however, readers can make widely different choices.

- Some may wish to jump directly to Chapter 6 (Integrating World Music), feeling that they wish to know more about the ways that cultural context can be brought into the lessons. To be sure, although the chapter on Integration is the penultimate chapter, issues of cultural context are woven throughout lessons of World Music Pedagogy, and not saved as an "add-on" at the end of the unit.
- Others may wish to dive straight into Chapter 4, the Performance chapter. Although public performance is not a dimension of World Music Pedagogy, it has been placed between the phases themselves as an interlude of sorts, partly because the Enactive Listening experiences that ended the previous chapter are the musickings that most closely parallel conventional performance practice. It is worth noting that the Performance chapter also contains references to the two dimensions of Chapters 5 and 6, to help teachers consider whether Creating World Music and Integrating World Music are appropriate for public performance.
- Still others may decide to move from Engaged and Enactive Listening to Chapter 5, Creating World Music. Creating World Music is the most logical extension of Enactive Listening, in that the experiences of that dimension most commonly take the principles of the pieces that were learned during Enactive Listening, moving them towards a new level of sophistication and personal expression. In many ways, this can be considered a choose-your-own-adventure process to reading!

Open Ears, Open Minds

As children begin their school years, they may not have had opportunities to explore the wide world of music that allows various groups of people to interact socially without speaking the same language, to communicate negative emotions or political concerns nonviolently, to provide solace or healing for those who are suffering, to celebrate life and grieve death within a supportive community, and to express and celebrate cultural values through creating works of art through the organization of sounds. Through World Music Pedagogy, teachers can offer children the gift of honoring the diversity of cultural expressions while gaining a better understanding of our shared humanity through extensive listening experiences.

Teacher Feature: Jeremy David

Jeremy David has been teaching general music and chorus to children in kindergarten through sixth grade for seven years. His public school in a suburb of Cincinnati, Ohio, has a student body that is 88% White. He is American-born and ethnically Liberian and Lebanese. He typically sees his general music students for one 45-minute class per week. He has also served on staff for the Cincinnati Children's Choir for five years.

Q. Describe your philosophy of listening to world music.
A. I believe that students need to engage with a variety of musical styles. There are plenty of songs, games, and other musical repertoire from within a child's own culture that can develop his musical ability over time. In my opinion, a music curriculum is most fulfilling and meaningful when music is presented to children as a window through which we can glimpse into parts of the world and moments of history that are otherwise unfamiliar to us. Gaining an understanding of music in relation to history

Jeremy David, Elementary School Music Teacher

and culture affords children a deeper insight into the music they learn and, in turn, a greater level of enjoyment, appreciation, and retention. An added extra-musical benefit is the chance to show my students that they have more in common with people from different cultures than they might realize.

Q. How do you encourage elementary school children to listen attentively to unfamiliar music?
A. I like to incorporate movement into listening activities when possible, so that students can physically respond to specific elements of the music that are most relevant to our class in the moment. When students are participating in a seated listening activity, I often give them multiple chances to listen to the music in sound bites of varying lengths, with specific listening prompts: "Which instrument begins playing first? What do you think this piece of music is about? What are you hearing that tells you that? Where in the world do you think this music comes from?"

Q. How do children of different ages respond when they are listening to world music?
A. I think children's responses vary, based on the particular style of a piece. Younger children tend to be much less inhibited in their initial responses: If it has a fast tempo or a "danceable," energetic rhythm, those children will usually start dancing without

any prompting from me. In general, students may do a "double-take" if a song contains lyrics in a different language and the sung part is very pronounced in relation to the instruments. Sometimes they giggle; sometimes they try to sing along; sometimes they pick out words that sound like English words and sing those English words along with it: in the French Canadian folk song "J'Entends le Moulin," "tique-tique-taque" becomes "tika-tika-TACO," and so on. As students get older, some of them tend to be more critical of a piece of music, the more unfamiliar it is. It then becomes my job to draw connections between that music and some other musical experience that is familiar to and beloved by my students. That opens the door to engagement, enjoyment, and new learning. An example of drawing connections to prior knowledge in this manner would be playing the opening sequence of the 2011 American animated film *Rio* (in which the song "Real in Rio" is performed by the main cast) as an introduction to Brazilian *samba.*

Q. Do you see yourself or anyone in your family as a "culture-bearer" (someone who knows a musical culture from being raised in it)?
A. Within my family, I see my father (Bai) and his cousin Joseph as musical culture-bearers. I grew up through my grade school years listening to Liberian *soca* and highlife music on my father's cassette tapes; in college, I would always be delighted to hear that same music played on my father's stereo, whenever my father's cousin Joseph would visit with his vast collection of music CDs. My father is also the one I credit with my affinity for wearing Liberian dashikis. To this day, he still makes requests to some of his family members back in Liberia to mail him some authentic dashikis large enough for me and my older brother to wear.

At the school where I teach, I most definitely consider myself as a culture-bearer. I am the only black teacher in my building, and the only music teacher of color in my school district. My district is predominantly white, in terms of students, staff, and community. Since my first year teaching, I have felt a responsibility to educate my students (and, by extension, their families and my fellow staff members) about African American music and culture, and about "brown" minorities in general. I often think to myself that "if I don't teach my students about how black music is intertwined with all American musical genres, where else are they going to learn it?"

References

Banks, J. A. (2013). Approaches to multicultural curriculum reform. In J. A. Banks & C. A. McGee Banks (Eds.), *Multicultural education: Issues and perspectives* (8th ed., pp. 181–199). Hoboken, NJ: Wiley.

Campbell, P. S. (2004). *Teaching music globally*. New York: Oxford University Press.

Campbell, P. S., & Scott-Kassner, C. (2018). *Music in childhood: From preschool through the elementary grades (Edition 4D)*. New York: Schirmer/Cengage Learning.

Gay, G. (2010). *Culturally responsive teaching: Theory, research, and practice* (2nd ed.). New York: Teacher's College Press.

Guidelines of the Orff Institute. (2011). *Orff Schulwerk Informationen: Special Edition: 50 Jahre Orff-Institut 1961–2011, 85*, 273–276.

Kodály, Z. (1964). Children's choirs. In F. Bónis (Ed.), *The selected writings of Zoltán Kodály* (L. Halápy & F. Macnicol, Trans., pp. 119–127). London: Boosey & Hawkes.

Midgley, R. (Ed.). (1976). *Musical instruments of the world: An illustrated encyclopedia.* Oxford: Facts on File Publications.

2

Attentive Listening for Cultural Awakenings

As recess ends, a gaggle of third grade students make their way into the music classroom, instinctively looking to the list of activities for the class period marked on the whiteboard. Seeing the unfamiliar words El Carnaval de mi Tierra, one child pipes up, "What's that? A carnival? Day . . . my . . . terror? Wow, a terror carnival, sounds fun!" Ms. Doquilo silently shrugs and smiles, and the other children laugh, turning their attention to the board. As the rest of the children stash their coats and lunchboxes in the corner and make their way to their assigned spots, more children join in, laughing good-naturedly while they do their best to sound out the word "tierra." "Guys, it's TIERRA—it means earth," declares a Spanish-speaking girl, somewhat impatiently. Once seated, Ms. Doquilo calls for their attention, waits for quiet, then simply says, "Listen to this new music. Think: What instruments are you hearing, and where do you think it might be from? Save your answers in your head until I stop the recording." The up-tempo music begins, and as the sound of two violins and a pulsing percussion section flows throughout the space, the children start dancing in their seats. Within ten seconds, some children begin excitedly calling out their answers ("Mexico!" "Spain!"), causing other students to shush them, and the teacher to arch an eyebrow at those children too excited to keep their ideas quiet. After 30 seconds, the teacher stops the recording and asks the children to raise their hands if they have ideas to share. A flurry of hands shoot into the air, and the class is underway.

Listening in Children's Lives

Music surrounds children, filling their ears with a wide range of sound. Parents often croon lullabies to ease their young children towards sleep, while televisions, computers, and internet-connected technologies envelop them in a broad swath of musical expression—cereal commercials may accompany their viewing habits, chorales may surround them as they squirm in the pews at Sunday morning church services, and anything from kiddie pop to contemporary hip hop may boom through car speakers as their parents ferry them from one activity to the next. As children mature through the elementary school years, they begin to identify their preferred musical styles and take ownership over their listening habits, often streaming popular music through phones and tablets. Listening happens in elementary schools, too, as their general classroom teachers may play calming background music or select music to supplement a social studies lesson. They may have a music teacher who leads them through structured lessons with recordings that are designed to teach about famous composers from the Western classical tradition or different instruments in the orchestra. The world is filled with music, and from their earliest moments in the world, children are surrounded by it. In all of these experiences, listening stands at the center.

An internet search using the terms "children and music" typically elicits images of children actively participating in musical expression, engaged in activities such as playing instruments or singing into a microphone. However, music making can be considered more broadly, as well. Christopher Small (1998) coined the term "musicking," and while this term incorporates active ventures into sound creation, it also includes the more introspective, inspiring, and imaginative process of listening.

Attentive Listening in World Music Pedagogy

When listening experiences originating from various cultural groups are brought into the music classroom and given directed questioning and guidance from the teacher, they comprise the first dimension of World Music Pedagogy, Attentive Listening. Campbell (2004) defined Attentive Listening as "directed listening that is focused on musical elements and structures, and that is guided by the use of specified points of focus" (p. 55). Attentive Listening activities are designed in a way to draw in children's ears and minds, providing experiences in which they listen with focus and imagination, without being distracted by the effort made to recreate the sounds. Indeed, while Attentive Listening activities typically lead to more participatory musicking, it is the fact that the children are not making music that makes this dimension a core aspect of the overall pedagogy of WMP. As they listen to the music multiple times with specific questions in mind, the music becomes embedded in their minds, allowing them to gradually grow to learn the nuances of the musical genre. When children are engaged in thoughtfully sequenced questions to a well-selected piece of music, their natural curiosity can be piqued in ways that allow them to learn about specific aspects of novel musical genres while also thinking creatively about the range of musical ideas that they are hearing.

This chapter first describes the characteristics of repertoire that can lead to successful Attentive Listening experiences, and then highlights the types of activities and questions that comprise this dimension. Following this, pedagogical techniques for designing lessons are addressed, including issues such as effective approaches to questioning and response modalities that lead to growth on the part of the children. Throughout the chapter, "episodes" contain learning activities that attend to each of these points in turn. Of the six episodes in the chapter, three are explicitly labeled "Learning Pathways," the musical examples that will return in later chapters to highlight other dimensions of World Music Pedagogy. The remaining episodes contain musical examples that will only be used in this chapter.

Topics for Attentive Listening Experiences

Sonic Qualities of the Music

Attentive Listening experiences focus primarily on the sonic structures of the musical examples. The range of topics that can be addressed is vast, and the appropriateness of various principles will vary widely based on the nature of the recording. An introductory list of experiences for Attentive Listening is provided here.

INSTRUMENTATION

Novel sounds typically fascinate children, and perhaps no aspect of the world's musical cultures can elicit as much interest on the part of children as new instruments or new instrumental techniques. Teachers may ask focusing questions about the register of the instruments ("Does that instrument sound high or low compared to the other instruments?"), the material that the instrument is made of ("Do you think this *embaire* barred instrument from Uganda is made of wood or metal?"), or particular playing techniques ("Is that Egyptian *oud* plucked or bowed?"). Children can also be prompted to listen for entrances of particular instruments in a piece, or listen in order to categorize the instruments into different families based on the material used to construct the instrument or the way it is played.

VOICES

Vocal traditions are found throughout the world, and teachers can ask questions to probe at the children's understanding of a group of singers. In a polyphonic choral piece from the Cook Islands, children can identify whether they are hearing men, women, or both, or attempt to predict the age of the singers based on the sound recording that they hear played in class. Older students can articulate what it is that they hear about particular vocal qualities as well, such as focused tone, breathiness, or vowel pronunciation.

ENSEMBLE SIZE

At times, a teacher may play a recording of a solo *pipa* performance from China, an informal presentation of a father and son playing on the banjo-like *cümbüs* and *darabuka* drum in Turkey, or a Japanese *gagaku* ensemble populated by distinct wind, string, and percussion instruments, none of which may be known by the students. Each of these varying ensembles can prompt a series of focusing questions or activities.

STRUCTURAL ORGANIZATION

Music the world over is often characterized by structural principles that elementary children may already know. They can listen for alternating sections of solo and ensemble in a jazz standard from the United States or call-and-response vocal lines in a *bomba* from Puerto Rico. More complicated structures can be a source of fascination as well, such as the 16-beat *colotomic structure* found in Javanese *gamelan* ensembles. In their all-subjects classroom, younger elementary children often identify patterns, especially in math and language arts. In Attentive Listening experiences, they can be invited to listen for patterns of melodies or rhythms, or text that repeats at different points in a song.

OTHER MUSICAL CHARACTERISTICS

The possible musical characteristics that might serve as a basis for Attentive Listening experiences are extensive and depend upon the nature of the recording. Dynamics, intonation, tempo, ornamentation, and range are just some of the characteristics that may engage children's ears and minds.

OTHER NON-MUSICAL CHARACTERISTICS

At times, a recording may feature extraneous sounds that do not appear to the children to be musical, but will draw their attention. In recordings that are made outside, students may hear the sounds of people laughing or cars driving by on a highway, all of which can give them clues in order to deduce the location of a musical performance or the purpose of the music. Attentive Listening questions might prompt children to listen for the clank of a metal hammer knocking against stones in *Song of a Stonemason*, a work song from Japan, or to identify the animal that is crowing in *Las Mañanitas*, a Mexican birthday song often sung in the morning (Answer: a rooster!).

Other Attentive Listening Activities

QUESTIONS TO PROMPT IMAGINATION

At times, it can be appropriate to ask more open-ended questions that are intended to provoke children's thinking and imagination. For example, when listening to the *gamelan* music that accompanies the puppet play *wayang kulit* from Java, children can imagine what the story might be before being told by the teacher. Other open-ended experiences might include questions such as "What do you think the performers might be feeling?" It is important to note that the responses by children are inevitably framed by their own cultural background and knowledge, and that their interpretation of the meaning of particular musical sounds may be vastly different from the understanding of those who have grown up in the musical culture. It is imperative that the teacher inform the children about the reasons that the culture-bearers' interpretation might be similar or different from that of the listening children. This provides a valuable opportunity for children to begin to understand various perspectives.

VIDEO RECORDINGS

Most experiences of World Music Pedagogy utilize audio recordings, but increasingly teachers find videos that can be shown to children. These can allow the children to more easily learn about characteristics such as the attire worn by the musicians or dance moves that might be seen on a visual display of the music. In addition, viewing a video may allow children to more accurately identify other aspects of a musical example, such as the materials used to make particular instruments.

In the preceding examples of Attentive Listening, the children in the class are asked to listen to the recording without engaging in music making. This is characteristic of Attentive Listening experiences. In fact, it could happen that some children will begin to hum and drum, sing, or otherwise express themselves musically, especially with every additional opportunity to listen. That happens, as children enjoy chiming in. Still, that's not the point of Attentive Listening. Rather, they can give their focus to listening, encouraged by teachers to get their ears up and give full

Figure 2.1 Dragon shadow puppet

Photo courtesy of Julie Froude

focus to the sounds of the music. Other steps within World Music Pedagogy invite more musically active engagement on the part of the children, but in Attentive Listening, the focus is on the sound source. Repeated listenings to a recording with specific questions in mind allows children to get the flavor of the music, gradually understanding the nuances of the performance practice.

Episode 2.1 portrays a teaching and learning episode (called just "episodes" throughout the rest of the volume) using Attentive Listening that is inspired by the music in Learning Pathway #1, *Maburu We (Oh, a Shoe, a Shoe)*, from Botswana. *Maburu We* is a children's game song from the Bakgaladi people of Southern Botswana. The lilting melody and clear singing voices of the children provide an engaging recording that allows the students to envision life of their same-aged peers in another part of the world. This episode of Attentive Listening begins with basic questions about the gender and age of the performers, then moves into a question to prompt their imagination before ending with specific questions and tasks related to the musical characteristics of the melody and rhythm.

Episode 2.1: Botswana: "Maburu We" (Learning Pathway #1)

Specific Use: Upper Elementary General Music Class

Materials:

- "Maburu We (Oh, a Shoe, a Shoe)," young children of the Bakgaladi culture group (from *Traditional Music of Botswana, Africa: A Journey with Tape Recorder along Southern Botswana from Mochudi to Kang*), Smithsonian Folkways Recordings

- Visual map of the melodic contour

Procedure:

1. Invite children to listen to the recording, identifying the different sounds that occur in the performance. (Answer: Singers, clapping, a whistle.)
   a. Play track (0:00–0:30), then field responses. Repeat to check answers.
2. Listen to the recording again, attempting to determine whether the performers are men, women, or children. (A: The liner notes report that the performers are children, although their specific ages are not provided.)
   a. Play track (0:00–0:30), field responses. Repeat to check answers.
3. "Listen again, and think: How do you think that the children might be feeling as they are singing the song? Why do you think so?" (A: This can be interpreted in a variety of ways.)
   a. Play track (0:00–0:30), then field responses.
4. Inform the children that the sung word "*ijoo*" means "ouch" to the Bakgaladi people. Listen to the recording to identify the number of times that the word is sung. (A: Four in first two lines.)
   a. Play track (0:00–0:30), then field responses. Repeat to check answers.
5. Show the pattern of the melody with a hand, while looking at a visual map of the melodic contour.
   a. Play track (0:00–0:30). Repeat if necessary.
6. Listen to the recording, trying to determine the rhythmic pattern of the clapping that accompanies the singing.
   a. Play track (0:00–0:30), field responses. Repeat to check answers.

Figure 2.2 "Maburu We (Oh, a Shoe, a Shoe)" from Botswana

x = hand claps

Traditional Music of Botswana, Africa *(FW album 4371), Collected by Elizabeth Nelbach Wood, 1963*

The Attentive Listening experiences posed in the episode above would not occur one after the other. Often, Attentive Listening activities are followed directly by an activity in which children are more actively engaged in making the music. For example, after suggestion 6 in Episode 2.1, in which children listen to the recording and try to determine the rhythmic patterning, it would logically follow that after discovering the pattern they would then attempt to imitate it by tapping along with the recording. Replicating an aspect of the music qualifies as Engaged Listening, which will be addressed in detail in the next chapter. Additionally, after asking the children to describe the affect of the children's singing, a teacher could provide the translation, which consists of the words *shoe*, *jail*, *ouch*, *from the back*, and *Boers* (i.e. the white South Africans, who created and instituted apartheid, a racist system of government that was in place in South Africa until the 1990s). More of this way of Integrating World Music will be addressed in Chapter 6.

Selecting Repertoire for Attentive Listening

When designing Attentive Listening lessons of world musical cultures, the first issue that emerges is the repertoire. What music will work? As mentioned in Chapter 1, teachers do well to consider children's musical interests in terms of tempo, tonal center, and timbres, particularly in the early stages of introducing very unfamiliar musical examples. In addition to the qualities of the music that influence children's affective response, there are traits of the music that lend themselves to more successful Attentive Listening lessons.

Shorter Excerpts

When children first hear a recording in a listening lesson, teachers often ask them to listen for specific aspects of the music, such as the number of performers, the types of instruments, or the region of the world from which they think the piece originated. Ideally, the musical excerpts should last between 30–60 seconds. By using brief examples, children can consider the question while listening, brainstorm answers to the question, then listen again. Shorter examples also allow children to listen multiple times with different questions, participating in some active way during some of the later repetitions. With repeated listenings, children gain a deeper understanding of the nuances of the music, a particularly important factor when the music is far from their experience. In addition, the increased familiarity derived from repeated hearings can lead to greater preference for the piece of music.

Thinner Textures

Listening experiences with the world's musical cultures often focus on instrumental genres because they provide sonic experiences that may be furthest from the students' previous experiences. Sometimes, though, the music can be incredibly complex. While richly textured music can be gorgeous (and compelling for teachers), when answering questions about the sonic properties on a recording, music with fewer voices or instruments will often be easier for children. If music has only two to four instruments and voices, young listeners can more easily discern individual parts. As children move through elementary school, they develop more acute listening skills and will become better at differentiating between more instrumental and vocal parts.

Music with Contrast

In addition to thinner textures, performances that contain contrasting musical parts can also lead to more successful Attentive Listening experiences. This contrast can take a variety of forms. A listening excerpt with instruments or voices that are extremely dissimilar in their sonic properties can lead to successful responses to the questions that follow. For example, children will have a more difficult time distinguishing the separate parts in a recording with three mildly different voices in a Bulgarian women's singing group than they would in a recording of a flute and a stringed instrument in a Chinese ensemble. Other musical contrasts that can lead to effective listening are changes in dynamics and tempo.

Music with Repetition

Musical repetition within an excerpt often provides a foundation for children when learning a novel piece of music. Repetition can occur with melodies, rhythms, or text. For example, if a 45-second excerpt contains a recurring vocal ostinato, a class can be asked to listen for "a voice part that repeats" before the song is played. Further Attentive Listenings can focus on other related questions, depending on the nature of the excerpt. Questions can include, How many times does the vocal pattern occur? Raise your hand when it changes. Can you draw the contour of the melody in the air? Additionally, musical repetition excerpt will allow for more successful experiences further on during the lesson or unit, when children participate in Engaged Listening or Enactive Listening, because the children will have internalized the music more deeply due to the fact that the melody repeats multiple times.

Musical Qualities That Relate to the Curriculum

Finally, Attentive Listening experiences with the world's musical cultures in an elementary music class do not take place in a vacuum, but in the broader context of the curricular goals of the music and general classrooms. Music curricula emphasize particular skills and forms of knowledge, and incorporating musical examples that allow the teacher to connect to these principles can lead to successful Attentive Listening experiences. For example, a music class that emphasizes xylophones, metallophones, and glockenspiels might lead a teacher to search out musical examples that precipitate questions about the type and timbre of barred instruments on a recording from Indonesia, Cambodia, or Uganda. Similarly, many elementary music classes include songs that are characterized by call-and-response form, a pattern that arises in music in other parts of the world such as sub-Saharan Africa.

Many of these characteristics can be incorporated into a series of Attentive Listening activities in the learning episode that follows (Episode 2.2) for *El Carnaval de mi Tierra* (Learning Pathway #2). The song was recorded in Washington, DC, by Los Hermanos Lovo, a group of immigrants from a mountainous, rural region in the southern part of El Salvador. In the liner notes, the performers state that they enjoy gathering together to make music with other immigrants from their country. This particular song from the *chanchona* musical tradition includes lyrics that refer to the joy that can come when attending a "carnival of my homeland."

El Carnaval de mi Tierra begins with an instrumental introduction that lasts 26 seconds, followed by the voices singing the verse and chorus. Initial Attentive Listening experiences can restrict their questions to the first section, before the singers enter, with later questions addressing the vocal portion. There are five instrumental parts, but each one is distinct and distinguishable. Repetition can be heard in both the violin melody that leads off the piece and also in the shaker that plays a consistent rhythmic pattern underneath it. Additionally, the melody played by the violin in the introduction returns in the chorus that occurs later in the song. Curricular connections are always specific to the school and music class, but the song is sung in Spanish. In the United States, Spanish is the most commonly spoken language after English, and most classes will hold children who either speak some Spanish or are able to recognize it, which can provide another entry point for Attentive Listening.

Episode 2.2: El Salvador: "El Carnaval de mi Tierra" (Learning Pathway #2)

Specific Use: Middle or Upper Elementary General Music Class

Materials:

- "El Carnaval de mi Tierra," Los Hermanos Lovo (from *¡Soy Salvadoreño! Chanchona Music from Eastern El Salvador*), Smithsonian Folkways Recordings

Procedure:

1. Identify the different instruments on the recording. (A: Bass, two guitars, two violins, shaker, drum.)
   a. Play track (0:00–0:26), then field responses.
   b. Repeat to check answers.
2. View short videos of each of the instruments (found online), then listen to the recording and pretend to play one of the instruments.
   a. Play track (0:00–0:26).
3. After imitating the teacher's clapping of the following pattern or reading notation, identify the instrument that is playing the rhythm. (A: A shaker or *guiro*; the term in this area of El Salvador is *media caña*.)
   a. Play track (0:00–0:26), then field responses.
   b. Repeat to check answers.

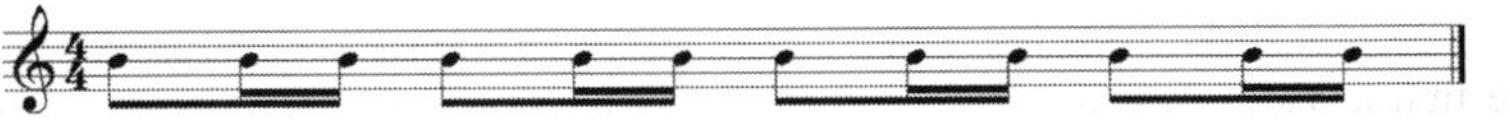

4. Identify the number of times the violins repeat the melody before changing the pattern. (A: Two.)
    a. Play track (0:00–0:26), then field responses.
    b. Repeat to check answers.
5. "Listen again, and raise your hand when you hear a sound that we haven't heard in this song yet." (A: Voice.)
    a. Play track (0:00–0:30, or until hands are raised), then field responses.
6. Starting the recording when the voice enters, identify the language that is being sung, and the number of singers. (A: Spanish; two.)
    a. Play track (0:26–1:03), then field responses.
7. Listen to the recording with the song text displayed on the board. Identify any Spanish words that are already known.
    a. Play track (0:26–1:03), then field responses.
8. Listen to the song from the beginning, raising a hand when the tune on the violins repeats later in the song. Provide the hint that the tune will be played on a different instrument. (A: The chorus.)
    a. Play track (0:00–1:03), observing student response.
    b. Repeat, if necessary.

Va-ma-nos a car-na- val..... al car - na-val de mi tier - ra Va-ma-nos a dis-fru- tar..... Y a go - zar nue-vos a- mo - res.

Figure 2.4 "El Carnaval de mi Tierra" from El Salvador

As with the other listening examples in this chapter, these Attentive Listening experiences should not follow each other, one after the next so that children are sitting and listening to the same selection over and over without engaging in music making for extended periods of time. After some of the steps in the episode, there are logical follow-up activities that incorporate other dimensions of World Music Pedagogy. For example, after the children identify that a shaker instrument played the notated rhythm, the next step might be to perform the rhythm while the recording sounds, by either playing it on an instrument or using their mouths to make a similar "ch-ch-ch" sound. When children perform an aspect of a recording while the sound is playing, it qualifies as Engaged Listening, to be addressed in Chapter 3. Also, after the children identify the Spanish words that they recognize, the teacher would be wise to provide the rest of the translation and then engage in a discussion of the text's meaning in the lives of the performers, a form of the dimension of Integrating World Music.

Designing Lessons for Attentive Listening

The first steps in creating Attentive Listening lessons within the context of World Music Pedagogy are to choose the music and identify the particular musical and non-musical issues that the musical selection suggests might be addressed. In creating cohesive lessons that lead to musical growth on the part of students, other principles apply.

Let the Recording Guide the Lesson

Effective lessons that incorporate Attentive Listening begin with the recording or live musical performance, not with an objective selected to fill a preconceived educational objective. Lessons are best designed when the teacher knows the recording inside and out, due to multiple repeated listenings. Transcribing parts of the recording into Western notation can help the teacher become more deeply familiar with the music as well. The repeated listenings allow the recording to become more fully known, which in turn allows the teacher to take a more critical eye to the lesson planning that follows. During these periods of listening, it is effective to jot down various musical and non-musical aspects of the recording that may ultimately serve as focal points for Attentive Listening.

Think Like a Child

Once the music is well known and a list of possible lesson topics for Attentive Listening has been created, teachers should attempt to revisit the recording with "the ears of a child" to as much a degree as possible. What characteristics of the recording will draw children's attention first? It can be tempting to design lessons in which the objective is set solely by the curriculum of the district, or by the facet of the recording that the teacher finds most compelling. However, when designing Attentive Listening lessons for children, it is essential to focus on the children's perception of the sound that they will be hearing for the first time. For example, if a Palestinian wedding song contains the sounds of *ululation*, the high-pitched trilling sound that can be heard in much of the Middle East, children who have no experience with the vocal phenomenon will find it fascinating and worthy of discussion. Although the teacher may want to move towards a discussion of the qualities of the wedding song itself, an initial discussion about the ululation will follow the child's way of thinking.

Pose Questions Before Listening

When teachers ask a question before pressing "play" on the sound system, it gives the children something specific to listen for as the music resounds through the room. It focuses their attention on a particular element of the music. Conversely, if the teacher plays a recording of a *bachata* piece of music from the Dominican Republic, and follows up by asking the children to name the different instruments that they heard, they essentially have to replay the music in their mind in order to answer the question—an advanced musical skill even if the music were well known.

Convergent and Divergent Questioning

Questions that teachers pose during Attentive Listening experiences can engage and motivate children, keep them on task, encourage them to share their opinions about what they are listening to, and allow teachers to check for understanding. Once teachers have determined the elements of the musical selection that should be the focus of the lesson, questions can be formulated to direct children's attention to those elements, and also to encourage further critical thinking about the music and cultural context of the music. Two types of questions lead to different types of thinking on part of the children.

Convergent or "closed-ended" questions usually have a clearly defined correct answer. They can help children discover basic knowledge about the music and the musical context for a musical selection. Examples of such questions that might be posed during an Attentive Listening lesson include:

- What instruments/voices are being used in this performance?
- How do the instruments and voices relate to each other (texture, harmony, etc.)?
- What is the form of the piece (where is the repetition and contrast)?

Divergent questions, on the other hand, are more open-ended, can have multiple answers, and require children to think critically about and apply previous knowledge to explain, extrapolate, or further analyze a topic or problem. Divergent questions to further engage children in Attentive Listening might include:

- What clues does the music give us as to where it might be from?
- What might the musicians be doing while they sing/play?
- What does the quality of the voices suggest to you about how the musicians might feel?
- How do you think people would respond if this music were performed in a different context (football game, wedding, etc.)?
- What is your favorite (or least favorite) part of the music and why?

Both convergent and divergent questions offer distinct benefits for students. Convergent questions can be particularly effective for factual information that has a limited range of responses. They encourage succinct responses, which often allows the teacher to play the recording more often since the amount of discussion required to address the question is limited. Divergent questions encourage discussion, allowing children the chance to think creatively and apply analytical thought to a question that may have many responses. Although the time required to answer the question is more extensive, children's thinking is typically more complex, and the questions may lead to deeper understandings.

Ideally, teachers should provide a balance of convergent and divergent questions in order to elicit different types of thinking on part of the students. Once the questions are posed and the music has been played, children benefit from "wait time," so it is typically effective to provide three to five seconds to allow children to formulate answers before providing a response. Teachers can then follow up to encourage children to complete, clarify, expand, or support answers. Additionally, children can be allowed opportunities to develop and ask their own questions about the music.

Episode 2.3 offers listening activities that feature both convergent and divergent questions as further learning prompts that fit well within the Attentive Listening experience. *Suwa Onbashira Kiyari-Taiko* (Learning Pathway #3) is a *taiko* drum piece that originated in the Shinto tradition common in Japan. The song is traditionally performed as part of the "Festival of Honorable Pillars," in which large trees are felled in a mountain forest, then moved down to the town of Suwa, Japan. The portion of the recording selected for the episodes in this volume can be found on the YouTube recording of *Suwa Onbashira Kiyari-Taiko,* originally recorded by Ensemble O-Suwa-Daiko on the Smithsonian Folkways Recording collection.

Episode 2.3: Japan: "Suwa Onbashira Kiyari-Taiko" (Learning Pathway #3)

Specific Use: Upper Elementary General Music Class

Materials:

- "Suwa Onbashira Kiyari-Taiko," Ensemble O-Suwa-Daiko (from *Japan: O-Suwa-Daiko Drums*), Smithsonian Folkways Recordings

Procedure:

1. Identify the instruments that can be heard on the recording, and the country that they think it might be from. (Convergent; Answer: Drums, clicking instruments, jingling instruments; the song hails from Japan.)
   a. Play track (3:15–4:10), then field responses.
   b. Repeat to check answers.
2. "Listen again, and note the similarities and contrasts: What is staying the same? What is changing?" (Convergent; A: Similarities: instruments, rhythmic patterns; Differences: tempo is gradually getting faster.)
   a. Play track (3:15–3:44), then field responses.
   b. Repeat to check answers
3. "Listen to a longer section this time and raise your hand when you hear something other than the tempo change. Also, how many 'sections' do you think this listening selection has, and how would you describe the musical differences between the sections?" (Convergent)

   (**A:** 3:44 New syncopated rhythmic pattern begins.)

   (**A:** 4:02 Beat stops and individual instruments take turns shaking/rolling.)

   (**A:** 4:12 New beat begins on clicking rim and drum head, and a new syncopated rhythmic "solo" begins, passed from high drum to the rim of drum to the low drum.)

   a. Play recording (3:15–4:49), then field responses.
   b. Repeat to check answers.

4. "What is your favorite and least favorite part of this music and why?" (Divergent)
   a. Play track (3:15–4:49), then field responses.
5. Listen, identifying an activity that the musicians might be doing, beyond playing instruments. (Divergent)
   a. Play track (3:15–4:49), then field responses. Inform the children that *taiko* performers typically move around the drums with specific choreographed movements.

Children's Responses

In addition to the manner in which questions are asked, teachers can also utilize various response modalities to help children externalize what they are hearing internally. Oral, visual, and kinesthetic modalities should be considered while developing Attentive Listening lessons.

ORAL RESPONSES

It is often most expedient for children to answer questions orally. Most commonly, one individual student will answer a question that has been posed to the entire class. When this transpires in a typical whole-class context of 20 to 30 children, the teacher only really knows the idea of that one respondent. It is common for the teacher to inform the student whether the answer was correct, and then move on to the next step in the lesson plan. However, greater learning for all students will occur if the teacher resists providing the answer, but instead plays the recording a second time, asking all students to listen to the recording with the particular answer in mind. In this case, those students who did not know the answer the first time they listened to the recording are afforded another chance to listen and determine the answer for themselves. Once the recording has been played the second time, additional discussion can ensue.

Other discussion protocols exist as well. In some teaching and learning contexts, children learn discussion protocols such as "think-pair-share." In this particular approach, one child turns to another student to discuss their answers to a question. Checking with the children's classroom teacher to determine the sort of language that is used in their classroom for this type of experience can make the transition easier when it is brought into the music classroom. This can be a particularly productive approach with divergent questions, in which children have to take a stance on an issue. For example, when listening to a drumming tradition that has historically been the province of males, the teacher might ask, "What do you think about women not playing the drums?" In a typical group discussion that is led by a teacher, only a few children would be able to share their thoughts. In the think-pair-share approach, all children are able to communicate their ideas, which can be particularly important when children may have different opinions. After discussion in pairs, they can listen to the recording again, thinking about the recording in light of their classmate's perspective.

VISUAL RESPONSES

Utilizing visual aids such as listening maps or picture books that follow the story of the music or show performers in action can be motivational for visual learners, can guide children through the formal structure of the music, and can help them maintain focus on particular musical elements during listening experiences. Technology can facilitate visual possibilities, such as viewing videos of musical performances or watching animated listening maps. Teachers might also set up iPads so that children can draw the melodic contour or other patterns heard while listening. Children could also be asked to interpret what they hear through drawing or writing, using prompts such as:

- Draw the arc of the dynamics.
- Write answers to specific questions, such as "What instruments do you hear?"
- Draw or write what you feel as you listen to the music.
- Draw what you think the sounds would look like if you could see them.

In some situations, written responses can help teachers understand children's thinking. With paper and pencils or their technological equivalent, children can scribble down thoughts that they have while the music is playing. They can respond to either divergent or convergent questions, and the act of writing down answers can keep them engaged and focused on the task at hand. In addition, this can allow teachers to quickly assess the children's understanding. Of course, writing works better for upper elementary children, due to the development of writing skills.

KINESTHETIC RESPONSES

While listening to the music of a particular culture, children can be asked to perform eurhythmic activities such as moving to show the melodic shape or the rhythmic phrasing. They can raise hands or touch noses when they hear a particular musical event, instrument, or pattern. An entire class of younger children can answer a question regarding form by holding out matching fists to show "same," and holding up one fist and one flat hand to show "different." Younger elementary students can "pretend play" an instrument, and older children can work together to create movement or dance forms to represent musical patterns. For a greater challenge, or in order for teachers to evaluate individuals, children can close their eyes when they kinesthetically respond to questions about repetition and contrast in the musical selection.

The following episode from Ukraine (Episode 2.4), *Zaporozhetz (Sabre Dance)* illustrates oral, visual, and kinesthetic responses in an experience of Attentive Listening. The rollicking tune features Michael Skorr, a United States citizen of Ukrainian descent, performing on the *bayan*, an accordion-type instrument that can be found in Ukraine, Russia, and other parts of Eastern Europe. When people emigrate from one country to another, they often bring with them aspects of their folk culture as a way of preserving their cultural identity, as is the case here.

Episode 2.4: Ukraine: "Zaporozhetz (Sabre Dance)"

Specific Use: Middle Elementary General Music Class

Materials:

- "Zaporozhetz (Sabre Dance)," Michael Skorr (from *17 Popular Ukrainian Dances*), Smithsonian Folkways Recordings
- Two small pieces of paper per student, one red with the letter "A" on it, and one blue with "B"

Procedure:

1. Identify the instruments on the recording and the continent the song might be from. (A: Accordion and drum set; Ukraine, in Eastern Europe.)
   a. Play track (0:00–0:20), then field responses. Inform students that the accordion is called a *bayan* and that the song is from Ukraine.
2. Listen, brainstorming ideas for an activity that people might be doing while this song is being played. (A: Folk dance.)
   a. Play track (0:00–0:29), then field responses. Lead to correct answer.
3. Identify the musical aspects that suggest that this might be accompanied by a folk dance. (Possible answers: the tempo is lively; the melody repeats; the melody moves at a fast clip.)
   a. Play track (0:00–0:29), then share answers with a neighbor in think-pair-share protocol. After 30–45 seconds of interaction, play track again.
4. Display musical notation below. Teacher sings the pattern (more slowly than the recording) while students track the notation by pointing from their seats.

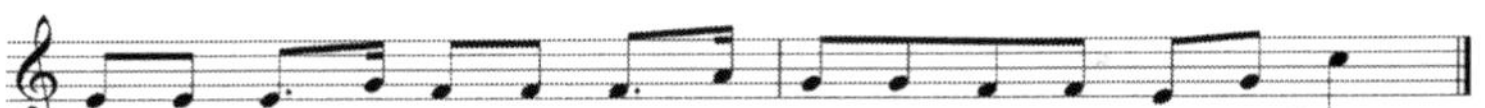

5. Distribute small red paper to the students. Raise paper in air when the pattern occurs.
   a. Play track (0:00–0:29), observing children's responses. Repeat if necessary.
6. Distribute blue pieces of paper. "Raise red paper on first tune, raise blue paper on the other part."
   a. Play track (0:00–0:29), observing children's responses. Repeat if necessary.
7. Raise the papers again the same way. Note how many times each pattern repeats before the section changes. (Possible answers: Two; or one, if they hear that upon repetition there is melodic ornamentation.)
   a. Play track (0:00–0:29), then field responses.

8. "When the tune in each section repeats, is it identical, or does it change? (A: It changes.)
   a. Play track (0:00–0:29), then field responses. In discussion that ensues, identify and define *ornamentation*. Repeat to check answers.
9. Write the form of the song, noting each change. (A: Probably: aabb^1 a^{1}a^{2}b^{2}b^3)
   a. Play track (0:00–0:29), then field responses.

CONSIDER THE RESPONSE MODALITY MOST APPROPRIATE FOR THE TASK

In a lesson that incorporates Attentive Listening, a skilled teacher constantly assesses the children to determine what types of activities are most successful at leading to growth. In some cases, a quick kinesthetic response ("raise your hand when you hear . . .") will be the most expedient at assessing student understanding, and it also provides the children with a specific task, lessening the likelihood that they will call out. With written responses, the physical engagement of writing combined with the mental engagement of Attentive Listening can require enough focus that children may be less likely to abruptly verbalize their thoughts. In other contexts, the think-pair-share approach can allow children the chance to express themselves, particularly when a divergent question is posed. When children know that they will have an opportunity to share their opinions once the listening example has ended, they may be more willing and able to sit quietly.

These approaches can have downsides, as well. With written responses, passing out materials necessarily takes time, lessening the time the children can listen to the recording. With think-pair-share protocols, the children are engaged in discussion with each other, but the teacher may be unable to detect the content of the conversations. Additionally, once children begin talking with each other, the conversations can get extensive, and some children may have a difficult time returning to a group-centered discussion. This can limit the opportunities that the children have to hear the excerpt, simply because the think-pair-share requires time to execute.

Episode 2.5 provides an Attentive Listening episode for early elementary-aged children. The clearly discernable steady pulse and rhythmic patterns of the music makes it ideal for first graders to focus on the rhythmic structure of the piece. Recorded in 1949, this historical recording of Aboriginal music comes from the Northwest Territory in Australia. The *didjeridu* (or *didjeridoo*) in the song's title is played by a "puller" while the clapsticks that can be heard are performed by the "Songman."

Episode 2.5: Australia: "Didjeridu"

Specific Use: Early Elementary General Music Class

Materials:

- "Didjeridu," two Aboriginal songmen (from *Tribal Music of Australia*), Smithsonian Folkways Recordings

Procedure:

1. "Touch your nose if you can tell me the name of the instrument that you hear first, but don't say the name of the instrument until I say 'go.'" (A: *didjeridu*, sticks.)
   a. Play track (0:00–0:30), then field responses.
   b. Repeat recording so that children can check the answers.
2. Raise hands when the sticks begin to play.
   a. Play track (0:00–0:30), observing children's responses. Repeat if necessary.
3. Listen to see if the *didjeridu* plays any repeated patterns. (A: Yes, beginning at 0:03.)
   a. Play track (0:00–0:30), then field responses. Listen again to check answer.
4. "Touch your head when the pattern changes."
   a. Play track (0:00–0:30), observe children's responses. Repeat if necessary.
5. Identify the number of times the *didjeridu* plays the repeated pattern before it changes. (A: 14.)
   a. Play track (0:00–0:30), then field responses.
   b. Repeat to check answer, showing each repetition of the *didjeridu* pattern on fingers.
6. Listen for other sounds on the recording (A: Unclear; it sounds like there may be insects in the background.)
   a. Play track (0:00–0:30), then field responses.
   b. Repeat to check answers.
7. "Does it sound like this song is performed inside or outside?" (A: Outside.)
   a. Play track (0:00–0:30), then field responses. Repeat to check answers, if necessary.

Responding to Personal Preferences

Young children in the early stages of elementary school typically hold positive attitudes about most things that happen in school—they love just about everything they do, from reading and math to recess and lunch. As children move from early through middle and on to upper elementary grades, they develop stronger personal values about the makeup of their school day, with specific subjects and topics that become their most and least favorite. This is true of music in particular, with children in grades 1 through 6 developing tastes that diverge from their parents and teachers, as they try to stake out their own perspectives on the musical world. Indeed, many children develop decreasing levels of "open-earedness" as they age through elementary school, with a narrowing of tastes that often begins to expand in later periods of adolescence.

World Music Pedagogy most commonly seeks to expose children to musical cultures that are unfamiliar to them—just at the time when some children are becoming more resistant to novel musical genres. Children may react negatively, and during Attentive Listening question-and-answer lesson segments, they may express these unfavorable opinions. However, there are tactics that a teacher can consider employing to address these issues.

RESPECT THEIR PERSPECTIVES

Typically, a teacher will label students' laughter or unfavorable comments to unfamiliar music as disrespectful. But these responses to new music should be recognized as age-appropriate for children in elementary schools. To some extent, antipathy towards the recording can be avoided by considering the musical characteristics of the piece when selecting music, as noted earlier in the chapter. But even when a teacher carefully considers the musical example, children may exhibit adverse reactions. If children laugh at an excerpt, one approach could be to acknowledge that the music is different and ask them to articulate the musical reasons that the music sounded funny to them. Was it the vocal timbre? The combination of instruments that struck them as weird? Straightforward discussions about their perspectives, without judgment on part of the teacher, can allow children to feel that their views are honored in the music class. After a brief discussion, they can be guided towards a more open-minded approach, in a variety of ways: Asking them to consider aspects of their own music that others might find unusual, describing the reasons for the particular musical styling that was problematic for them, or providing other cultural context about the recording may serve to redirect the children towards acknowledging other valid viewpoints. Recognizing that their resistance is natural can be an essential part of the process of leading them towards acceptance of something unfamiliar.

HEAD OFF THE PROBLEM

If a teacher anticipates that a particular recording might have musical characteristics that could elicit negative comments, posing questions before the first listening can focus the children's thinking towards a particular end. These questions can refer to the specific musical characteristic, asking the children to describe it, or compare it to other music that they know. If they are faced with a particular task when listening, children may be distracted from making negative comments and directed into solving a musical problem instead. For example, before listening to the recording of *Pahan Chunariya*, a song from India that includes melodic and rhythmic material that may be very unfamiliar to the children, a teacher might challenge the students to guess which instruments they hear.

Sometimes an unfamiliar listening example can be preceded by another recording or video that is more closely related to something that the children are familiar with. Episode 2.6 describes a lesson in which a traditional Lebanese *oud* piece (Middle Eastern stringed instrument) is introduced to children ages eight to ten. The children watch a video of two musicians in a recording studio performing *Rast*, an upbeat *dumbek* and *oud* duet, to "hook" the children's attention before they listen to the more traditional Lebanese *oud* piece.

Episode 2.6: Iraq and Lebanon: "Taqsim on the 'Oud-Andalusian Style'"

Specific Use: Middle Elementary General Music Class

Materials:

- "Rast," (Video), Rahim Alhaj and Souhail Kaspar (no album), Smithsonian Folkways Recordings
- "Taqsim on the 'Oud-Andalusian Style,'" performers unknown (from *Melodies and Rhythms of Arabic Music*), Smithsonian Folkways Recordings

Procedure:

1. Watch the video of "Rast," with two questions in mind: "Is there a steady beat? How are the two instruments in this recording similar to what we know?" (A: The beat is steady; the *oud* is a stringed lute, which many students will think resembles a guitar; the *dumbek* is a drum.)
   a. Play video (0:00–0:45), then field responses. Inform them of the instruments' names.
2. Play track and listen to "Taqsim on the 'Oud-Andalusian Style.'" Identify whether the beat stays steady, and identify the instruments. (A: The beat is not steady; *oud*.)
   a. Play track (0:00–0:40), then field responses.
   b. Repeat, if necessary.
3. "Compare these two pieces. What else might be happening while the music is playing?"
   a. Play video (0:00–0:45), then play track (0:00–0:40). Field responses, ultimately informing the children that video is a piece for dancing from Iraq and the second piece is an example of a *taqsim* from Lebanon. *Taqsim* is a melodic musical improvisation that usually precedes a traditional composition in parts of the Middle East (including Lebanon, where this recording is from). The *taqsim* is in a particular mode that informs the performer of the scale, melodic patterns, and rhythmic structure to use. The performer can then determine how to change certain parts to make it more interesting and exciting for the audience.
4. Identify the musical characteristics that make it an effective piece for dancing.
   a. Play track (0:00–0:40), field responses.
5. "Which recording do you prefer, and why?"
   a. Play video (0:00–0:45), then play track (0:00–0:40). Field responses.

It is important that a teacher not assume that children will respond negatively to new sounds. In many teaching situations, particularly ones where the music teacher regularly incorporates a variety of musical traditions into the class, children welcome the novelty that often comes with new and diverse musical genres. But if past experience with a particular group of students leads a teacher to believe that respect will be a problem, these strategies above can be effective.

Let's Listen!

Within World Music Pedagogy, Attentive Listening is often the first step in expanding children's musical and social perspectives. Wise teachers will recognize that children bring a wealth of musical experiences to the music classroom through their exposure to media, music, and movement both inside and outside of school, and will find ways to help children compare and contrast familiar with unfamiliar musics. The choices that teachers make in terms of listening examples, approaches to questioning, and assessment techniques can motivate children not only to expand their musical knowledge, but also to develop skills in various ways of listening and communicating about music. Vocabularies expand as children are encouraged to use language to describe musical elements, performance techniques, and other thoughts about the listening material. Thoughtful teachers will also call attention to the social aspects of the music, ideally by inviting a culture-bearer into the classroom to present and discuss practices with the children. As children listen and respond to music through verbal, visual, and kinesthetic means, teachers can assess student progress, and move on to develop further curriculum that also includes participatory musicking and performing music of various world cultures, as well as composing and improvising.

Teacher Feature: BethAnn Hepburn

BethAnn Hepburn, Elementary School Music Teacher

BethAnn Hepburn teaches general music, Orff Ensemble, and choir to children ages nine through twelve in Streetsboro, Ohio. She has had the opportunity to teach Orff Schulwerk courses and workshops across the United States, Singapore, China, Scotland, and Malaysia. She is in her 20th year of music education and is the co-author of *Purposeful Pathways, Possibilities for the Elementary Music Classroom.*

Q: Describe your philosophy of listening to music.
A: I love listening to music that is non-western, and very much enjoy fusion music, bands like Dr. Didg, or Afro-Celt Sound System, which fuse together musics of several cultures in a new way. As a teacher, I believe listening activities should be engaging for students, active, and constitute a huge variety of music, various genres, and infused into each class period.

Q: How do you encourage elementary school children to listen attentively?
A: I often use a listening activity to demonstrate form or another musical concept, such as dynamic changes or legato vs. staccato. Depending on the goal of the listening, I may use movement through eurhythmics exercises, or creative movement for students to demonstrate form. I also have listening activities that involve props, such as cotton balls and white cloth to accompany Vivaldi's *Winter*: Students must actively respond to the dynamic changes as they listen with the cloth and cotton. I use Chinese fans and rice umbrellas when students are demonstrating phrase form with a slow legato motion to various Chinese songs like recordings of the Beijing Angelic Choir. The listening is usually active to keep students engaged.

Q: How do children of different ages respond when they are listening to world music?
A: I think this varies, depending on the expectation set by the teacher when it is introduced. I tell my students they are going to hear a new, exciting style of music, but they will not understand the words because it is in another language, so I need them to be mature about it, but I think they are ready to handle it. This sets the tone that the music should be taken seriously. I often use the music during beat activities, so listening to music of other places is just something we do. Because they become accustomed to it, it becomes second nature in our classroom. I find with upper grade students they enjoy singing in another language, and I often get requests for songs from their particular heritage. Even if songs are in the English language, knowing the meaning, or where a song is from creates more interest. When I taught K–2, there were often giggles, but at the same time, an excitement. I can recall listening to an *mbira* player from Zimbabwe, Ephat Mujuru, and his singing-story tale "Jamakina," and the first graders giggling at the accent, but then simply engaged in his story telling. Students also respond to the "quality" of the music, if the music has a new tonality and a slow tempo, they respond differently in their body than to music that is very rhythmic and upbeat. They also respond very differently when given a task to complete, for example, students holding sticks asked to respond with a sudden motion on a particular rhythm during a Japanese *taiko* activity feel very strong, and have bold posture during the activity compared to moving with bamboo sticks to flowing flute tones of *Shakuhachi* music. I use the later activity before I introduce the Japanese folk song, *Deta, Deta*. The first activity is good as a set up to Chinese drums and gong music or *taiko* style drumming. We may not have the exact equipment, but we go for the same effect with our classroom drums.

References

Campbell, P. S. (2004). *Teaching music globally*. New York: Oxford University Press.

Small, C. (1998). *Musicking*. Middletown, CT: Wesleyan University Press.

Recording List

"Didjeridu," two Aboriginal Songmen (from *Tribal Music of Australia*), Smithsonian Folkways Recordings, www.folkways.si.edu/didjeridu-puller-with-rhythmsticks/didjeridu/world/music/track/smithsonian

"El Carnaval de mi Tierra," Los Hermanos Lovo (from *¡Soy Salvadoreño! Chanchona Music from Eastern El Salvador*), Smithsonian Folkways Recordings, www.folkways.si.edu/los-hermanos-lovo/el-carnaval-de-mi-tierra-the-carnival-of-my-land/latin/music/track/smithsonian

"Maburu We (Oh, a Shoe, a Shoe)," young children of the Bakgaladi Culture Group (from *Traditional Music of Botswana, Africa: A Journey with Tape Recorder along Southern Botswana from Mochudi to Kang*), Smithsonian Folkways Recordings, www.folkways.si.edu/young-school-children-of-the-bakgaladi-group/tribal-songs-of-batswana-oh-a-shoe-oh-a-shoe/world/music/track/smithsonian

"Rast," (Video), Rahim Alhaj and Souhail Kaspar (no album), Smithsonian Folkways Recordings, www.folkways.si.edu/recording-song-rast/world/music/video/smithsonian

"Suwa Onbashira Kiyari-Taiko," Ensemble O-Suwa-Daiko (from *Japan: O-Suwa-Daiko Drums*), Smithsonian Folkways Recordings, www.folkways.si.edu/ensemble-o-suwa-daiko-under-the-direction-of-oguchi-daihachi/suwa-onbashira-kiyari-taiko/music/track/smithsonian

"Taqsim on the 'Oud-Andalusian Style,'" performers unknown (from *Melodies and Rhythms of Arabic Music*), Smithsonian Folkways Recordings, www.folkways.si.edu/melodies-and-rhythms-of-arabic-music/islamica-world/music/album/smithsonian

"Zaporozhetz (Sabre Dance)," Michael Skorr (from *17 Popular Ukrainian Dances*), Smithsonian Folkways Recordings, www.folkways.si.edu/michael-skorr-and-his-ukrainian-ensemble/zaporozhetz-sabre-dance/world/music/track/smithsonian

3

Participatory Musicking

The children in Ms. Andrews's third grade music class finish playing the rambunctious Anglo-American singing game Weevily Wheat *and noisily make their way to sit on the floor in their assigned row spots. When the recording of* El Carnaval de mi Tierra *begins to boom through the speakers, they immediately begin grooving with the music, some children patting their legs in time with the beat of the song, others making a "ch-ch-ch" sound with their mouths to mimic the sound of the media caña, a shaker-like instrument heard in this song from El Salvador. As the children settle down to the floor with their legs crossed, Ms. Andrews stops the music, saying, "I see that some of you remember the new mouth pattern we did last class! This time, everyone try that." She starts the recording again, and the students' mouths pucker up as they "ch" along with the recording. Ms. Andrews's critical eye scans the class and, satisfied that the students have retained this skill, she stops the recording after 30 seconds. "All right," she tells the class. "Today, we're going to work on the words of the chorus." A slide flashes up on the interactive whiteboard, showing the Spanish-language text of the song; she comments, "I don't speak Spanish. Can someone pronounce the words for me, and tell us what it means?" In this particular class, six students speak the language with their families, and four of those children volunteer. Ms. Andrews asks each of the four to read one line aloud "very slowly!" The class echoes, stumbling over some of the words now and again. After this is completed, the teacher sings each line, more slowly than the recording, and the class sings it back to her. After a few minutes of this, they sing the chorus straight through, with most students singing most of the words correctly. Ms. Andrews expects that mental fatigue is setting in after the pronunciation work, so she says, "OK, challenge time! We're going to try to sing it along with the recording." She starts the recording, cues the children just before the text starts, and they jump in, trying to sing along with the music. The words on the recording come at a much faster clip than the children just practiced, and many of the students immediately begin struggling in their attempt to sing along. The native Spanish speakers and the teacher, however, sing well, and as the chorus finishes, the class starts to laugh. "I know, not so good, huh?" says Ms. Andrews. "It's part of the process—we'll work on it next time! If you're a superstar, you can take a copy of the words home to practice on your own."*

Participatory Musicking in Children's Lives

When children hear music in their everyday lives, their natural instinct is to join in. Driving in the car on the way to sports practice or dance class, many elementary-aged children plead for their parents turn on the latest pop station. Often, they sing along—sometimes under their breath and sometimes at the top of their lungs; sometimes with correct words and sometimes with misunderstood texts; sometimes to the annoyance of their parents and sometimes as a full-throated family sing-along. Parents looking in the rearview mirror may see them idly drumming the beat on the car window or trying out some of the moves that they have seen on a music video. At professional sporting events, when the home team's theme song is blasted at top volume on scratchy loudspeakers, children may try to sing along with the crowd, moving in time to the music. In religious services, too, children in elementary school may hum along with songs that are common, but for which the words are not yet known. In all of these experiences, the music that surrounds children elicits their response, and participation ensues.

At other times, children recreate the music that they have previously heard, working to perfect it. After hearing pop songs in the car earlier in the day, a boy may start singing a favorite song while playing outside, and then scurry to the computer to search for the correct lyrics when he realizes he does not know them. In the privacy of her bedroom, a girl may work on dance moves, practicing over and over in front of the mirror then comparing her moves to those of the video that she sees online, planning to show off to her friends in the after-school program the following day. The girls on a local basketball team may recall the theme song they heard when their team attended the women's professional basketball game in the nearby city, and start singing it raucously on their journey home after a game, good-naturedly debating each other as to how much they sound like the recording at the arena. Families, too, may sing church songs together before meals, as a form of giving thanks. In all of these experiences, the young musicians have developed a fuller working knowledge of the same music. As they become more familiar with the music, they work towards recreating it, trying to attain the ideal sound as much as possible.

Participatory Musicking in World Music Pedagogy

These musical experiences spring organically in the lives of many children, unbidden and unplanned. When a teacher incorporates these modes of teaching and learning into the classroom, using them as a way to teach novel musics to children, then they become examples of World Music Pedagogy's second and third dimensions, Engaged Listening and Enactive Listening. According to Campbell (2004), Engaged Listening consists of "the active participation by a listener in some extent of music-making while the recorded (or live) music is sounding" (p. 91). Here, children are *doing* something musical, fulfilling the natural desire of children to actively engage in their learning. In the first dimension of WMP, Attentive Listening, children listened to music with particular questions in mind, but with Engaged Listening they move into what is naturally exciting for them, participating in the music making—they sing, they move, and they play instruments. At this juncture, the degree of their participation in the musicking is introductory and partial, as they do not yet know the music well enough (or have the musical facility) to be able to recreate the music exactly. Therefore, one of the principal features of Engaged Listening is that children hear music and participate in some aspect of musicking at the exact same time, because without the support of the sound source, the music would fall apart.

In some cases, these introductory experiences in which the children are only able to participate minimally in the musicking is as much as is possible. At other times, the recording may match the children's skills so that they are able to move into Enactive Listening, in which they work to recreate the music. In Enactive Listening, children alternate between sometimes performing with the recording, sometimes without the recording, all the while considering the ways in which they can render their performances to be more like those of the culture-bearer(s). Engaged Listening experiences are introductory activities in which the support of the sound source is absolutely necessary, but when children enter into Enactive Listening, they have heard the recording so many times that they have developed a fuller understanding of the music, with a deeper knowledge of all of the musical parts. During Enactive Listening, it becomes possible for the volume to be turned down and the music to continue, emanating completely from the children. The ultimate goal of Enactive Listening is to recreate all of the parts of a recording, reflecting the musical styling of the performers as closely as possible. Of course, children are typically less musically skilled than the adult musicians that they will often be attempting to imitate, and so modifications to meet the level of the students are always appropriate and continue to characterize the dimension of Enactive Listening.

This chapter addresses participatory musicking as it occurs in Engaged Listening and Enactive Listening. This section of the book will identify means by which to select music, design lessons involving Engaged and Enactive Listening, suggest assessment possibilities, and propose specific strategies for success to address potential challenges that may emerge. In the episodes that highlight specific aspects of participatory musicking, some incorporate solely Engaged Listening, others include solely Enactive Listening, and still others encompass both dimensions.

Engaged Listening in World Music

The types of activities that comprise Engaged Listening experiences are seemingly endless. In the Attentive Listening of Chapter 2, children are typically brand new to the music and are not invited to participate in music making. Rather, they listen, attempting to answer specific questions posed by the teacher. Here, the recording still sounds, but children respond with musical participation. In Engaged Listening, the students have now heard the music enough times to actively participate—but not enough to be successful in performing it by themselves. The support of the sound source is there for them in repeated attempts to listen and "join in" with the recording.

The following section provides an initial set of possible activities for teachers to consider when creating Engaged Listening activities involving world music. However, the options are extensive, and teachers should consider the various skills that their students possess when creating lessons and units for their classes.

Singing

In most elementary schools, vocal development is a central curricular goal, and verbally performing aspects of a recording is a common means by which to participate in Engaged Listening experiences with world music.

"LOO" ALONG WITH A SONG

In early stages of learning a song in a foreign language, children may know the tune of the song, but not well enough to sing the words. When initially singing along with the *conjunto* song *El Coco Royado*, it is easier for non-Spanish speakers to initially hum with the recording or sing on a neutral syllable such as "loo."

SING LYRICS ALONG WITH THE RECORDING

When children know the words of a song, they can sing with the recording. Singing the lyrics leads to a deeper experience with the music than "looing." At times, a teacher may decide that the effort required to learn the lyrics is too great to merit the time required to be successful, but singing with the words of the original language is preferred practice.

SING THE RESPONSE IN A CALL-AND-RESPONSE PIECE

Some musical forms lend themselves to partial participation in the piece. If children learn an African American spiritual in call-and-response form, they can perform the simpler response part along with the recording, while the performer on the recording sings the call.

HUM THE MELODY OF AN INSTRUMENTAL PIECE

When teachers select a piece of world music that is solely instrumental, humming a melody can be an effective first step towards performing the piece on a melodic instrument. Once children can hum the melody, they can work on transferring the melody to an instrument. In other cases, children may not have the instrumental skills to be able to perform the piece of music, and simply humming the melody can allow them to participate musically, even if it won't lead to instrumental performance.

SING THE FUNCTIONAL HARMONY UNDERNEATH THE MELODY

For musical cultures in which functional harmony is implied, such as Mexican or European folk songs, the children can use the word "bum," chord numbers, and/or *solfège* to sing the root of a chord that underlies a tune. This strategy can allow children to continue to hear a complex melody while participating vocally. Often, a teacher will model and perhaps sing along with the students.

SING IN PARTS

Common elementary music curricula include skills in which children maintain their musical part while simultaneously hearing another, typically beginning in second or third grade. Sometimes, the teacher might divide the class, with half singing the melody, while the other half sings the functional harmony along with the recording. At other times, the form of a piece of world music naturally lends itself to move beyond Engaged into Enactive experiences, such as the Russian vocal canon *Beriozka* (often called *The Birch Tree* in English), in which the children can eventually sing without the recording.

Playing Rhythms

For children, it is difficult to imagine music without rhythmic pulse and patterns. Class-based experiences that engage children in rhythmic performances along with the recording can often be initial forays into participatory ventures with the music that lead to children's success.

PERFORM THE BEAT

Music across the world often features a consistent and steady pulse, and "keeping the beat" is a core foundational skill for elementary students. Students can perform the beat in a variety of ways—patting their laps or other parts of their bodies, taking pencils to tap on the chairs or the floor, or performing the beat on non-pitched percussion instruments.

PERFORM THE DOWNBEAT

The musical concept of strong-weak is one that is salient across many musical traditions, and children can work on finding the downbeat, then express it through patting or playing instruments. Some genres, such as Balkan folk musics, contain meters that are less common to many children, with five, seven, or nine (or more!) beats per measure. In the *colotomic structure* of Javanese *gamelan*, a gong articulates the primary beat in a metrical format that is commonly 16 beats long. Finding the downbeat for those pieces can be an enjoyable challenge for students in upper elementary. Other musical cultures express the various beats in the meter in more complex fashion. In classical Indian music, for example, a person may represent the beats of the rhythmic cycle called the *tala* through movements such as hand clapping, touching fingers to hand, and waving. Children can be musically engaged in clapping and waving the *tala* while listening to a complex recording of music that they would not be able to perform themselves.

PERFORM THE RHYTHM

If a particular rhythmic pattern repeats throughout a piece of music, children can clap the rhythm along with the recording. Sometimes, these may be rhythms that are specific to the particular piece, or they may be a core aspect of a musical tradition. The *clave* rhythm that is common in many Latin American traditions can be easily performed by upper elementary children to accompany a Cuban *son*.

PERFORM RHYTHMS ON BODY PERCUSSION

Some musical traditions may contain percussion instruments or percussion patterns that contain more than one sound. In the Middle East, for example, some drum traditions incorporate contrasting sounds that are referred to as *dum* and *tek*, which to children unfamiliar with the tradition often sound like "high" and "low." In an attempt to replicate these musical expressions, children can use body percussion—snapping, clapping, stomping, or patting their chest, cheeks, head, lap, or bellies—in an effort to reproduce the music in a child-friendly fashion that nonetheless reflects the musical principles. Similarly, the higher and lower sounds produced by double bells such as the *gankogui* or *agogô* from West Africa can be simulated by patting different parts of the body.

Playing Melodies

In many schools, elementary-aged children are developing skills on instruments such as recorder, xylophone, ukulele, or guitar. When the melodies of world music are played on novel instruments with unique sounds, children's eyes open wide and their ears stay on high alert. What *is* that sound, they wonder, and can I do it? Generally speaking, the ability of elementary children to perform instrumental melodies on instruments is more challenging than either singing or playing rhythms. However, depending on the skill of the children, they can participate in introductory fashion by performing along with a recording in a variety of ways.

PLAY A SIMILAR INSTRUMENT

Some curricula in the upper elementary include a unit in which children learn guitar. In addition to classic folk songs from traditional textbooks, students can also learn chords to accompany *mariachi* music, which typically incorporates two guitar-like instruments (the *guitarrón* and the *vihuela*) in addition to the guitar. This might be simulated in the classroom by a ukulele. Other musical genres use instruments that are similar to those that are used in a given music class. For example, children can play Peruvian panpipe melodies on recorders, Shona-style *marimba* tunes on xylophones, or Egyptian *oud* pieces on guitars.

PLAY A DIFFERENT INSTRUMENT

Sometimes, a musical genre highlights an instrument that children do not know or cannot play. To engage all children in participatory musicking, it can be appropriate to allow them to play a given part on an instrument that they *do* know. A steel pan tune from the Caribbean can be performed on xylophones or a Mongolian horsehead fiddle tune can be played on a recorder. This recontextualization makes for a substantially different sonic experience—but can lead to discussions about what can make the music sound "good," and what that means.

PLAY A SIMPLIFIED PART ON AN INSTRUMENT

Often, recordings of world music feature performances that are beyond the competence of elementary students, particularly when it comes to instrumental skill. Simplifying an instrumental part so that they can play along with it is an effective way to provide students with the opportunity to actively participate. Parts can be modified in a variety of ways: (a) fast runs can be simplified to play only the melodic skeleton; (b) the functional harmony can be simplified by performing only the chord roots or playing each chord less frequently; or (c) one part can be broken up into multiple parts, so that individual students are responsible for only a portion of the performance. For example, in a unit on *mariachi* music, fifth grade children studying guitar are not likely to have developed the facility to play their instruments as quickly as the recording. Instead, they can play the chords on the downbeat of each measure.

Caution! In participatory musicking experiences, the students are often playing while the recording occurs. With instruments, tuning can be an issue—if classroom instruments are a quarter step different from the recording, the resulting musical experience will be highly unsatisfying for all. When this occurs, options are to (a) limit instrumental accompaniment to instruments that do not require specific tunings, such as nonpitched percussion, or (b) transfer the musical recording to a computer program that can modify the pitch of the recording to match the instruments in your classroom.

Moving

When elementary children are asked about their favorite part of the school day, their immediate reply is often "Recess!" During this period of life, many children seem to be in constant movement, running at top speed on the playground or bouncing their feet while sitting at their desks. To capitalize upon this natural inclination, elementary music classrooms often include folk dance, creative dance, singing games, and other forms of movement that provide children the opportunity to express themselves physically. Selecting world music experiences that naturally incorporate movement or finding ways to create movement activities can be engaging for all children, even if they are unable to sing or play instruments with the musical recording.

STEP OR MARCH THE BEAT

In addition to patting the beat on their lap or an instrument, children can demonstrate the beat by moving throughout the space while the music is playing. Those in early

Figure 3.1 American children playing a *tinikling* game from the Philippines

Photo courtesy of BethAnn Hepburn

elementary will be more apt to be successful with a piece that has a steady, pulsive quality, while older students may be challenged by a piece with a beat structure that is harder to hear, such as an Afro-Peruvian *landó*.

STEP OR CONDUCT THE METER

If students have developed skills at marching the beat, they can kinesthetically represent the meter, either by stepping only on the downbeats, or by stepping deeply on the downbeats and more lightly on the off-beats. In classes where children have learned basic conducting patterns, they can conduct along with the recording. Students who need a still greater challenge can conduct while they step the beat. For children in upper elementary, a piece in changing meters such as Botswana's *Maburu We* (Learning Pathway #1) can provide an extra challenge.

PLAY A SINGING GAME ALONG WITH A RECORDING

Since singing games come from children's cultures, they typically involve songs that children can learn, regardless of their culture of origin. While ultimately they will likely be able to sing a song and play the accompanying singing game, an introductory step can be for students to play a game along with a recording. The singing game *Kye Kye Kule* (sometimes spelled *Che Che Coolay* or *Cooley*), for example, has been found in Ghana as well as other places in Africa. Recordings and videos of culture-bearers can be found online, and the children can play the game while listening to the singers from the culture of origin. (See end of the chapter for an abbreviated list of singing games with links to recordings.)

PERFORM A FOLK DANCE

Folk dances from around the world can afford children the opportunity to learn the nuances of a musical culture, even if the music is challenging enough that they cannot perform any of it themselves. Further, the movement involved in folk dances often reflects the melodic form of the music, leading to logical connections to concept-based curricular goals. If students learn a Greek dance in the meter of 7/4, the dance may help them internalize the unfamiliar meter.

DEMONSTRATE MUSICAL ELEMENTS THROUGH CREATIVE MOVEMENT

Some aspects of music will lend themselves to creative movement. If a piece contains a recurring melodic motif, for example, students can work in groups to create a movement to represent that motif, and then perform it when they hear the part.

Combine Any of the Above

Musicians around the world often engage in multiple musical activities at once, such as the dancing and singing that is common in the contemporary *K-Pop* performances in South Korea or the singing and guitar playing that characterizes old-time folk performers in the United States. As children move through the elementary grades, their musical sophistication and abilities expand, and many are able to perform two musical acts at the same time. Children may simultaneously sing and pat the beat, step the beat while clapping the rhythm, or sing one part while playing a different instrumental part.

The two episodes that follow offer introductory Engaged Listening experiences, the first in which the primary form of participating is singing and the second in which the primary form is playing instruments. Episode 3.1 highlights a sequence for Engaged Listening using music from the American popular music artist Taylor Swift. The vast majority of episodes in this book incorporate musical genres from folk, indigenous, and classical traditions from around the world, but World Music Pedagogy can be used in virtually any musical context. To make this episode successful, precede the experience with Attentive Listening activities that address the verse-chorus structure, listening for the repeated text in the chorus.

Episode 3.1: United States: "Welcome to New York"

Specific Use: Upper Elementary General Music Class

Materials:

- "Welcome to New York," Taylor Swift (from *T.S. 1989*) American popular song available on iTunes and Spotify
- Song lyrics, printed on paper or projected on the board

Procedure:

(Engaged)

1. Sing the chorus with the words (with lyrics provided).
   a. Play track (0:42–1:25).
2. Clap on the off-beat during the introduction and first verse, then sing chorus with words.
   a. Play track (0:00–1:25).
3. Sing first verse (with lyrics provided) and chorus, clapping on the off-beat, "if you want the challenge."
   a. Play track (0:00–1:25), observing children's responses. Repeat if necessary.
4. Repeat (3), while teacher sings a bass line accompaniment using *solfège*.
   a. Play track (0:00–1:25).
   b. Bass line *solfège*, starting at the chorus (0:45):

      d—s,—f,—f,— (repeat four times)

      d—d—s,—s,—f,—f,—

      f,—s,—l,— l,—s,—s,—f,—f,—f,—f,—

      d—s,—f,—f,— (repeat two times)

5. Sing bass line accompaniment (with *solfège* posted on board).
   a. Play track (0:00–1:25), observing children's responses. Repeat if necessary.
6. Split the class in two parts: half sing bass line; half sing verse and chorus.
   a. Play track (0:00–1:25), observing children's responses. Repeat if necessary.
7. Optional: Sing the verse and chorus, showing Curwen hand signs for the bass line at the same time.
   a. Play track (0:00–1:25).

The following episode (Episode 3.2) brings back Learning Pathway #3, the *taiko* percussion piece *Suwa Onbashira Kiyari-Taiko* from Japan. This particular experience with Engaged Listening follows the Attentive Listening activities in the episode in Chapter 2, offering children the opportunity to participate kinesthetically before moving to the percussion instruments. Additionally, it provides the opportunity for children to experiment with sounds by asking them to determine the best way to represent the music of the recording, rather than relying solely on the teacher. Upper elementary students almost always enjoy drumming activities, and those who may be reticent to participate in other activities in music class will usually enthusiastically join in when drumming is involved. The increasing tempo renders a typically simple experience such as patting or walking the beat more interesting for children in upper elementary school.

Episode 3.2: Japan: "Suwa Onbashira Kiyari-Taiko" (Learning Pathway #3)

Specific Use: Upper Elementary General Music Class

Materials:

- "Suwa Onbashira Kiyari-Taiko," Ensemble O-Suwa-Daiko (from *Japan: O-Suwa-Daiko Drums*), Smithsonian Folkways Recordings
- Tambourines or jingle bells (optional)
- *Taiko* or other drums, with felt mallets or drumsticks (optional)

Procedure:

(Engaged)

1. Pat the beat.
   a. Play track (3:15–4:10), observing responses. Repeat if necessary.

2. Walk the beat.
   a. Play track (3:15–4:10), observing responses. Repeat if necessary.
3. Walk the beat, moving arms low for the low drum sound and high for the high drum sound.
   a. Play track (3:15–4:10), observing responses. Repeat if necessary.
4. Repeat (3), shake different body parts during the "roll" section.
   a. Play track (3:15–4:10), observing responses. Repeat if necessary.
5. Standing still, "clap a repeated rhythmic pattern that stands out to you" during the first part of the excerpt.
   a. Play track (3:15–3:45), observing responses. Repeat if necessary.
6. Standing still, play the high drum sounds on the chest and low drum sounds on the legs.
   a. Play track (3:15–3:45), observing responses. Repeat if necessary.
7. Repeat (5) and (6), with the second part of the excerpt.
   a. Play track (3:45–4:10), observing responses. Repeat if necessary.
8. Distribute drums. "How might you imitate the sounds of the drums on the recording with the instruments that we have?"
   a. Give 30–60 seconds to explore. Field responses from individuals.
9. "Listen to the recording: Which suggestion sounded the most like the Ensemble O-Suwa Daiko?"
   a. Play track (3:15–4:10), field responses. Coalesce around a decision.
10. Perform rhythm with recording. "Don't play too loudly, so that we can hear the music."
   a. Play track (3:15–4:10), observing responses. Repeat, if necessary.
11. (Optional): Add tambourines or sleigh bells on beat, "rolling" when that sound occurs.
   a. Play track (3:15–4:10), observing responses. Repeat, if necessary.

Many classrooms will not own *taiko* drums, but may have other options such as frame, tubano, or *djembe* drums. In schools that have more than one type of drum, the teacher can ask the children to choose the classroom drum that most resembles the recording. If only frame drums are available, groups of three children can play; one holds a larger drum, one a smaller drum, and one plays with mallets.

Enactive Listening in World Music

When children have listened repeatedly to a piece of music, typically through Attentive and Engaged Listening experiences, they grow to know the music. The natural inclination is to turn off the music and try to replicate the sound of the recordings. This dimension is Enactive Listening, which Campbell (2004) has called "the third and potentially deepest level of listening" (p. 126). Enactive listening not only emphasizes recreating music from a recording, but doing so in a manner that pays explicit attention to the nuances of the performance practice, moving towards a performance that is as reflective of the culture-bearers as possible. Depending on the piece of music and age of the children, this may be as simple as trying to emulate the specific pronunciation of words in an unfamiliar language or as complex as working towards an exact replication of a complex rhythm that cannot easily be notated in Western notation. To do this, children alternate between performing with the recording and without the recording. They grow in their ability to replicate significant aspects of the music without the support of the recording, but regularly refer back to the sound source to check their progress, asking questions such as, What can we do differently? How can we change our performance to more accurately reproduce that of the culture-bearers? Thus, the major differences between Engaged and Enactive Listening are two: First, in Enactive Listening, the children have a much deeper understanding of and ability to perform the music; and second, the ultimate goal of Enactive Listening is to perform as many of the sonic qualities of the recording as possible without the sound source. To the children, the significance of this second difference is immense. With Enactive Listening, they develop a sense of ownership over the music, as they incorporate the sounds into their beings, and begin to see themselves as independent musicians—a goal of music educators everywhere.

Without the Recording, What Sounds Good?

Some Engaged Listening activities cannot effectively be turned into Enactive Listening. Without the recording sounding, some experiences will not be musically satisfying. For example, patting the beat—a common activity with Engaged Listening—does not have any musical meaning without a fuller sound source to surround it. Similarly, Engaged Listening experiences such as conducting a song or singing functional harmony will appear to have little musical purpose without the melody. However, when joined together in sequence, Engaged and Enactive Listening can produce musically satisfying experiences for children. Similarly, it is possible to perform parts of Taylor Swift's 2014 pop hit *Welcome to New York* without the recording, but it may be more enjoyable to sing it with the accompaniment.

At times, one aspect of an Engaged Listening experience will not be successful by itself, but if joined with other parts, it will lead to a pleasing musical experience. In *El Carnaval de mi Tierra*, for example, playing the beat on rhythm sticks will not produce a satisfying sound without the recording. However, if a small group of children plays the beat on rhythm sticks, while three other small groups sing the melody, sing the harmony, and make the "ch-ch-ch" rhythmic sound of the shaker, the sonic result will be musically rewarding. The combination of parts renders it more of an Enactive experience, as the piece begins to take shape.

Practice a Part

Enactive Listening experiences at the elementary school level usually include practicing one or more parts. For example, in the opening vignette, Ms. Andrews' goal was that the children begin to learn the words of the chorus of *El Carnaval de mi Tierra*. The song occurs at a fast clip, and for students who were not Spanish speakers, learning the words was challenging. In this case, Ms. Andrews stopped the recording and taught the music by rote at a much slower speed than they are sung on the recording. In future classes, the children's growing familiarity with the text would allow the tempo to increase, even without additional conscious work on the lyrics. In the dimensions of World Music Pedagogy, learning the text without the recording is typically Enactive Listening because the activity works towards fully learning the piece by way of the oral/aural tradition.

Modify a Part

With some music, children can recreate the sounds exactly as they are heard on a recording. Singing games, for example, come from children's cultures, and although it may be challenging to learn the words if they are in an unfamiliar language, the musical characteristics usually do not pose extensive challenges to students. When performing other music, particularly adult music, there may be musical characteristics that render Engaged Listening experiences musically challenging. In these situations, teachers can make modifications through Enactive Listening experiences. For example:

- When practicing a challenging drum rhythm on a *djembe* from a Ghanaian drumming tradition, the teacher can slow the tempo to allow children a chance to perform it perfectly, and then gradually speed it up.
- If an educator is teaching a Mexican *marimba* piece that falls in B Major on a recording, children with xylophones typical in elementary schools will not have all of the bars to be able to perform in that key. With Enactive Listening, after numerous Attentive and Engaged Listening activities, the recording can be turned off, and the children can practice the piece with C as the tonic.

Modify a Part Digitally

Technological means exist to alter recordings. For example, there are apps and other computer-based programs that allow listeners to change the tempo of a recording or change the key. After working on the piece in a more accessible tempo or key, the recording can be converted back to its original state to compare the differences and ground the children's musicking in the musical source.

Episode 3.3 offers an episode that features both Engaged and Enactive Listening experiences with the song *Rocky Road*, a children's singing game from Jamaica. The Engaged Listening that begins the episode highlights the introductory nature of this dimension of World Music Pedagogy, with activities that, at this point in the children's learning, can only be performed while the recording is sounding. After repeated experiences with Engaged Listening, the children begin to know it well enough that they can perform the piece without the recording—but with a caveat. On the recording, the singing game is accompanied by a guitar, an instrument that children in the middle elementary grades likely will not have learned. Therefore, the instrumentation can be modified so that the children can play instruments that they are more likely to know, such as ukuleles, recorders or xylophones. Although the sound of recorders playing functional harmony will produce a sound that differs greatly from the recording, the reflective nature of the end of the lesson renders this a classic example of Enactive Listening in action.

Episode 3.3 suggests that children play an engaging singing game with the song "Rocky Road." The game begins with two lines of partners, facing each other. Each pair joins hands to form an arch. The couple at the top of the line drops hands, ducks their heads, and walks through the arches to the other end, forming an arch again when they get there. The other couples follow in succession, until all have gone under the arches. When the first couple is once again at the top of the set, each pair then drops hands and walks down the outside of the lines, making an arch when they make it to the bottom. Repeat until song is complete.

Episode 3.3: Jamaica: "Rocky Road"

Specific Use: Middle Elementary General Music Class

Materials:

- "Rocky Road," Louise Bennett (from *Children's Jamaican Songs and Games*), Smithsonian Folkways Recordings
- Lyrics of song, posted on the board
- Guitars (if available, and if students have the necessary skills), or
- Xylophones (if available, and if students have the necessary skills)

Procedure:

(Engaged)

1. Sing response along with the recording.
   a. Play track (0:00–0:34).
2. Sing call with the recording (with lyrics provided).
   a. Play track (0:00–0:34), observing children's responses. Repeat if necessary.
3. Half the class sings call, the other half sings response.
   a. Play track (0:00–0:34), observing children's responses. Repeat if necessary.
4. Sing functional harmony, either *solfège* (do/so/fa) or on numbers (I/IV/V).
   a. Play track (0:00–0:34), observing children's responses. Repeat if necessary.

      Lines 1–4: I-I-V-I (each chord held for a measure)

      Line 5: IV-I-V-I (each chord held for a measure)

5. Play the singing game along with the recording, singing a preferred part.
   a. After explaining game directions, play entire track (0:00–1:32)

(Enactive)

1. Sing with the recording: Half the class sings call, the other half sings response; switch.
   a. Play track (0:00–0:34).
2. Sing without the recording: Half the class sings call, the other half sings response; switch.
   a. Play track (0:00–0:34). Repeat, if necessary.
3. With the recording sounding (0:00–0:34), split into three parts: 1/3 sing call; 1/3 sing response; 1/3 sing functional harmony.
   a. Repeat, without the recording sounding.
4. Transfer the functional harmony to an instrument (I = C chord; V = G chord; IV = F chord).
   a. Guitar or ukulele (to most aptly reflect the recording)
   b. Xylophone or recorder (if students have those skills instead)
5. Without the recording, perform the piece: 1/3 sing call; 1/3 sing response; 1/3 play functional harmony on an instrument.
6. "Think about what our performance sounds like as we listen to the recording again. What is the same? What is different? What could we do in our performance to sound more like the recording?"
   a. Play track (0:00–0:34), then field responses. Repeat to check answers.
7. Without recording, perform piece again, implementing students' suggestions.

Figure 3.2 "Rocky Road" from Jamaica

Bennett, L. (1957). Childrens' [sic] Jamaican Songs and Games. *Sound Recording, FW 7250. Note: The lyrics are presented here as in the liner notes.*

Selecting Musical Material for Participatory Musicking

Many of the principles that warrant consideration when selecting music for Attentive Listening experiences are also relevant for both Engaged Listening and Enactive Listening. As noted in Chapter 1, children are more motivated and attentive when they are making music that holds most of the following characteristics: steady beat, faster tempo, clear tonal center, and melodic consonance. However, many other key aspects come into play when choosing music for students to be successfully involved in participatory musicking, particularly for Enactive Listening in which children might be challenged to sing or play what they hear on the recording.

Repetition

Examples that contain musical repetition lead to more successful participatory musicking with world music. Repetition not only elicits enthusiasm and stimulates children to focus their attention during Attentive Listening, but it also facilitates a more time-efficient learning process during Engaged and Enactive Listening. If children are learning a xylophone piece from the Ivory Coast in West Africa, for example, they will be able to master a repeating melody much more quickly than one that is through-composed. Repetition does not have to be exact. In some traditions, there is a core musical pattern, but then improvisation occurs around it. For example, drummers in the Middle East often incorporate two main performing techniques; a *dum* stroke is produced in the center of the drum, and a *tek* stroke is played on the edge. The following rhythm is common:

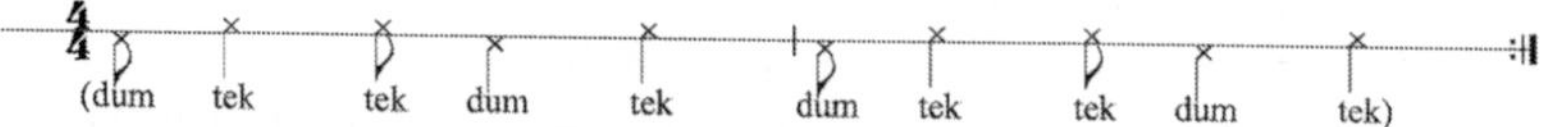

Often, though, a drummer will perform similar rhythms that deviate slightly from that pattern. Working to decode all the patterns to exactly replicate the performance can be overly time consuming. Instead, the children can perform the characteristic pattern along with the recording. The teacher can lead the students to discover that the performers on the recording are improvising, telling them that this is a common musical experience—thereby providing some relevant information about the musical culture while also allowing them to be musically engaged. This knowledge sets the stage for improvising their own music in a similar style, as will be discussed in Chapter 5.

Song Texts

Lessons in which children learn a song in another language can be tedious and time consuming, due to the challenges of learning how to pronounce words and remembering the sounds that carry no meaning for non-speakers. Some factors to consider when determining how to teach song texts:

SELECT MUSIC WITH ENGLISH-LANGUAGE COGNATES

Some languages contain words that sound very much like their English equivalent. In *El Carnaval de mi Tierra* (Learning Pathway #2), for example, the Spanish word "*carnaval*" does indeed translate to "carnival." Knowing even one word can serve as an anchor for students, and they can more easily recall the unfamiliar words around it.

SELECT MUSIC WHERE THE TEXT IS NOT TOO FAST

When the words fly past at the speed of a bullet train, it is very difficult for students to replicate them. When possible, teachers can select songs in which the texts are sung at a slower pace.

LYRICS: SHOW THE WORDS ON THE BOARD

To help students learn texts in unfamiliar languages, a variety of strategies can help speed the process. Often, music teachers want to focus on skills of aural learning and musical memory, asking children to use their ears and minds to learn music. However, with words in unfamiliar languages, this can be challenging. Providing children with the song texts makes it much easier for them to replicate the music. When the lyrics are displayed in the front of the classroom on a whiteboard (rather than on individual pieces of paper), the teacher can also point to specific words, making connections for the students.

LYRICS: LINE OUT THE WORDS

There are two common ways to teach songs. In the "whole song method," a teacher can sing the whole song multiple times, and over time the students will join in, first singing the parts they know, and eventually singing the whole song. In the "phrase-by-phrase approach," the teacher can sing one line at a time, asking the children to repeat it. Once each line is learned, the teacher then joins some of the lines together in longer phrases, and eventually the children learn the whole song. The whole song method tends to be a more musical experience for the children (and the teacher), because the song is not broken down into small bits. With songs in other languages, however, the complexity of the lyrics makes the phrase-by-phrase method typically more effective. The children may simply need to hear the individual words in order to retain them.

SING A PORTION OF THE LYRICS

If a song has a great deal of complicated text, a teacher can decide to ask the children to sing only part of it. In *El Carnaval de mi Tierra*, for example, students can learn the words of the chorus, but sing the verses on "loo."

The Brazilian song *O'Embole, Embole—Embolada* comes from an improvisatory tradition in which singers make up verses about contemporary issues. In Episode 3.4, the lesson begins with Engaged Listening, as the children play small percussion and sing various parts along with the recording. It becomes Enactive as the children develop the skill to sing the piece without the music playing. The episode highlights choices a teacher makes when selecting songs in foreign languages. In this case, the children sing the repetitive portion of the text in Portuguese, while the more challenging sections are in English. It also represents the Enactive process of singing without the music and then turning the music back on to compare their performance with that on the recording, ultimately culminating in a more representative performance. In the episode, the children sing a chorus that has been pre-composed by the teacher. The genre more typically requires improvisation on part of the performers, the type of activity that will be included in Chapter 5, Creating World Music. To be successful, this episode would have been preceded by experiences in which the students listened for repeated patterns in the vocal line and discovered the language, culture of origin, and instrumentation through Attentive Listening experiences.

Episode 3.4: Brazil: "O' Embole, Embole—Embolada"

Specific Use: Middle Elementary General Music Class

Materials:

- "O' Embole, Embole—Embolada," performers unknown (from *Songs and Dances from Brazil*), Smithsonian Folkways Recordings
- Tambourines (or sleigh bells)
- Xylophones (optional)

Procedure:

(Engaged)

1. Sing along with the chorus ("Oy bole, bole, Oy bole, bola").
   a. Play track (0:00–0:56).
   b. Repeat (1), starting directly before the chorus (0:22–0:56).
2. Play tambourine or sleigh bells on the beat.
   a. Play track (0:00–0:56).
   b. (Note: The instruments play twice as fast as this on the recording, but most children will not have the facility to play instruments at such a rapid pace.)
3. Sing functional harmony, beginning when chorus starts.
   Chorus: I-V-V-I (repeated)
   Verse: V-I-V-I
   a. Play track (0:00–0:56).

(Enactive)

1. Without the music playing, sing the words of the chorus, working on the words as necessary.
2. Listen to the chorus on the recording, checking the pronunciation of the text and the vocal "sliding" into the first word of the phrase.
   a. Play track (0:22–0:56), field responses.
   b. Without the music playing, sing the chorus.

3. Sing functional harmony with recording.
    a. Play track (0:00–0:56).
    b. Without the music playing, sing chorus and functional harmony.
4. Listen to recording, checking pronunciation and vocal styling.
    a. Play track (0:22–0:56).
    b. Without the music playing, sing chorus and functional harmony.
5. Learn a teacher-composed verse concerning a topic of the students' interest.
6. Without the music playing, sing the verse, chorus, and functional harmony during the chorus.
7. Listen to recording, then compare the class's performance to those of the culture-bearers.
    a. Play track (0:00–0:56), field responses.
8. Final performance: Select one child to sing the verse, while the rest of the class performs the verse and chorus.

Putting It Together: Designing Lessons of Participatory Musicking

A well-selected musical example is the first step, but to create a successful lesson that incorporates participatory musicking with world music, it is essential to thoughtfully create a sequence that will lead to students' success. The following section uses Learning Pathway #2, *El Carnaval de mi Tierra*, to highlight a process of created a series of lessons for Engaged and Enactive Listening.

Brainstorm All Possibilities

The first step is to listen to the recording and write down everything possible that the students could do. Teachers can start with the list from earlier in the chapter and consider: Is this idea appropriate for this particular piece of music? For most pieces, tapping or patting the beat will be an option in Engaged Listening, since most pieces incorporate a steady beat. However, playing the functional harmony on an instrument will only work if the harmonic progression is fairly consistent and repetitive.

Decide: What Makes "Musical Sense?"

All ideas are not equal, and some possible musical activities do not reflect important aspects of the musical culture, would not be musically satisfying, or are simply too difficult for students. For example, in *El Carnaval de mi Tierra*, the song holds a pulsive quality right from the beginning, and performing the beat in some way will be a musically satisfying experience in an introductory way. Patting the downbeat, on the other hand, would be less enjoyable and musically relevant. While the music possesses a strong-weak metrical pattern, identifying and performing the beat to represent the meter is not central to the musical experience from the children's perspective.

What Will Children Enjoy?

After winnowing down the list of possible musical activities, the teacher can determine if there are some options that merit inclusion because the students would find them enjoyable. For example, chanting the rhythmic ostinato of the *media caña* shaker on "ch-ch-ch-ch" would be enjoyable for most students. On the other hand, the tune of the violin part is played very rapidly. While it is conceivable that children could learn to play the violin part on a xylophone, a teacher would need to decide if it was worth investing the time to teach that particular part, given the musical outcome. If the school has a strong orchestra program or a *mariachi* band, children who are members could play a simplified version on their stringed instruments.

Select the Activities

At this point, the teacher will still have a large number of options and must identify the possibilities that are best for this lesson. There is no set number of activities that is appropriate; it will depend on the time that a teacher wants to spend on the lesson, the curricular goals, and the musical skills of the students. Below, see a winnowed list of activities to include in the lesson.

LIST OF ACTIVITIES: *EL CARNAVAL DE MI TIERRA*

Included Activity	**Rationale**
*Sing I-V harmonies with the chorus	*Pattern of I-V is repetitive and easy to learn
*Pat the beat	*Pulse is strong; easy first activity
*Play the beat on rhythm sticks	*Gives children a chance to play an instrument, and is easy
*Say the rhythm pattern of the shaker ostinato with "ch-ch-ch"	*Fun!
*Sing the chorus with words	*Singable words, repeating text, core musical element of the song

Excluded Activity	**Rationale**
*Sing the verses with words	*Text would take too long to learn
*Play I-V harmonies on xylophone	*Tuning is not the same
*March downbeat	*From third grader's perspective, meter is not as salient an issue as other ideas

Organize the Activities in Order of Difficulty

Some activities will be easier than others. In the list for *El Carnaval de mi Tierra*, the two singing activities will be more difficult than the rhythmic work, due to the time it will take to learn the text. Logically, those experiences would occur after the rhythmic activities. Additionally, the fact that the students will hear the text and melody while working on rhythmic aspects will allow the words and chords to become unconsciously embedded in their ears. An order for the activities can be found below.

ORDER OF ACTIVITIES: *EL CARNAVAL DE MI TIERRA*

1. Keep the beat along with the recording (0:00–1:01).
2. Perform the beat on rhythm sticks (0:00–1:01).

3. Speak the rhythm pattern of the shaker ostinato with the syllables "ch-ch-ch" (0:00–0:30).
4. Sing chorus with words (0:43–1:01).
5. Sing I-V harmonies during the chorus (0:43–1:01).
6. Half the class sings chorus with the words, while the other half sings I-V harmonies (0:43–1:01).

Shift Between Attentive, Engaged, and Enactive Listening

Attentive Listening will almost always precede Engaged Listening. To effectively reproduce sounds on recordings, children need to listen to the recordings first—if they join in too quickly, they are likely to perform incorrectly. Similarly, Engaged Listening will almost always precede Enactive Listening. Before reproducing the sounds without a recording, it will almost always be more successful if they have performed the music with the recording first. However, an effective lesson will iteratively shift between all three dimensions, allowing children a chance to exercise different types of thinking and musicking.

Episode 3.5 provides a final list of activities for participatory musicking with the song *El Carnaval de mi Tierra* (Learning Pathway #2). This episode can be seen as the first lesson in a series of lessons, one that incorporates Attentive Listening, Engaged Listening, and Enactive Listening in a way that will elicit and maintain children's interest with incremental steps. These steps will lead the children towards the ability to fully know and perform the piece.

Episode 3.5: El Salvador: "El Carnaval de mi Tierra" (Learning Pathway #2)

Specific Use: Upper Elementary General Music Class

Materials:

- "El Carnaval de mi Tierra," Los Hermanos Lovo (from *¡Soy Salvadoreño! Chanchona Music from Eastern El Salvador)*, Smithsonian Folkways Recordings

Procedure:

(Engaged)

1. Pat the beat on different parts of the body, copying the teacher.
   a. Play track (0:00–1:01).

(Attentive)

2. Identify the instruments in the introduction. (A: Bass, two guitars, two violins, shaker, percussion.)
    a. Play track (0:00–0:26), field responses. Repeat to check answers.

(Engaged)

3. Lightly pat the beat on laps and identify which instrument is playing the beat during the introduction. (A: It sounds like a wooden instrument.)
    a. Play track (0:00–0:26), field responses.
4. Play the beat on the rhythm sticks, through the chorus.
    a. Play track (0:00–1:01).

(Attentive)

5. Listen to the teacher clap the following pattern, then identify the instrument playing it on the recording. (A: A *guiro*-like instrument called a *media caña*.)
    a. Play track (0:00–0:26).

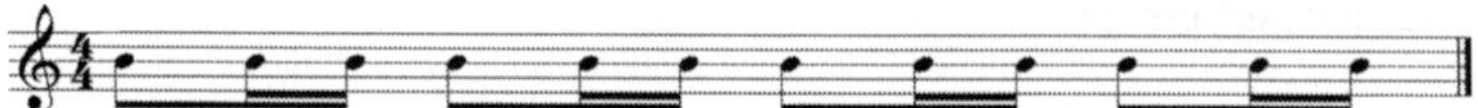

(Engaged)

6. Echo the teacher, who models the modified rhythm of the *media caña* shaker on the consonants "ch":

7. Chant the ostinato of the *media caña* rhythm on "ch-ch-ch" with the recording.
    a. Play track (0:00–0:26), observing responses. Repeat if necessary.

(Engaged and Attentive)

8. Repeat step (7), but play the recording further. Raise hand when a new voice or instrument enters, and identify the sound. (A: Male voice enters at 0:26.)
    a. Play track (0:00–0:40), field responses.

(Attentive)

9. Listen to the voice, identifying the language in which the performers are singing, and the number of singers. (A: Spanish; two.)
   a. Play track (0:26–1:01), field responses.
10. Listen to the chorus, following along with words posted on the board. Identify any known words. (A: Students may recognize "carnaval" as "carnival.")
   a. Play track (0:43–1:01), field responses.

(Engaged and Enactive)

11. Learn words by rote, echoing the teacher.
12. Sing chorus with recording.
   a. Play track (0:43–1:01), observing responses. Repeat if necessary.

(Enactive)

13. 1/3 class sings chorus; 1/3 class keeps beat on sticks; 1/3 class chants rhythm on "ch."
14. Check performance against recording, identifying areas to improve.
   a. Play track (0:00–1:01), field responses.
15. Repeat (13): Perform all three parts without recording, with student suggestions in mind.

As noted earlier, other aspects of World Music Pedagogy may be brought in at different points in this lesson segment as well. For example, in the above lesson, the students have not learned anything about the cultural context of the song—not even where it is from. That information is almost always provided early in a lesson, but it qualifies as Integrating World Music, so it has been saved for that chapter.

Other Considerations for Participatory Musicking

Consider Spreading a Lesson Over Multiple Days

Many elementary classroom teachers structure their lessons with multiple short activities that address different objectives. In a 30-minute third grade lesson, for example, a teacher might plan a segment that includes singing in a round, learning a xylophone piece, working in small groups on a composition activity, and practicing a newly learned *solfège* note. The *El Carnaval de mi Tierra* episode would likely take 20–25 minutes, after fielding various responses from students and ensuring that each step of the sequence is mastered.

Teachers may find it more successful to take a plan like the episode for *El Carnaval de mi Tierra* and break it into two or more classes. One option for the above lesson episode would be to dedicate 10 minutes on the first day, ending when the children chant the ostinato of the shaker (steps 1–7). The second lesson could begin on step 7 as a review, and then continue on through learning the words of the chorus (steps 8–12). On a third day, after a brief review, all three parts (the beat, rhythmic ostinato, and chorus) could be performed at once.

Processes of Learning: Listening, Watching, Imitating, or Reading

When children are taught music of the world's cultures through World Music Pedagogy, the goal is not only that they learn to perform the music itself, but also to understand cultural aspects of the music. This includes acquiring information about the people who are making the music, the role that the music plays in the culture, and the context in which it occurs. Part of this also includes the way that it is taught: In the home culture, how does one learn the music? Ideally, teachers should strive to teach the music in a fashion that is as culturally appropriate as possible. When the teacher decides on a particular musical response from the children, there are often multiple ways that it can be taught. Some of these may be culturally representative, and some may not. In *El Carnaval de mi Tierra*, the rhythm of the *media caña* shaker could be taught in at least five different ways:

LISTENING

Students can listen to the recording to "figure out the rhythm that the shaker is playing." Once they note the repeated rhythmic pattern, they can lightly tap along with the recording. One overarching principle of World Music Pedagogy is to ground the experience in the sounds of culture-bearers, so this is often an effective way for children to begin to get a feel for the music.

LISTENING, TAKE 2

Alternatively, the teacher can demonstrate the pattern, and then challenge the children to identify the instrument that is playing the rhythm. After playing the recording once to decide the answer, the children can clap along. This still grounds the activity in the recording, but is perhaps slightly easier.

LISTENING AND WATCHING

In the particular case of *El Carnaval de mi Tierra*, there is a video of the song that can be freely viewed through the Smithsonian Folkways website. The teacher can clap the pattern for the students, and then the children can watch the video, using their eyes and ears to "find the instrument."

IMITATING

At times, teachers just tell the students what they need to know! Here, the teacher can demonstrate the rhythmic pattern, inform the students that it is the shaker playing the part, and then lead them in performing the pattern along with the recording. This is the most time-efficient way for children to become actively engaged in musically performing with the recording, although it does not require them to think or listen critically to a recording; it only requires them to copy the teacher.

READING

If the students have notational literacy skills, the teacher can show students the rhythm, have the students read it with rhythm words or claps, and then have them listen for the pattern in the recording. For classrooms that include conventional music literacy skills as central to their curriculum, this can be an effective way to tie the WMP activity into their previous skills.

So, how should this rhythm for *El Carnaval de mi Tierra* be taught? In the home culture, the musicians would most likely learn the music by rote, so that would be the mode that is most representative of World Music Pedagogy. However, the use of Western notation might conceivably bridge the divide between the learning culture of the particular music classroom and the musical culture of the novel musical tradition. Ultimately, there is no correct choice. It depends on the children's skills, the teacher's perceptions of the students' interests, and the length of the lesson segment. In addition, a teacher may know that in their particular teaching context, students may respond better to "joining in," while others may learn more easily through more specific and direct instruction.

Consider the Noise

One major reason to program lessons of participatory musicking is so that students can continue to hear the sound of the culture-bearers while also becoming musically active. Sometimes, the music making on part of the children can be very loud. Imagine, for example, a full class of 25 students playing *djembe*-style drums along with a recording of drumming from Nigeria. The recording will have to be at tip-top volume for children to hear the recording over the din of their own playing. Options for addressing this issue:

- Provide drums to only a portion of the students at a given time. The rest of the class can either perform on body percussion or listen critically to the recording to think about how they will try to perform it. Then, switch parts, so that eventually all students receive a turn.
- Select instruments that are softer for use during Engaged Listening -—even when more culturally representative instruments are available. During Enactive Listening, when the sound is turned off and the students are working on recreating the music, the other instruments can be brought out.

Length of Participatory Musicking Excerpts

The Attentive Listening lessons of Chapter 2 were most effective when the length of the listening excerpt was relatively short, between 30 and 45 seconds. With Attentive Listening, children sit quietly and listen for specific musical or non-musical aspects of the recording. Maintaining mental focus while sitting quietly for long periods of time is challenging for many elementary children, particularly when high-energy music is booming over speakers.

Engaged Listening and Enactive Listening do not require that the listening excerpts be kept so concise, since children are actively participating in the music making. For example, if a teacher teaches a Cuban *son* with a clave pattern that repeats for the entire song, 10 sets of claves can be passed around the room, and children can alternate playing the instruments with listening. In that scenario, the music can last for 2 to 3 minutes, with a high level of musical engagement on the part of the children.

There are distinct benefits to a longer excerpt. First, a protracted selection affords children more opportunities to practice the musical skill, as they take turns playing along with the recording. Second, and perhaps more importantly, the extended period of listening allows the children to "get into the groove" more than they can when they are listening for short bursts. The short length of the listening examples in Attentive Listening leads to tightly run classes in which the children can learn a great deal in a short amount of time, but that often comes at the expense of a deep feel for the music.

The length of Engaged Listening experiences, however, always depends on the characteristics of the music. If students are learning the words to the chorus for *El Carnaval de mi Tierra*, they should not listen from the beginning, waiting silently until the chorus begins, 44 seconds in.

Consider Involving Students in the Decision-Making

One of the primary purposes of working with world music is to provide children the opportunity to engage with novel musical genres. By definition, they know little about the musical culture. It is natural for teachers to rely solely on direct instruction or to provide students with information about the musical culture. However, children must be actively engaged in participating with the music in order to maximize motivation and learning. In addition to physical and musical engagement, mental engagement is also essential—and providing children with choice is an effective way to accomplish this goal. At some points during lessons, teachers must direct the participatory musicking, but at others, children can make choices themselves and exercise their opinions. Some possibilities for student choice in Engaged and Enactive Listening lessons include the following:

ASK CHILDREN TO SELECT THE INSTRUMENT TO PLAY

Engaged Listening experiences frequently involve replicating an instrument from a recording. More often than not, classrooms do not possess the instruments from the recording. In this case, students can consider various options from a classroom instrumentarium, providing their input for the instrument that they think "sounds the most like the one on the recording." For example, if children have listened to a recording of a *fangxiang* (a suspended metallophone) from China, they can decide whether the metallophones or glockenspiels that they have in their classroom better represent the sound.

ASK CHILDREN TO SELECT THE PART(S) THAT THEY WANT TO PERFORM

As children progress through Engaged and Enactive Listening lessons, they often learn different parts to a piece of music. When appropriate, teachers can provide them with the choice to "perform their favorite part." For example, in *El Carnaval de mi Tierra*, children could choose to chant "ch-ch-ch" or sing the words, once both parts are learned. Children in upper elementary are often working on performing two parts of a piece at the same time. They can self-select their level of difficulty for a performance. For *El Carnaval de mi Tierra*, they can stomp the beat, play the rhythmic ostinato on a shaker, or sing the words—or try any combination of those three. Many children will find the challenge of attempting all three of them at the same time to be an enjoyable experience. Even if they cannot perform all of them accurately (it's hard!), the experience can be engaging.

ASK CHILDREN TO ENGAGE IN CREATIVE MOVEMENT

When children create movement to imitate a melodic line, they are able to engage in personal expression while also responding to the music in representative fashion. This idea will be addressed in greater detail in Chapter 5.

ASK THE CHILDREN TO LISTEN CRITICALLY AND GIVE FEEDBACK

Instead of relying on the teacher to provide feedback as to the degree of their success, the students can be asked to assess their performance in the context of the performance. Episode 3.6 features a sequential set of activities that offer children the opportunity for decision-making, experimenting on their own and working in small groups to determine the best way to play a melody. The song "Wau Rauh (Just Arrived)," from the Indonesian island of Lombok, close to Bali, comes from the *gamelan angklung* musical tradition. It uses a four-note melodic scale called *slendro* that differs from the diatonic scale with which most children in the West are familiar. The main instrument in this recording is the *gangsa jongkok*, a metallophone with keys placed over a wooden case. After introductory matter lasting approximately two seconds, the music features a repetitive 16-beat cycle that is marked by a gong. For this episode to be effective, it would have been preceded by Attentive Listening experiences, focused on the instrumentation, intonation, and repetition within the instrumental parts, and Integrating World Music activities, which provided further information about the nature of the *gamelan* ensemble. Additionally, students would have participated in introductory Engaged Listening experiences such as patting the beat and singing the principal tune along with the recording. In the transcription that follows the episode, the short introduction at the beginning has been omitted. For teachers interested in working to more closely approximate the intonation of the *gamelan*, it is possible to apply a putty-like substance to the bars to slightly alter the tuning of conventional metallophones found in schools.

Episode 3.6: Bali: "Wau Rauh (Just Arrived)"

Specific Use: Middle or Upper Elementary General Music Class

Materials:

- "Wau Rauh (Just Arrived)," Sekaha Angklung Murni (from *Bali: Balinese Music of Lombok*), UNESCO Recordings
- Xylophones, enough for one instrument per every two or three children

- Metallophones and/or glockenspiels
- Gong (optional)

Procedure:

(Engaged)

1. Sing the *gamelan* part in Figure 3.6 below, with the recording.
   a. Play track (0:00–0:28).

(Enactive)

2. Divide the students into groups of two or three, then inform the children that they will play the piece starting on an A. Sound out the melody on xylophones. (Note: Because the intonation differs from school xylophones, children, particularly those in upper elementary, may experiment with different notes, including accidentals.)
3. Small groups share with the class.
4. Compare with recording.
   a. Play track (0:00–0:28). Discuss differences, then decide on one part to play.
5. Practice in small groups, then play as a group.
6. When successful, transfer the tune to metallophones and/or glockenspiels. Discuss the difference with the sound. Compare with recording.
   a. Play track (0:00–0:28). Discuss differences.
7. Demonstrate "dampening" technique, or observe videos. In this process, one hand strikes a note while the other hand grabs the previous note to stop the sound from ringing.
8. Repeat steps 2–6 with Part II.
9. Play parts I and II together.
10. (Optional): As an extension, add the gong that occurs on the first beat of measure 7 (the X in the notation below), and the metallophone part labeled Part III. Further discussion about the style of the drumming may lead to student arrangement of the percussion portion.

    Note: Transcription below is approximate.

Figure 3.6 "Wau Rauh (Just Arrived)" from Bali (continued on next page)

Figure 3.6 (Continued)

As with all of the episodes, each teacher should consider the best way to modify the plan to meet the skills of the students in a class. For example, in "Wau Rauh (Just Arrived)," one teacher might choose to teach the instrumental parts by direct instruction, while another teacher might ask them to decode traditional Western notation. Yet another teach might decide to differentiate instruction by splitting the class in half, asking lesser skilled students to figure out the easier Part I while more skilled students determine the more challenging Part II. Regardless of the approach to sequencing instruction, all teachers can decide how far to extend the lesson. In a performance context, for example, teachers might ask the children to create an arrangement of the song, referring to this recording and other similar ones to determine a culturally appropriate structure. This type of activity will be discussed more extensively in Chapter 5, Creating World Music.

Episode 3.7 provides an episode for *Maburu We* (Learning Pathway #1), from Botswana. The episode highlights the ability to shift recursively between Attentive, Enactive, and Engaged Listening, and also demonstrates the self-evaluation that can occur during the process.

Episode 3.7: Botswana: "Maburu We" (Learning Pathway #1)

Specific Use: Upper Elementary General Music Class

Materials:

- "Maburu We (Oh, a Shoe, a Shoe)," young children of the Bakgaladi culture group (from *Traditional Music of Botswana, Africa: A Journey with Tape Recorder along Southern Botswana from Mochudi to Kang*), Smithsonian Folkways Recordings

Procedure:

(Engaged)

1. While the recording sounds, softly imitate the clapping of the performers.
   a. Play track (0:00–0:48).

(Attentive)

2. While the recording sounds, listen for pronunciation of the first two verses of the song text.
    a. Play track (0:00–0:30).

(Engaged)

3. While the recording sounds, sing the first two verses.
    a. Play track (0:00–0:30).

(Enactive)

4. With the recording turned off, sing the first two verses.

(Attentive)

5. Listen to the first two verses again, considering what might sound more like the recording. (A: Answers will vary, but may include a discussion about whether the words "chang chang" at the end of the line are actually present on the recording; the slight vocal descending slide at the end of the words "we" and "*ijoo*"; the emphasis on the word "*ijoo*.")
    a. Play track (0:00–0:30), then field responses. After one or two answers, listen to the recording again to check if other students in the class agree.

(Engaged and Enactive)

6. Sing along with first two verses (0:00–0:30), trying to implement the suggestion from the Attentive Listening step above.
    a. Play track (0:00–0:30), observing response.

(Enactive)

7. Sing the first two verses without the recording, implementing the suggestion from the Attentive Listening step.
8. Repeat steps 5–7, above, taking another suggestion from a student.

Assessment

During lessons involving participatory musicking, the students are "doing it"—they're actually making music. The new learning always involves musical participation on their part. Thus, the assessment should consist of an examination of the degree to which they were successful on the musical skill that they were performing—that is, the assessment should be of what students can do musically, rather than what they know about it. During Engaged Listening, it is often difficult for a teacher to hear how accurately the students were performing the specified skill, because the music is playing at the same time. Most assessment within Engaged Listening, then, is formative rather than summative, and is based on teacher observation of the students' responses. For example:

- If they are clapping an ostinato, are their hands moving at the correct time?
- As the teacher walks by individual students, are they playing or singing what is expected?
- If they are working on the words of a song, does the movement of their mouths appear to represent accurate singing?
- Does their performance reflect the tone and/or technique that emulate the sounds they are hearing on the recording?
- If they are imitating a video for instrumental technique, are the children holding and playing the instrument correctly?
- If they are creating movements to reflect a musical aspect of the piece, is it an accurate portrayal?

In addition, individuals or small groups might be asked to do something different from the rest of the group in order to assess individual performance. In Engaged Listening lessons, creative movement activities are perhaps the best way to assess understanding. When children work together to come up with movements that reflect form, for example, the teacher can easily assess the degree to which it was successful.

With Enactive Listening, assessment can be much more straightforward for the teacher, because students have learned the music well enough that the music can be turned off. The teacher can ask the children to perform the musical aspect of focus in the lesson, either as a whole class, in small groups, or individually. The teacher should not participate in the musicking during assessment, to determine whether the children (either individually or collectively) have developed independence.

Let's Participate!

The shift from Attentive Listening into Engaged and Enactive Listening is an exciting one for children—now they are able to actively make music! Elementary children often find World Music Pedagogy lessons that incorporate Engaged and Enactive Listening to be the most satisfying and enjoyable of all the dimensions, due to children's natural inclination to be participatory. When a series of lessons are structured in such a way that a well-selected musical choice can provide children with the opportunity to develop the ability to perform a piece by themselves, sounding like culture-bearers, it can be a transformative experience for them. The children experience feelings of pride at their newfound skill, feeling special because they are able to perform a style of music that other children and family members may know nothing about. At the close of a class, when children finish their final run-through of a piece that they are soon to perform for their parents, there can be a pause at the end, with comments ("that was cool!") quietly voiced by the students.

Teacher Feature: Stephanie Magnusson

Stephanie Magnusson, Elementary School Music Teacher

Stephanie Magnusson is in her 25th year as a full-time music teacher. A flute player, Stephanie initially intended to be a band director, but when she tried out elementary school music teaching, she was hooked. She has taught in various parts of Washington State, in schools with different populations, and is presently in her 11th year in the Puyallup School District, a diverse area in which 40% of the students are people of color. At Stephanie's current elementary school, almost half of the students are classified as minorities, with most of those students holding Hispanic heritage.

Q: Why do you do world music with your students?
A: I started doing world music with my students because at the time I lived and worked in a community that was not terribly ethnically diverse, it was mostly white

kids. For them, I thought that there was no way that they were going to get to experience this music outside of the classroom, so I really tried to do music that was outside the norm. But I've also taught world music in schools that were much more diverse, and I thought it was important there, too, for students to see the different music in the world.

Q: How do you choose the cultures to teach?
A: I have done it in several ways. One year, I took the demographics from my school and did two weeks for each culture. Some of them were hard to find. Cambodian? Very cool music, not easy to locate. And I did two styles of music of India because I had Punjabi *and* Hindi in the same school, sometimes in the same classroom. That was the year that we did a performance of musical cultures based on the demographics of the school—I think it was an Olympics year. Other times, it is music that I have studied in a class or figured out on my own by listening and watching videos.

Q: What is one benefit of teaching world music?
A: I think my biggest benefit has been making those cultural connections with students of that culture in my room. The smile you get when a child hears music that they have heard at home or that they can relate to, is really just the best. That year that I had Punjabi and Hindi kids in my school, there was one Hindi boy. When he realized I knew a little about his culture, he literally shared something about India with me every single music day for the whole year. It is something I will never forget, and I think he'll remember too.

Q: One challenge?
A: The biggest challenge is getting kids to have "open ears." When they haven't been exposed there can be a lot of laughing and sometimes making fun. I always tell them that people laugh because it's new and they don't understand it yet. That's OK, I tell them, we'll learn. And they're fascinated by things that aren't their everyday, once they get past the giggles. Really, it's just exposure. The more you do it, the more comfortable they get.

Q: How do you find the music that you do?
A: It really varies. I like to find a culture-bearer, and sometimes that's a kid in my school. Once I taught a singing game from China, and a girl from China told me the words were wrong and corrected me! I had a principal from Trinidad, and I asked him to sing some songs. I videotaped him singing, and then notated the songs so that I could remember them. I knew a little bit about Trinidadian music from a class I took, and so I ended up having my kids write *lavways*. I use YouTube, too.

Q: Do videos work well?
A: Whenever, possible, I show a video of the authentic instruments in action. A true cultural viewing can't be replaced, and the video really helps a lot. Sometimes it's hard to figure out what's good, but usually you can tell if it's a guy in his house that is actually in the country. I'll also ask other people, if I'm not sure. I got in touch with an ethnomusicologist who knew a lot about music from Trinidad, and he sent me links to some good videos. Same with Korean drumming.

Figure 3.8 Drum made by students and teacher

Photo courtesy of Stephanie Magnusson

Q: Do you think you do more Engaged Listening or Enactive Listening?
A: Definitely Enactive. Engaged is great, but sometimes the recordings are too much for kids to do. But I definitely want them to hear it, and get a sense of how it sounds, then try to recreate it.

Q: Have you modified music that you have learned in order to fit the skills of your students?
A: Yes, I often have to adjust. My motto is to make it as authentic as possible. If they are feeling and hearing and doing something from another culture, I want them to see how difficult it is, within reason. If it is so hard that they can't do it without a *ton* of time (which we don't have) then I will alter it. I had to do this with Korean drumming specifically. Some of the patterns are just really rough, even for me.

Q: What about instruments? Have you ever modified them?
A: All the time! With Korean drumming, I couldn't buy the instruments, so I made them. I took a world music class where I learned about Korean drumming, and I carpooled with a guy. We brainstormed what would work for cymbals, so I literally went to a thrift store with my mom and pounded on kitchenware to see what made the best sound. And then I painted them all black and my husband drilled holes in them for handles. I *do* make sure that the students hold them as authentically as possible though.

Q: Any last words of advice?
A: Just do it! Try it out. Don't try to be perfect, but do try to be as authentic as possible. I am constantly learning new things.

Reference

Campbell, P. S. (2004). *Teaching music globally*. New York: Oxford University Press.

Recording List

"El Carnaval de mi Tierra," Los Hermanos Lovo (from *¡Soy Salvadoreño! Chanchona Music from Eastern El Salvador)*, Smithsonian Folkways Recordings, www.folkways.si.edu/los-hermanos-lovo/el-carnaval-de-mi-tierra-the-carnival-of-my-land/latin/music/track/smithsonian

"Maburu We (Oh, a Shoe, a Shoe)," young children of the Bakgaladi Culture Group (from *Traditional Music of Botswana, Africa: A Journey with Tape Recorder along Southern Botswana from Mochudi to Kang*), Smithsonian Folkways Recordings, www.folkways.si.edu/young-school-children-of-the-bakgaladi-group/tribal-songs-of-batswana-oh-a-shoe-oh-a-shoe/world/music/track/smithsonian

"O' Embole, Embole—Embolada," performers unknown (from *Songs and Dances from Brazil*), Smithsonian Folkways Recordings, www.folkways.si.edu/o-embole-embole-embolada/latin-world/music/track/smithsonian

"Rocky Road," Louise Bennett (from *Children's Jamaican Songs and Games*), Smithsonian Folkways Recordings, www.folkways.si.edu/louise-bennett/rocky-road/caribbean-childrens-world/music/track/smithsonian

"Suwa Onbashira Kiyari-Taiko," Ensemble O-Suwa-Daiko (from *Japan: O-Suwa-Daiko Drums*), Smithsonian Folkways Recordings, www.folkways.si.edu/ensemble-o-suwa-daiko-under-the-direction-of-oguchi-daihachi/suwa-onbashira-kiyari-taiko/music/track/smithsonian

"Wau Rauh (Just Arrived)," Sekaha Angklung Murni (from *Bali: Balinese Music of Lombok*), UNESCO Recordings, https://folkways.si.edu/sekaha-angklung-murni/wau-rauh-just-arrived/music/track/smithsonian

"Welcome to New York," Taylor Swift (from *T.S. 1989*), American popular song available on iTunes and Spotify

Recording List: Singing Games

French Canada: "Promenons-Nous Dans le Bois," a chase game about a wolf, performers unknown (from *Game Songs of French Canada*), Smithsonian Folkways Recordings, www.folkways.si.edu/promenons-nous-dans-le-bois-the-wolf-song-singing-game/childrens/music/track/smithsonian

Ireland: "Wallflowers," a free movement game, performers unknown (from *The Clancy Children—So Early in the Morning*), Tradition Records, available on iTunes and Spotify.

Japan: "Maritsuki-Uta," a ball bouncing game, performer unknown (from *Folk Music of Japan*), Smithsonian Folkways Recordings, www.folkways.si.edu/maritsuki-uta/world/music/track/smithsonian

Mexico: "El Lobo," a chase game about a wolf, Cathy Illsey and other unnamed children (from *Children's Songs and Games from Ecuador, Mexico, and Puerto Rico*), Smithsonian Folkways Recordings, www.folkways.si.edu/TrackDetails.aspx?itemid=17678

Native Americans/First Nations: "Inuit Children's Singing Game," a breathing elimination game, Kasugat and Ishmatuk (from *The Eskimos of Hudson Bay and Alaska*), Smithsonian Folkways Recordings, www.folkways.si.edu/TrackDetails.aspx?itemid=41798

Scotland: "PK Penny Packet," a ball-bouncing game, performers unknown (from *Singing in the Streets: Scottish Children's Songs*), Rounder Records, http://research.culturalequity.org/rc-b2/get-audio-detailed-recording.do?recordingId=12198

Trinidad and Tobago: "Gypsy in the Moonlight," a choosing game, performers unknown (from *Caribbean Voyage: Brown Girl in the Ring*), Rounder Records, available on iTunes and Spotify.

United States: "London Bridge Is Bouncin' Down," a free-movement game, performers unknown (from *Songs for Children from New York City*), Smithsonian Folkways Recordings, www.folkways.si.edu/london-bridge/childrens/music/track/smithsonian

4

Performing World Music

The 25 children of Ms. Hamblet's fifth grade class stand in the school hallway, impatiently hopping from one foot to the other. They hear the low hubbub of their family and friends in the cafeteria that lies on the other side of the wall, the sounds of parents catching up with each other on the latest events of their lives as they wait for their children's performance. One four-year-old dashes into the hall with the bigger kids, and Jasmine whisper-yells at him, "Jonah! Get out of here!" As he scampers away, she turns to her friend Jasper, saying, "I'm so embarrassed!" Jasper nods and rolls his eyes, then replies excitedly, "I just hope we get all these words right!" As they hear their music teacher Mr. Ramirez begin speaking, they check that their shirts are tucked in and quietly enter the cafeteria, remembering his instruction to ignore their parents' attempts to gain their attention.

The students move into their assigned positions, standing in a semi-circle that surrounds the audience. After Mr. Ramirez finishes his general announcements to the parents ("try to keep your young children from running up to the performers"), Lucy takes her turn at the microphone. She informs the audience that the first song they will perform is a firefly-catching song from Japan and that they listened to a recording of Japanese singers many times to try to sing with perfect pronunciation. She challenges them to imagine fireflies as they listen. Mr. Ramirez raises his tuning fork to his ear, hums a note into the microphone, and cues the students to begin singing. The children's voices fill the room with the words that are unfamiliar to most in the audience, "Ho- ho- ho-ta-ru koi," first in unison, then in a two-part round, then in three parts. Finally, they repeat the three-part round, but this time bring out the tiny flashlights that have been concealed in their school sweatshirts, and the room explodes as random flashes of light simulate the experience of a field of fireflies. As the singers finish their last sung word "koi," the audience sits in silence for a beat, stunned by the surprise and the beauty, and then bursts into applause. The children make their way onto the temporary stage, and Jasper whispers to Jasmine, "I remembered all the words!" As the class walks onto the risers, they get into position for the next part of their 30-minute concert.

Performance in Children's Lives

"Look at me, Mom!"

One of the principal ways that childhood can be distinguished from adulthood is the vast and consistent growth that occurs as children age. Change in children is seemingly nonstop, with each passing year finding children growing bigger and stronger, thinking more deeply and creatively, and interacting with a wider swath of the world in self-sufficient ways. Children hold deep feelings of pride as they develop new knowledge and skills, and often want to "show what they know." This pride often emerges in a desire to demonstrate their new abilities through performance. Children's musical performances are typically thought of as a public demonstration of ability, such as the fourth grade girl in private piano lessons who excitedly wears a new dress and shiny black shoes to demonstrate her facility on Bach's *Prelude in C*, while an audience of parents looks on with love and admiration. Additionally, performances can be more private and informal. A fifth grade boy may spend a great deal of time recreating the dance moves from a music video so that he can perform for his friends in an after-school program, while his third grade sister may demand their mother's attention as she cooks dinner, intent on performing the new song that she learned in music class. These, too, are forms of performance.

The drive to demonstrate competence through performance occurs as an important aspect of musicking throughout much of the world. The ways in which performance can occur vary widely depending on culture and context. In some cases, these performances may come across as formal and presentational. Contemporary pop stars in Japan perform in large amphitheaters to hordes of teenagers, a university in Namibia hosts a choir competition for choirs from around the region, and a teenager in Singapore live-streams his newly composed guitar piece through social media. Performance can also occur in ways that are less presentational but more participatory, experiences that invite audience members to join in with the music making. A congregation in an African American church joins in with the chorus of a gospel song performed by the choir, and everyone joins in singing and clapping as the band plays an Afro-Peruvian *festejo* at a *peña* (a grassroots community meeting place) in Lima, Peru. All of these examples remind us of the various ways in which musical performance can occur throughout the world, with varying degrees of participation on the part of the audience.

Performances are also common in elementary schools, not only in music but in school overall. In a child's general classroom, the teacher will often plan a final presentation at the end of a major unit, with dioramas of the solar system exhibited for third grade parents, or sixth graders' research studies on the geography of Southeast Asia displayed on posters taped to walls in the school's hallway. It is music and other arts, however, in which performance often stands as central to one's ability to demonstrate the growth made in the subject matter. In language arts classes, students can show their knowledge by writing a paper, and in math class, they can demonstrate understanding of a mathematical principle by applying it to a new problem. At its core, though, music is a demonstrative discipline, in which the best way to show growth is not by *talking* about music, but by *doing* it; it is the actions of our bodies—our vocal cords vibrating, our hands striking drums or xylophones, our fingers strumming guitars—that make sounds come together to make rich and compelling music. Performance allows these skills to be demonstrated in real time.

This chapter will address issues related to performance in the context of World Music Pedagogy. Of the five dimensions of WMP, all can be incorporated into performance in some way, but some dimensions are more likely to lead to successful performances.[1] Other issues to be discussed include characteristics of repertoire that can be effective in performance, types of performance spaces, and the role of the audience. Specific performance themes will be suggested, and the issue of aesthetic and ethical compromises that must be made in order to move musical products to new performance contexts will also be addressed.

Models of Performance in Elementary Schools

When designing a performance that incorporates World Music Pedagogy, a variety of factors contribute to a successful presentation. First, the teacher must determine the best model for the performance. In elementary schools, these will be either multi-grade performances or single-grade performances. In addition to public performance, these may also occur as a cross-grade sharing.

TRADITIONAL PERFORMANCES

In some contexts, all students in a school gather together in a cross-school musicking extravaganza. These may occur at an assembly during the day, with the primary goal to share music with other students in the school, or in the evening, to perform for extended family and friends. In these settings, each grade will typically perform one song, or two songs at the most. An appropriate length of a concert is an hour; any longer than that, and the younger siblings of the school-aged performers will likely grow restless. When a performance is comprised of two or three grades rather than the entire school, each grade can perform between three and five pieces. In this format, the musicking can highlight more than one skill or type of music. In other contexts, a performance will feature one class, or multiple classes from one grade that perform together. These performances typically last 20–30 minutes, providing the children with enough time to demonstrate a variety of music they have been working on in class, typically between five and seven pieces of music.

INFORMANCES

The term "informances" was created to transform the idea of "performances" to become less focused on perfect performance, with greater attention given to the process of learning. In informances, parents and guardians are invited to come and observe what is essentially a typical class, as a way to highlight the learning processes rather than the musical product. In these sessions, children will engage in a variety of normal classroom activities, with the teacher or students occasionally providing a description of the skills or knowledge being gained by the children through each experience.

CROSS-GRADE SHARING

In some teaching contexts, it is difficult for parents, guardians, and other special people in a child's life to attend a concert. It is still important for children who have been working towards particular musical goals to have some way to demonstrate their newfound abilities. Inviting another grade to 10 or 15 minutes of a music class can be a way for children to experience performance. These are generally most successful when the difference in grade levels is two years or greater. If a first grade class observes a group of fifth graders, they will likely be impressed by the skill of their older peers. If a fifth grade class watches a first grade class, they are likely to recall the skills that they learned when they were that age with fondness. If those same fifth graders observe fourth graders, they are more apt to look down on their slightly younger peers.

These models of performance are found in many elementary music classes and are not specific to World Music Pedagogy. However, deciding the best format for a performance has implications for the types of WMP experiences that a teacher will choose to include in performance. For example, in a "cross-grade sharing," in which older students performed for younger children, the degree to which the performance should be polished is not as great as an evening event in which each grade level performed only one piece of music.

Enactive Listening: Classic Performance Practice

While all dimensions of World Music Pedagogy can be incorporated effectively into performance contexts, the outcome of Enactive Listening is the central approach to performance. Performance is about demonstrating musical skill, and that performance is rooted in an effort to recreate an ideal sound of a particular type of music. For example, in a typical elementary choir in which World Music Pedagogy is not utilized, the students might work on a set of pieces for two or three months—perhaps paying attention to typical musical dimensions such as phrasing, intonation, and dynamics. In some cases, the teacher may have also played a recording of the English folk song that they are performing in order for the children to render their performance sound as much like the quintessential sound as possible, or the children may have watched a video on YouTube of a similar choir. In other cases, they may not. But in all cases, there is an ideal sound that is the target for the teacher and choristers.

Enactive Listening in the context of World Music Pedagogy has the same outcome—that of a performance that is as top-notch as possible. Where it differs is in the execution: in WMP, Enactive Listening *always* includes conscious and explicit effort to create a sound that is as much like a recording as possible, recognizing that the teacher (and students) may not have a solid knowledge of the intricacies of the musical styling to be able to recreate it without extensive experience listening to the recording. Repeated listening, performing with and without the recording, all the while referring back to the performance of culture-bearers in order to note the nuances and characteristics of their rendition—this is what makes it Enactive Listening. In a performance context, it may not appear to the audience that listening has occurred at all, because the children are the ones who are performing, usually without any recording. But the performance is the result of repeated experiences with the original sound source.

Enactive Listening: From Classroom to Performance

When working in the classroom, teachers have student learning at the forefront of all decisions. Lessons and curricula are constructed around ideas of what will be best for the students—how they will grow in their skills and knowledge, creating community through joyful musical interactions with others. More and more, contemporary curricula in music emphasize thought processes (see, for example, the current National Core Arts Standards in the United States), with more time in class spent in analysis and class-based discussions, sometimes with writing prompts, small group work, and other activities designed to improve critical thinking skills. These types of experiences can lead to great growth on the part of children, in terms of their musical skills, social skills, and general thinking skills.

However, these are not the types of experiences that generally make for effective performance—at least not as far as the audience is concerned. Think of the popular music concerts that we see on television and the live arena, in which the explicit focus is almost always to be as musically satisfying and visually pleasing as possible. At its pinnacle, an outstanding performance means excellent music making that is enjoyable for the audience to observe. If popular musicians put on shows that are lackluster musically (or, in some cases, lackluster visually), audiences will decline, and the performers' careers will spiral downward.

Many performances in other parts of the world also emphasize an exhibition that is sonically and visually pleasing to an audience. For example, when the singers of the Wagogo culture group in central Tanzania ready themselves for the annual Chamwino Arts Festival, the performances have clearly been prepared in such a way so that choreography is perfectly aligned, attire is culturally appropriate and sharp looking, and the music locks in with itself, with the singers demonstrating perfect intonation and matched tone quality. This particular festival is one of the apexes of the music scene of the Wagogo people, with the final performances resulting in the largest crowd of the year. For musicians who want to share their music and demonstrate their love (and ability) in performing it, it is *the* place to be. Additionally, the performances must be excellent—it is a competitive event, with more groups vying to participate than there are slots available.

To be sure, school performances do not have nearly the same pressure for perfection, nor should they. However, working towards an exemplary performance reflects an essential broad principle of performance-based music programs and is typically the type of experience that is the goal for many music teachers. After briefly addressing the other dimensions of WMP and the ways that they work in performance, enactive experiences will be discussed more explicitly.

Other Dimensions of World Music Pedagogy in Performance

Although Enactive Listening experiences comprise the core of performance in a World Music Pedagogy context, other dimensions sometimes have their place in performance, depending on the characteristics of the performance and the music. This section considers the other four dimensions.

Attentive Listening

The Attentive Listening experiences of Chapter 2, when children listened to recordings with specific questions in mind, are rarely effective in performance. Parents want to see children perform, so watching them listen to a recording of a Thai *pi phat* ensemble and raise their hands when they hear the entrance of the *kakko* drum simply won't be of interest. It is an essential step in the sequence of World Music Pedagogy, but it does not fit well in a performance context.

The one exception to this general rule is to ask the audience to compare the children's performance to a recording. If the children have worked hard to recreate the bright, forward vocal sound of a women's Bulgarian choral piece, it may be a point of pride on part of the children. In these cases, it can be effective for the teacher to play a brief excerpt of a recording, and then inform the parents of the particular musical styling that the students have been attempting to imitate. In addition, if the demands of the music are such that the teacher has modified the instrumentation to reflect the skills of the children, playing a brief excerpt of the original recording can be an effective way to highlight the differing interpretation of the students. For example, the violins and bass on *El Carnaval de mi Tierra* (Learning Pathway #2) may have been replaced by xylophones and piano, leading to a significantly different sound. Thirty seconds of the recording can be played over speakers, to show the audience the ways that the children changed the music.

Engaged Listening

Similarly, Engaged Listening is typically not effective in performance. In Engaged Listening, children perform along with the performance of a live or recorded culture-bearer, with musickings that are introductory and partial. The focus of a performance should be the children. If children were to perform the steady beat on their laps along with a recording of a *samba* from Brazil, their performance would be of little interest and the recording would serve as distraction from the children.

One exception for this general principle involves folk dance. When children present a longer concert, folk dance is occasionally included. In a 30-minute concert that addresses the music of Lithuania, a folk dance performed along with a recording can provide an appropriate change of pace within the concert. The children participate kinesthetically (an enjoyable activity for most children), and the dance provides visual interest for the audience. In this case, the recording does not take away from the children's performance, but highlights a skill they have been addressing. The sound of the recording provides sonic interest, but the visual aspect of the dance still makes the children the focal point of the performance.

Creating World Music

In many ways, Creating World Music is the most advanced dimension of World Music Pedagogy, and it requires a deep working understanding of the musical culture. If a performance consists of one song from the given culture, then an Enactive Listening activity is most appropriate, accompanied by some integrative context. However, if children have studied a particular culture to such a degree that they have created new music in the style of a particular genre through composing, improvising, or songwriting, it can be a perfect aspect of performance. Indeed, it gives children a chance to demonstrate their personal creativity and solid understanding of a genre. Simpler forms of Creating World Music, such as an experience in which children have extended a brief listening example or have decided on the arrangement of a particular piece, can be effective as well, particularly if children explain the way in which the arrangement reflects the culture of origin.

Integrating World Music

Although set aside as its own dimension, Integrating World Music is a core aspect of WMP and must always be a part of any experience involving world music. This includes performance. If children are performing one song, this integrative material may be as minimal as informing the audience of the culture of origin and giving some brief context as to the way that the song is used in the culture. In a longer performance that highlights a variety of musical experiences of a particular culture, integrative experiences may take up a greater portion of the program and present more in-depth information. In a performance of music of Turkey, for example, one child might read a folk tale about the bumbling-but-wise figure *Nasreddin Hoca* while other children act out the story, or a group of students may provide their findings from a short research project on whether the confection Turkish Delight actually hails from Turkey (Answer: Yes!). Cultural and contextual information can also be provided in a written program to be distributed to audience members before the performance.

Figure 4.1 Indonesian shadow theater

Photo courtesy of BethAnn Hepburn

Selecting Musical Material for Performance

While all dimensions of World Music Pedagogy should be considered, Enactive Listening is the primary dimension that is incorporated in performance. Through a series of steps that incorporate other dimensions, Enactive Listening explicitly leads towards an effort to recreate the music of culture-bearers to the best of the students' ability, and as such, stands as the dimension of WMP that is most appropriate to present in public as a means of demonstrating students' learning.

What Sounds Good?

When selecting music for WMP in performance, teachers must consider the potential final sonic product. Performance is usually intended to highlight children's musical skills, and some music that will be enacted in class will not "sell" in a performance. It is important that children feel that they are successful, with a performance in which they are putting their best foot forward. A sonically pleasing performance does not necessarily mean that "perfection" is the goal—if that is even possible. Indeed, teachers often wish to demonstrate a particular process that occurred in class, a series of actions that led to growth in a particular area, or a greater understanding of a concept. However, if second graders are playing a *marimba* piece from Zimbabwe but do not have the ensemble skill for the overlapping ostinati to stay together on the beat, the performance will likely be deemed a failure—by parents and students alike.

For many elementary school music teachers, an ideal performance is one in which the children perform all the parts by themselves, without the support of the teacher or other musician. Ensuring that the music to be performed reflects the children's skills is particularly relevant with World Music Pedagogy. When teachers create or implement units of World Music Pedagogy for the classroom, the musical skills of the culture-bearing performers are often greater than the skills of the children. As noted in Chapter 1, the teacher may choose a culture for a variety of reasons that may be unrelated to performance goals. As such, the musical recordings that the teacher finds may be musically challenging for the students to perform, and the units may consist of musical experiences that never move beyond Attentive Listening and Integrating World Music. When a teacher knows that a performance looms in the future and that this WMP unit will comprise at least a part of it, the musical culture or musical examples may be chosen with those ideas in mind.

CHOOSE PIECES WITH MULTIPLE PARTS THAT ARE FAIRLY SIMPLE

Children in middle and upper elementary school are often working on part independence, where they are able to perform one part of a piece of music while also hearing another. Most adult music from around the world has more than one part (e.g. singers accompanied by percussion and a guitar). Music in which each of those parts are fairly simple will allow children the opportunity to be able to perform in such a way that reflects the musical culture while also being musically satisfying. For example, the Japanese song *Suwa Onbashira Kiyari-Taiko* (see episodes in Chapters 2, 3, 5, and 6) has multiple drum parts that are not overly complex, but when performed together confidently with choreographed and synchronized large, strong movements of the arms with drumsticks (*bachi*), it can be especially interesting for an audience to behold.

CONSIDER TEACHER ACCOMPANIMENT REFLECTIVE OF THE MUSICAL CULTURE

Preferably, the children are able to perform all parts of a piece by themselves, but there may be times when a teacher must provide musical support to create a performance that will sound good. For example, second graders performing a song from Senegal may not have the ability to play a complementary drumming pattern, simply because of their age and developmental skill. A teacher can accompany on a *sabar* drum, providing more musical interest for the audience and the students. Since the instrument comes from the *Serer* people of Senegal, it can be seen as culturally appropriate. Most commonly, the music teacher provides this musical support, but older students can also step in to demonstrate their skills. Whenever possible, a culture-bearer can also enter into a performance and provide the accompaniment.

CONSIDER TEACHER ACCOMPANIMENT *LESS* REFLECTIVE OF THE MUSICAL CULTURE

At times, students may need musical support, but the teacher may not have the musical skill or knowledge to be able to provide it. In this case, a simple acknowledgment in performance can ensure that the audience understands the difference. For example, the song *Embolada* (see the episode in Chapter 3) can be used as part of a broader unit on the Music of Brazil. This song is in call-response form, with the call being an improvisatory section performed by a soloist. On the recording, the song is accompanied by a guitar. In performance, the song can be modified in a number of ways. First, rather than asking children to improvise texts on the verses—a challenging skill for adult musicians, let alone children—the children can work in small groups during class to write verses to fit into the short call section. The children can decide on eight verses to be sung in performance to demonstrate the composition skills that they have developed. Second, if the teacher does not know how to play the guitar, the first step would be to try to find someone from the broader community. However, if that search is unsuccessful and the teacher knows no other string instruments, piano accompaniment would suffice, despite the radically different sound. A simple statement acknowledging the differences between the home culture and the performance can address the issues.

Choral Octavos

In many elementary schools, choral octavos are a staple of performance.[2] At times, these songs are pieces that a teacher found not because he was searching for music from a particular culture, but because he heard another choir perform the piece or sight-read the octavo at a choral reading session. In these cases, a teacher can research to learn about the song and the musical culture, and then teach the piece with those ideas in mind. The same steps that are utilized when selecting music for World Music Pedagogy broadly apply for octavos:

- find a field recording
- read the liner notes of the recording
- search out additional material about the musical culture, either from a culture-bearer or an ethnomusicologist

- play the recording for the students
- discuss with the students the ways in which they might most authentically perform the piece

Not all composers who create choral arrangements of world music songs are familiar with issues of World Music Pedagogy. Some arrangements, upon further investigation, may turn out to have melodies that have been modified by the arranger or accompaniment styles that are vastly different from the ways that the music is performed in the culture. If the text in the country of origin is in an unfamiliar language, the arranger may have used English transliterations to make the learning easier. Typically, if a non-culture-bearer arranges a song from an unfamiliar culture, he or she has selected a folk song to arrange. Folk songs are in the public domain, so a teacher is free to modify it to be more representative of the principles of WMP. Some specific suggestions follow:

SING IN THE ORIGINAL LANGUAGE

If the song is published with an English transliteration, the teacher can easily substitute the original text back in the octavo. This can be accomplished through notation software, or a teacher can use traditional means—either writing the words on the board (with the English text covered up in the octavo) or printing out the text and taping it into the octavo.

USE THE ORIGINAL MELODY AND RHYTHM

Upon searching, if a teacher discovers that the melody is inaccurate, it is fully appropriate to change it back to its original form. It is important to recognize that there are often slightly different versions of the same folk song, but more often than not, an arranger unfamiliar with WMP will have changed the tune to conform to her idea of an appropriate melody. For example, a song that has uneven phrase lengths in the original musical culture may have been altered to have phrases of consistent length to fit more conventional Western patterns. It is best to alter the performance to include the traditional phrasing.

CREATE AN ARRANGEMENT

If the accompaniment is vastly different from what would occur in the home culture, teachers can consider constructing an arrangement. This need not be difficult. If singing the Latin American lullaby *A la Nanita Nana*, the teacher can pay a simple a chordal accompaniment on a guitar rather than a virtuosic piano part found in an octavo, which will render the performance more reflective of the culture.

Putting It Together: Designing a Performance

In some cases, a class may present a concert in which an instrumental piece that incorporates WMP is one of many activities highlighted in a performance. For example, a third grade class may present a brief assembly that has four different activities representing multiple aspects of their curriculum, including a play party from rural United States, a European American folk song with a xylophone accompaniment, and a through-composed *a cappella* two-part choral octavo. The fourth performance piece may be a piece that they have been learning through World Music Pedagogy, such as a rendition of a Mexican *corrido*, complete with verses composed by the children. In these cases, a teacher can program the WMP activity wherever it fits best, and it becomes one of many experiences that are not connected by any particular concept beyond the general idea, "Here's what happens in music class."

In other cases, a teacher might plan a performance around a particular theme, all of which incorporates aspects of World Music Pedagogy. Theme-based performances should take place at the end of a unit, when individual classes or grade levels have been working on music of a specific region or a particular subject matter. They can also occur when the entire school has had music class that has been focused around a particular topic.

Themes for Performance

In elementary general music classes, performances that incorporate world music can be structured around a variety of themes.

MUSIC FROM A REGION OF THE WORLD

The most common organizing principle for concerts of world music is location. Either individual classes or an entire school may have had music classes devoted to studying the music of a particular culture. From a pedagogical standpoint, delving deeply into a singular culture by learning multiple pieces of music from an area can lead to a more substantive understanding of the music of a region. These experiences often warrant public performance, because the children have learned a great deal of music that likely differs from the genres known to their parents.

When thinking about creating a unit (and a performance) of a particular musical culture, a question sometimes arises as to how broad the culture can be. An effective frame can be to think of culture as a series of concentric circles, from the narrowest view of a culture group to the broadest regional frame—even, perhaps, moving towards diasporic traditions. For example, with *Maburu We* (Learning Pathway #1) from Botswana, the song could be part of a performance in any of the following circles:

Culture group

- The song comes from the Bakgaladi culture group of Southern Botswana, along the South African border. A performance of culture group could consist solely of music from the Bakgaladi people.

Country

- A broader performance could highlight music from different peoples of Botswana, including the Tswana and Kalanga peoples in addition to the Bakgaladi.

Region

- Botswana lies in south-central Africa, and as such, a performance could include music of Zimbabwe and Zambia, or Zimbabwe, Zambia, Namibia, Mozambique, and South Africa. (See the end of this chapter for a sample concert designed in this manner.)

Diaspora

- In some cases, emigration has led to a large group of people from one country moving to another country and creating new musical styles that incorporate multiple musical traditions. This is not the case with the Bakgaladi people or Botswana more broadly, but it could occur with other musics.

It is worth noting that "continent" is not included as one of the ever-expanding circles around which a concert can be organized. In many parts of the world, people mistakenly believe that cultures are the same throughout a continent. While Tunisia and Zimbabwe are both in Africa, their musical cultures bear limited similarity (and, indeed, are over 3,500 miles from each other—further than the distance between Chicago and Bogota, Columbia). Further discussion of "essentializing" (attributing the same cultural characteristics to all musical cultures in a particular sociopolitical area) is provided in Chapter 7 of this volume.

MUSICAL CONNECTIONS, CROSS-CULTURALLY

Performances can also be organized around themes or musical concepts that occur across cultures. Rather than focusing in-depth on the music of one particular culture or region, these performances highlight a unit of study in which students have explored principles of musical expression that occur in many cultures. For example, particular aspects of instrumentation may serve as a focusing theme. Xylophones are common in many elementary schools, and many musical traditions incorporate barred instruments. Wooden barred instruments include *marimbas* of Zimbabwe and Nicaragua, *embaire* of Uganda, and *ranat ek* and *ranat thum* from Thailand. Barred instruments made of metal can also be found in many parts of the world, such as the *gender wayang* from Balinese *gamelan* ensembles, the *vibraphone* found in many jazz ensembles, and *roneat dek* from Cambodia. If schools own metallophones or glockenspiels, these can be used to replicate the sounds. Similarly, if children in fifth or sixth grade are learning the guitar or ukulele, they can mount a performance in which they play their instruments using repertoire from a range of plucked *lute* traditions, from the *oud* of Turkey to the *jarana* of Mexico to the *pipa* of China. Drums are also common in classroom settings, and single-headed membranophones are often one of the first instruments that children play. Performances can highlight playing techniques or rhythmic forms that are common in different parts of the world. Although the children may only have access to one type of drum, they can nonetheless play music characteristic of goblet-shaped drums in the Middle East such as the *dombek* or *darbuka*, *djembe* drums from Ghana, or *changgo* drums from Korea—all of which have different sizes and sounds.

Performances with a focus on the way that one type of musical instrument occurs in different cultures are typically more effective if the concert occurs in a cross-grade format. For example, it is difficult and time consuming for one grade to learn about five different drumming traditions well enough to be able to represent them accurately. However, if each grade level focuses on a different tradition, the contrast will be more apparent to the audience and highlight the difference.

In addition to instrumentation, other musical similarities can be explored through cross-cultural study and can then lend themselves to performance. For example, music with a call-and-response structure is found throughout many musical traditions in the world, such as African American work songs, the *plena* from Puerto Rico,

Trinidadian Carnival songs called *lavways*, and the *kplanlogo* drum tradition of the *Ga* people of Ghana. Singing games form a staple of many elementary music classes, and a class in a lower or middle elementary grade can choose to highlight singing games that children play in a variety of cultures, from *Promenons-Nous dans le Bois* in French Canada, to *Gypsy in the Moonlight* in Trinidad and Tobago, to *Maritsuki-Uta* in Japan. An entire evening can be also be filled with folk dance from around the world. This crowd-pleasing performance can end with adults and other family members being invited to dance with the performers. In this way, the children serve as teachers to their parents, instructing them in the correct movements to the Cuban *son* and modeling the styling that they have been perfecting during class.

SOCIAL OR TOPICAL CONNECTIONS, CROSS-CULTURALLY

Music often serves similar purposes throughout the world, with many cultures using music as a way to mark particular cultural, religious, or personal experiences. In some cases, these connections can spring from the curriculum in the children's homeroom class. If a sixth grade classroom is comparing different religious traditions, the music teacher can teach music from each of those traditions, as a way of increasing the depth of the children's learning about the area of study. For example, students could perform a concert with a theme of "Songs of Celebration." Music often plays a role in celebrations throughout the world, to mark specific moments in time. Songs share the joy of a new marriage or birth, and are sometimes used in a celebration of the life of a recently deceased person. A concert incorporating "Songs of Love" need not reflect romantic love (which might cause giggling on the part of the children), but could reflect the emotions that one feels for a parent, a friend, or a sibling. "Songs of Protest" can highlight some of the many musical pieces that have been created to protest injustice. Issues such as slavery and authoritarian governments have inspired protest songs in various parts of the world. Elementary children often have a highly developed sense of right and wrong, and music that addresses inequity can elicit deep emotional and intellectual responses that can lead to a meaningful performance. A concert that consists solely of lullabies can be particularly successful in a cross-grade concert. In a single-grade concert, a group of second graders would likely find performing a set of exclusively slow pieces to be repetitive. But if each grade performs one lullaby from a different culture, the performance can be a parental favorite.

The social and topical connections that a teacher can make across cultures are seemingly endless and can provide an effective structure for a performance. There also may be surface-level topics that are central to a homeroom class's curriculum, subjects for which the music teacher can find a connection. If a first grade class spends extended periods of time studying animals, learning about the different categorization systems and creating individual reports on their favorite animal, they can perform a concert that incorporates animal songs from around the world. Such units are less centered on important musical understandings, but may nonetheless be an effective way for the children's cross-school experiences to connect with each other.

At the end of the chapter, see a worked example of a teacher progressing through the construction of a unit to connect with a fifth grade class's studies of the colonial period in the United States.

Introductions

Most performances (or informances) include short explanations of the musical material to be presented. Often, these are limited to a report of the title of the piece, along with the names of any students with solos or other special parts. In a performance that incorporates World Music Pedagogy, more extensive remarks can provide the audience with a broader understanding of the process of the children's learning. That said, each introduction should still be limited to 30–60 seconds, so that the focus remains on the children and the music. Possible topics to address might include:

- the meaning of the song in the culture
- a challenging element of the children's learning process
- an aspect of learning the piece that the students found enjoyable
- a comparison between the children's performance and the way the song would be performed in the home culture

To mention all of these aspects would take too long, so the teacher or students can decide the most important features to highlight.

Whenever possible, students should give the introductions, rather than the teacher. This provides them with an increased sense of ownership over the process and product, and allows children the opportunity to develop presentational skills.

Culture-Bearers in Performance

If a teacher has created a longer unit dedicated to the music of a particular people, a culture-bearer may enter in and work with the students. When this is the case, it is ideal for the culture-bearer to be a part of the final performance. It is rewarding for the students, who have usually learned a great deal from the performer; it is rewarding for the parents, who are able to see the teachers that have been working with their students (as well as experience the musical skill of the performer); and it is rewarding for the administration, who has most likely contributed funds to pay for the culture-bearer. If a culture-bearer is willing and able, he or she can perform, both alone and with the students.

Of course, the presence of culture-bearers at a performance is not always possible, due to financial issues or artist availability. When this is the case, the teacher can consider making a video recording of the culture-bearer. In the recording, the culture-bearer can introduce herself and give brief explanations of some of the music, or demonstrate some of the musical skills that are beyond the skills of the students. Alternatively, a video could show the artist working with the students in class, to provide the audience with a sense of the way that the process unfolded.

Traditional Attire

If a performance consists of music from one culture, teachers may wish to have children wear attire that reflects the culture. Finding (or creating) garb can be a time-intensive and costly process. At times, a teacher knows that the unit of study may

Figure 4.2 Children in traditional attire

Photo courtesy of BethAnn Hepburn

repeat each year. For example, if fourth graders at a school in Oklahoma always study Cherokee culture as part of their social studies curriculum, a unit on the music of the Cherokee may be a regular part of the curriculum. In these cases, an investment of time and resources may be worthwhile, knowing that the attire can be used each year. On the other hand, a unit that occurs only once may not warrant the time and expense required to make apparel for an entire class or grade level. However, it might be possible to borrow clothing that is culturally representative. Community centers, churches, or other organizations that are peopled by the culture group under study may have outfits that a school can borrow. Teachers can also utilize social media to see if other teachers or schools have attire to borrow, or enlist parents to assist in creating representative garments.

Traditional attire can be stereotypical when viewed as "costumes," and it is important that children appear in ways that are not seen as offensive. One thinks of movies of the mid-20th century in the United States, when Native Americans were invariably shown with face paint and feathers in their hair. Performances that include such visually stereotypical experiences can distract from the performance and detract from the intentions of the WMP experience. In order to ensure that attire is appropriate, teachers can check with culture-bearers. This can be as simple as taking a picture of an outfit and e-mailing it to a person from the culture, asking their opinion.

Physical Arrangement of Performance Space

Classic performance practice in many countries finds performers on a raised stage, with the audience seated in rows facing the performers. In other parts of the world, public presentations may occur in different ways. For example, musical artists may perform while standing in the middle of a circle, surrounded by the viewers on all sides. In other contexts, the audience may be expected to stand or sit on the ground, rather than remain seated in chairs.

In some elementary schools, the nature of the physical space in the performance venue limits the possibilities for altering the arrangement of the audience and performers. If performances occur in an auditorium where chairs are nailed to the floor, there is little a teacher can do to alter the physical makeup. However, when the performance space has more flexibility, such as in a cafeteria or gymnasium, the teacher can arrange the seating to reflect the typical performance practice of the home culture. For example, the audience could be arranged in a semi-circle, seated on the floor, to represent the way that a performance might occur in a rural area of Central Africa.

Role of the Audience

The role of the audience, too, differs based on context. Reflecting the Western classical tradition, many elementary schools explicitly teach "performance etiquette," in which children and other audience members are expected to sit quietly, providing polite applause at specific times in the concert. By no means is this a universal standard for performance. In *conjunto* music of Mexico, the audience expresses their enjoyment and approval by dancing in pairs while the performers play and sing. In performances of Western popular music, the audience often sings (or hollers) at top volume, accompanying the performance with rhythmic clapping and screams of approval. In South Indian concerts of *Carnatic* music, audience members may "count *tala*" while the performers play, expressing the metrical patterns by a series of light claps, taps, and hand waves.

When possible, the audience can be encouraged to participate in ways that are appropriate in the musical culture. This may require some education of the audience in the moment, to let them know what is expected. For example, if it is common for audience members to shout enthusiastically when they hear a musically pleasing excerpt, as in the case of the Mexican expression of joy or excitement known as *grito*, the introduction to the piece can let them know that this is appropriate—and, indeed, that it is expected. While some parents may not be comfortable with in-concert proclamations, the younger siblings of the performers likely will be. This can even be practiced during the concert; after informing the audience that they should yell "right on!" when they hear something that they like, teachers can invite them to try this out as a whole group, before the song begins.

In many cultures, the divide between the audience and musicians is not as great as it is in the Western tradition of symphonic orchestras, and concert attendees are encouraged to participate in the music making. In any concert of elementary music, this can be a meaningful way for parents and guardians to understand what children have learned, but it can be even more powerful in performances incorporating World Music Pedagogy. For example, after children have performed a particularly challenging piece of instrumental music that has many different parts, such as *El Carnaval de mi Tierra* (Learning Pathway #2), parents can be invited to go up to their child, and their child can teach them the part that they were playing. If the parents appear to be learning the parts effectively, the teacher can even lead the adults through a mini-performance of the piece, with the children serving as support, jumping in to take over if their parents err in their performance. The last activity of a concert can also be a folk dance or children's singing game, in which the parents are matched with their children. Once again, the children can instruct their parents, correcting them if they make mistakes. In addition to providing parents with the chance to actively participate and more fully understand what their children's experience in music class, such events also allow children to understand how much they have learned as part of a process.

For this to be successful, the teacher must be aware of students who may not have a parent or guardian attending the concert. These children may well be saddened by the fact that they do not have special guests in attendance, and asking them to watch their peers with parents can add salt to the wound. One possible solution to such a situation is to have parents be taught by a student other than their own child. In this way, parents can still learn the music that their child learned, but individual students will not be left out in the same way.

Let's Perform!

A half an hour after the fifth graders of Ms. Hamblet's class quietly stood in a circle, surrounding their parents and guardians with the sounds of the Japanese canon Hotaru Koi, *the children sing a three-part arrangement of the African American spiritual,* This Little Light of Mine, *with some of the children playing the school's djembe drums and a gospel pianist from the community offering a rousing accompaniment.*

Their performance on the theme of "Light in Times of Darkness" complete, the children greet their family members with beaming smiles and somewhat awkward hugs—appropriate for these pre-teens. "What was your favorite part?" they demand of their parents, and these queries are met with a range of responses. Jasper's mother notes the novel vocal style of the Thai song Ngam Sang Duan *("Yeah, we learned that from a Thai person in class," replies her daughter.) Jasper's grandfather also names that song as his favorite, but it is the accompaniment that was his focus—"I know that the xylophones are a different sound than you would hear in Thailand, but I couldn't believe that you stayed together so well!" Jasper nods his head in agreement, saying, "We worked hard on that!" The children and their parents walk out into the cool winter night, with the children continuing to hum some of the tunes from the show, peppering their adults with questions like, "Did you hear that triangle I played? It was supposed to sound like a star!" As they go home, parents and children alike are happy, satisfied that this performance allowed them to shine, just like the theme of the concert.*

Teacher Feature: Darcy Morrissey

Darcy Morrissey spent ten years as a public school music teacher in the Lake Washington School district, just outside Seattle, Washington. She taught every age group and nearly every type of music course, including general music, guitar, keyboard, orchestra, and choir. Her focus, however, has always been singing and choral environments,

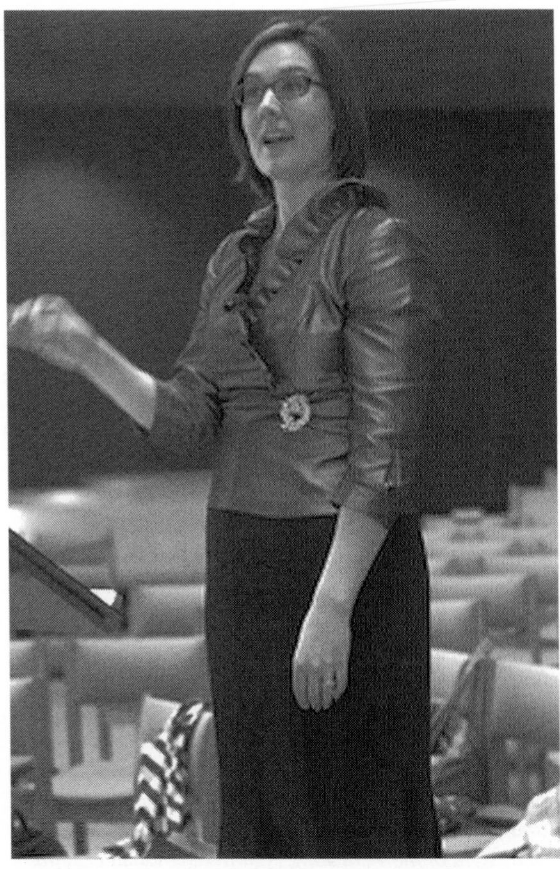

Darcy Morrissey, Vocal Music Teacher

and in 2012 she founded the Bellevue Girlchoir, growing from 80 choristers to 200 in the first five years. This expansion included the founding of the Bellevue Boychoir in 2015. Darcy continues to serve as a professional choral singer, as well as a highly sought after choral clinician and guest conductor.

Q: What were your first experiences with music of the world's cultures?
A: I started out in elementary choir, and we mostly sang in English, along with some songs from the generic "Africa." As if Africa was all once place. And I sung in Latin, but that doesn't really count [laughing]. When I was an adult, I was in a private choir, and we were singing a Balkan piece. The director insisted on that we sing with a "Balkan smile"—a bright forward sound that has a lot of chest behind it. I just loved the sound, and the experience. At first, I was worried that this style of singing would hurt my voice, but eventually it dawned on me that if people had been singing in this way

for hundreds of years, it was probably fine—I just had to think about breath support and vowel placement to make it work right.

Q: Can you tell me about experiences teaching unfamiliar musical traditions to children in choirs?
A: First of all, I have found it really important to bring in guests to help me out. Over the years, I have had a singer from Mongolia visit my choir, a former Russian boy choir member, and a visiting Chinese choral director. Of course, I can do research on my own, but there is nothing quite like having someone from the culture visit and work with the students.

Q: What do you mean by research? Can you give me an example?
A: Yes. A couple of years ago, I was attending another teacher's concert, and the kids performed a Thai song, *Ngam Sang Duan*. I loved the melody, and so I found a choral octavo and ordered it. When I was planning out how to teach it, I went to YouTube to listen for performances of Thai people. I had to wade through a lot of recordings of American choral groups, but eventually found videos of Thai people singing the song. I compared their singing to the octavo, and found a lot of differences in the words. So I put the lyrics into IPA format, to make the score like the recording. I also listened closely to the vocal quality, which was different than the *bel canto* sound I am used to—the tone was very nasal, and required the soft palate to be lowered to get the right sound. I worked on it by myself before demonstrating for the kids.

Q: How did it go with your students?
A: Good! They're great kids. But I thought a lot about how to present it to them. I was worried that they might think that the vocal sound was really weird, and so I decided that they would first learn the tune and text from my own singing, and not the video. After a couple of days, I shared the video, to show them what it really sounded like. Also, I said on the first day, "Who knows, maybe you'll become the ambassador to Thailand when you grow up! Then you could sing this song to them." It seems like a little thing, but that seemed to get their attention. And finally, I told them that there would be a solo, but only if *all* of them commit to sounding like the Thai singing style as much as possible. That group loved solos, so it worked.

Q: Were there any other issues that came up?
A: Yes. Initially, I planned to sing some of it in Thai and some in English. After they had worked so hard on the Thai pronunciation, I couldn't figure out what to do about the English. If they sung the tune like a normal American kid, the contrast would be jarring in the performance, but if they tried to sing English words with a Thai vocal quality, it might come across as disrespectful. Ultimately, I decided to just eliminate the English altogether, which was the right choice. The other thing was that I wish that I had had money so that I could have hired a Thai musician or two to accompany the group, but that didn't work out. You can't get everything right, I suppose.

Q: How did the concert go?
A: I thought they were fantastic. The kids threw themselves into it, and totally pulled it off.

Performance Program Examples

Table 4.1 One grade, musical-cultural theme: Grade 4: Music of South-Central Africa (Botswana, Zimbabwe, and South Africa)

	Country	*Tradition*	*Type of Performance*	*Dimension of WMP*	*Issues Highlighted*
"Manhanga"	Zimbabwe-inspired	Zimarimba song	Xylophones	Enactive	Xylophone performance skills
"Maburu We"	Botswana	Children's singing game	Singing/playing game	Enactive, Creating, Integrating	Creating a game based on context
"Chatigo Chinyi"	Zimbabwe	Story-song	Acting out story, with song	Enactive, Integrating	Folk tale with music
"Setinkane song"	Botswana	Mbira (setinkane)	Student demonstration of pieces composed in a culturally specific style	Creating	Modifying instruments for creative activities
Images of the region, written and narrated by children	South-Central Africa	N/A	PowerPoint presentation	Integrating	Student research
"Shosholoza"	S. Africa	Choral	Part singing	Enactive	Choral octavo

Table 4.2 Whole school, musical-cultural theme: Music of Spanish-Speaking Central and South America

Grade & Piece	*Country or Culture*	*Tradition*	*Type of Performance*	*Dimension of WMP*	*Issues Highlighted*
1: "El Juego Chirimbolo"	Ecuador	Ecuadorian children's singing game	A cappella	Enactive	Song to learn names of body parts in Spanish
2: "A la Nanita Nana"	Latin America	Spanish Lullaby	Perform with piano	Enactive	Some songs cross borders
3: "La Guacamaya"	Mexico	Folkloric dance	Folk dance to a recording	Engaged	Performing with a recording
4: Mambo composition	Cuba-inspired	Mambo	Unpitched percussion	Creating	Improvise in the style of the mambo
5: "Small Marimba"	Guatemala	Guatemalan *marimba*	Xylophone ensemble	Enactive	In concert, compare recording to children's performance
6: "El Carnaval de mi Tierra"	El Salvador	Chanchona	Large ensemble	Enactive	Changing instrumentation from original culture

Table 4.3 Whole school, topical cross-cultural theme: Songs of Social Justice

Grade & Piece	*Country*	*Tradition*	*Type of Performance*	*Dimension of WMP*	*Issues Highlighted*
1: "De Colores"	Mexico/United States	Mexican folk	Teacher accompanies on guitar	Enactive	Sung at rallies for unionization of farm workers in U.S.
2: "Ogaada"	Somalia	Somali Folk Song	Teacher accompanies on guitar	Enactive	Text stresses importance of education for new country to prosper
3: "We Shall Overcome"	United States	U.S. Civil Rights Song	A cappella	Enactive	1960s Civil Rights in U.S.
4: "Maburu We"	Botswana	Botswana children's singing game	Children demonstrate signing game	Enactive, Creating	Text concerns apartheid in South Africa
5: "Ballad of Springhill"	Canada	Singer-songwriter	Song, with mountain dulcimer	Enactive	Text concerns conditions in coal mines
6: "Sikalela Izwe Lakithi (We Protest for Our Land)"	South Africa	South African freedom song	2-part song with percussion	Enactive	Text concerns apartheid in South Africa
Gr. 1–6 Finale: "This Land Is Your Land"	United States	American folk	T. accompanies on guitar, with picture book	Enactive	Text concerns issues of poverty

Worked Example of a Performance: Colonial Fair

The fifth graders at Snow Elementary School in the Western region of the United States, like many fifth graders in their country, embarked upon an in-depth study of the Colonial period of American history. In the 21st century, such units are usually not restricted to history, but incorporate subjects across the curriculum. At Snow School, the fifth graders' study was framed through the perspective of the interaction of three different culture groups—Native Americans, European Americans, and African Americans. The study of colonialism was not limited to social studies class but was woven into much of the rest of the curriculum. The fifth graders read fictional accounts of children living during the 18th century, used math skills to create the dimensions of a typical colonial living structure, and performed scientific experiments in order to explore the effect of different types of soil on the crops during this time. Their culminating activity was a project in which they worked in small groups to research a subject such as food, housing, clothing, or leisure activities. They examined their topic from the perspective of each of the three culture groups. At the end of the unit, they put on a "Colonial Fair," dressing in garb typical of one of the culture groups while presenting the findings that came out of their small group work.

When the music teacher Mr. Newman heard about this, he jumped into action. This was a perfect opportunity to create a mini-unit that employed World Music Pedagogy to teach music from the Native American, European American, and African American traditions. Given all the work that was occurring in the students' daily general classroom, the experience integrated appropriately into the students' existing framework. The students were able to perform their pieces for the Colonial Fair, providing the students the opportunity for public performance.

Mr. Newman chose three pieces for the students to learn and perform. All had pros and cons, but ultimately he felt that these were the best choices.

Native American Tradition

To represent Native American traditions, Mr. Newman selected a flute piece from the Ojibwe people.

Pros:

- The piece was for the flute, and the students had been working on recorder in class. The song was easy enough so that the children could learn it and replicate it successfully. Connecting with their pre-existing curriculum allowed him to meet the broader musical goal of recorder skills.
- The recording of the song was readily available, and the students were able to listen to the recording, comparing the different timbre of the Ojibwe flute and the classroom recorders they used.

Cons:

- The Ojibwe people hail primarily from modern-day Canada, as well as parts of the United States that were not settled by Europeans or Africans during early parts of Colonialism. Nonetheless, Mr. Newman decided that the song itself and its ability to connect to the curriculum outweighed those concerns.

As the performance drew near, Mr. Newman penned the following introduction that was read by one of the fifth graders during the performance:

> When the Native Peoples of the New World came into contact with the Europeans, many died because of disease. Very little is known about their music from that time, though it likely included much singing and dancing, as well as drumming and flute playing. In this next song, we will perform a piece from the Ojibwe people. We will be performing it on our recorders, which sound similar to the flutes played in many Native American tribes. You will also see and hear Jamey, Sam, and Randy playing the beat on a large gathering drum, which is also common among many Native American groups.

African American Tradition

To represent African American traditions, Mr. Newman looked to traditions of West Africa. African American musical traditions developed over time, and during the early Colonial period, the musical traditions were likely mostly influenced by the cultures that the Africans had left behind. He chose a piece called *Kiembara Xylophone Ensemble*, from the Senufo people of the Ivory Coast.

Pros:

- The Ivory Coast is in West Africa, the homeland of many slaves.
- The song contained xylophones and drums—both of which the school owned, and both of which the students already knew how to play.
- The xylophone parts had two overlapping ostinati, both of which were fairly easy for the children to learn.
- The drum part also consisted of two parts, allowing the children to continue to work on part-work skills.

Cons:

- Some might find the focus on slavery and going all the way back to these "roots" to be offensive.
- There are many other rich African American musical traditions such as spirituals, gospel, and jazz that could have been selected.

During the performance, a different fifth grader read the following introduction:

> Most slaves in the United States came from the Western coast of Africa. This next piece is from the Ivory Coast, and is the type of music that you would hear if you went there today. You will hear xylophones and drums. These instruments

will play overlapping ostinati, which are patterns that repeat themselves over and over again. In West Africa, these ostinati have rhythms that are often similar, but not identical. Listen to the two xylophone parts, and note how they sound almost exactly alike—but not quite. Xylophones that you hear in many parts of West Africa often have a rattling sound to it. Our xylophones have a clearer sound, but the overall musical effect of the performance is similar.

European American Tradition

To represent European American traditions, Mr. Newman decided to select a work song, since it would highlight the kind of hard-working lives that many new immigrants have when then enter a new world, even to this day. He chose the classic sea shanty, *What Shall We Do with a Drunken Sailor*.

Pros:

- The work song would allow the performance to highlight the hard work that typically characterizes the experience of most immigrants when they come to a new world. The British colonists were no exception.
- Mr. Newman knew of a three-part arrangement that would allow the students to demonstrate the part-work skills that were a focus of the curriculum in fifth grade music classes.

Cons:

- The idea of "drunken sailors" might be offensive to some.

During the performance, a third fifth grader read the following introduction:

> The song *What Shall We Do with a Drunken Sailor* is a sea shanty, which is a kind of work song. People in many parts of the world have songs that they sing together to help the coordinate tasks when they are working. They also make the time go by faster! In class, we talked about the meaning of the word "stereotype," which is an oversimplified image of a group of people, one that is usually unfair. We decided that this stereotype was unfair. In our performance, see if you can hear the three different parts that we are singing without any help from the piano. We had to work hard to get them down perfectly!

Notes

1 Although the dimensions of Creating World Music and Integrating World Music are discussed in detail in Chapters 5 and 6, they will be addressed in this chapter in the context of performance.
2 World Music Pedagogy in choral settings is further discussed in Volume V of this series.

Recording List: Sample Concerts

Music of South-Central Africa

"Chatigo Chinyi," Adzenya K. Abraham, Judith Cook Tucker, and Dumisani Mararie (from *Let Your Voice Be Heard*), World Music Press, book/CD available online.

"Maburu We," Young children of the Bakgaladi culture group (from *Traditional Music of Botswana, Africa: A Journey with Tape Recorder along Southern Botswana from Mochudi to Kang*), Smithsonian Folkways Recordings, www.folkways.si.edu/young-school-children-of-the-bakgaladi-group/tribal-songs-of-batswana-oh-a-shoe-oh-a-shoe/world/music/track/smithsonian

"Manhanga," performer and composer unknown (based on a Zimbabwean wedding song in the "Zimarimba" style), numerous videos available online.

"Setinkane" (also called "Basarwa [Bushmen] Selections: Basarwa Instrumental Selection—Setinkane [Mbira]"), young Masarawa woman (from *Traditional Music of Botswana, Africa: A Journey with Tape Recorder along Southern Botswana from Mochudi to Kang*), Smithsonian Folkways Recordings, https://folkways.si.edu/young-masarawa-woman-recorded-in-the-village-of-kang/basarwa-bushmen-selections-basarwa-instrumental-selection-setinkane-mbira/world/music/track/smithsonian

"Shosholoza," from "Three South African Songs," arr. by Steven Fisher (simplified), Colla Voce Music; videos of South African choirs available on YouTube.

Music of Spanish-Speaking Central and South America

"A la Nanita Nana," Octavio Corvalan (from *Vamos a Cantar: Let Us Sing: A Collection of Children's Songs in Spanish*), Smithsonian Folkways Recordings, https://folkways.si.edu/na/a-la-nanita-nana/music/track/smithsonian

"El Carnaval de mi Tierra," Los Hermanos Lovo (from *¡Soy Salvadoreño! Chanchona Music from Eastern El Salvador*), Smithsonian Folkways Recordings, www.folkways.si.edu/los-hermanos-lovo/el-carnaval-de-mi-tierra-the-carnival-of-my-land/latin/music/track/smithsonian

"El Juego Chirimbolo," Elizabeth Villarreal Brennan (from *Roots and Branches: A Legacy of Multicultural Music for Children*) (Book/CD), World Music Press, www.worldmusicpress.com/detail.php?product_group=278

"La Guacamaya," José Gutiérrez and Los Hermanos Ochoa (from *La Bamba: Sones Jarochos from Veracruz*), Smithsonian Folkways Recordings, https://folkways.si.edu/jose-gutierrez-los-hermanos-ochoa/la-guacamaya/latin-world/music/track/smithsonian

"Mambo Composition by Fourth Graders," N/A (student-created piece).

"Small Marimba," Tzutuzil Indians (performer names unknown) (from *Music of Guatemala, Vol. 1*), Smithsonian Folkways Recordings, https://folkways.si.edu/tzutuzil-indians/small-marimba/american-indian-latin-world/music/track/smithsonian

Songs of Social Justice

"Ballad of Springhill," written by Peggy Seeger, videos of performers such as U2 and the Dubliners available on YouTube.

"De Colores," Baldemar Velasquez and Aguila Negra (from *Classic Labor Songs from Smithsonian Folkways*), Smithsonian Folkways Recordings, https://folkways.si.edu/baldemar-velasquez-and-aguila-negra/de-colores/american-folk-struggle-protest/music/track/smithsonian

"Maburu We," Young children of the Bakgaladi culture group (from *Traditional Music of Botswana, Africa: A Journey with Tape Recorder along Southern Botswana from Mochudi to Kang*), Smithsonian Folkways Recordings, www.folkways.si.edu/young-school-children-of-the-bakgaladi-group/tribal-songs-of-batswana-oh-a-shoe-oh-a-shoe/world/music/track/smithsonian

"Ogaada," Abdullah Kershi and Ahmed Sherif (from *The Freedom Songs of the Somali Republic*), Smithsonian Folkways Recordings, https://folkways.si.edu/abdullah-kershi-and-ahmed-sherif/ogaada/historical-song-islamica-struggle-protest-world/music/track/smithsonian

"Sikalela Izwe Lakithi (We Protest for Our Land)," South African refugees in Tanganyika (modern-day Tanzania), recorded in 1965 (from *This Land is Mine: South African Freedom Songs*), Smithsonian Folkways Recordings, https://folkways.si.edu/sikalela-izwe-lakithi-we-protest-for-our-land/historical-song-struggle-protest-world/music/track/smithsonian

"This Land Is Your Land," Woody Guthrie (from *This Land Is Your Land: The Asch Recordings, Vol. 1*), Smithsonian Folkways Recordings, https://folkways.si.edu/woody-guthrie/this-land-is-your-land-the-asch-recordings-vol-1/american-folk-struggle-protest/music/album/Smithsonian

"We Shall Overcome," The Freedom Singers (from *Voices of the Civil Rights Movement: Black American Freedom Songs 1960–1966*), Smithsonian Folkways Recordings, https://folkways.si.edu/the-freedom-singers/we-shall-overcome/african-american-music-documentary-struggle-protest/track/smithsonian

5

Creating World Music

A cacophony of sound fills the music room as 24 sixth grade children sit on the floor, two children behind each of 12 Orff xylophones and 12 hand drums that are placed on the floor, scattered around the room. Earlier in the class period, the music teacher, Mr. Rossol, had led a discussion in which he reviewed the characteristics of the culture and xylophone music of the Bura people (which they had been listening to and performing for several weeks) and asked the children to talk about their thoughts regarding how the music that they make up in their music classroom might be different and how it might be similar to the music that they might hear if they were at a dance in Nigeria. He had given directions to "work with your partner to create a new xylophone and drum piece that you can remember based on melodic and/or rhythmic ideas from the Nigerian xylophone music that we've been listening to."

Some of the children are exploring playing different musical patterns on the instruments, and others are glancing up at the list of Nigerian xylophone music characteristics written on the board and saying, "it was really syncopated, and there's lots of repetition. Let me try to play . . . " After a specified period of time, Mr. Rossol turns off the lights signaling for the children to stop playing. He says, "Now it is time to make some decisions and practice your piece together. Decide who will play which parts, and in 4 minutes, the first partner groups who are ready will perform for us." The children get back to work, busily talking and practicing, and when the lights go off again, over half of them are raising their hands with excitement to share their new xylophone pieces. After each pair performs, the teacher asks the rest of the class to comment upon what made it sound similar to and different from the Nigerian xylophone dance piece that they had learned earlier, then he asks the children who have not performed to make sure they have their piece memorized so they can perform for the class the next time they meet.

Musical Creativity in Children's Lives

Throughout their early years, children spontaneously make their own music, humming new melodies to themselves, drumming with wooden spoons on metal kitchen pots and pans, or blowing across bottle tops. As children get older, the spontaneous creativity of free-form chants and songs from early childhood give way to the tendency to create parodies of common songs and explore other new ways of changing or expanding upon familiar singing games and other music. Even at the age of seven, children are likely to be interested in popular music, and their created songs may reflect the influence of Disney, Broadway musicals, and popular genres such as rap (Gluschankof, 2016).

Technology is also often a rich source for creative expression. All children who have access to apps enjoy playing musical games and exploring and arranging sounds on cell phones and other electronic devices. As they move into upper elementary years and beyond, they may take more interest in using computer programs or instruments with MIDI attachments to organize, perform, and record their own music.

Musical Creativity in the World

Exploration, improvisation, and composition are the most common terms used to describe creative musical activity. There are various definitions of these terms, but within much Western music education scholarship, they are often conceived of as a continuum from free-play (exploration) through creating music during performance (improvisation) to solidifying a finalized piece that is memorized and/or notated (composition).

From a Western analytical perspective, exploration usually involves "playing with sound" or trying out various ways to organize elements of music such as timbre, melody, rhythm, harmony, and form. Most elementary music teachers agree that exploration is an important prerequisite for children to learn to improvise and compose. In much music education literature, improvisation is defined as the act of creating music *during* performance, whereas composition is distinguished as the process of developing and refining a musical work *before* the work is performed or notated in its final form. This is not to say that improvising musicians do not plan ahead, because in many musical cultures, improvisation is an advanced skill that requires learning and practicing melodic, rhythmic, and/or harmonic structures in preparation for various ordering of musical patterns during performance.

Much ethnomusicology research does not support the notion of improvisation as completely extemporaneous performance. Ethnomusicologist Bonnie Wade (2004) argues that all music improvisation is based upon pre-existing musical material. She also suggests that, rather than distinguishing between improvisation and composition based on whether the performance occurs during or after the creative process, it might be more appropriate to consider the various levels of flexibility that are exercised in music around the world, so that improvisation might be defined as a high level of flexibility demonstrated during the process of performing.

All musical performances require at least a minimal amount of creativity in which there are varying degrees of musical flexibility on the part of the performers, from making expressive choices while interpreting a previously composed piece to a much more extemporaneous performance in which the musical material is treated with extreme flexibility. Different solo performers of the same Chopin nocturne may make different expressive choices regarding dynamics, tempo, phrasing, etc., demonstrating that even when "compositions" are notated and recreated, there is some flexibility in performance through interpretation.

Creative musical behaviors are common throughout the world, and in many musical cultures, improvisation and composition are central to a genre. In Hindustani music of North India and many sub-Saharan African musical practices, the performers are expected to treat musical material with a great deal of flexibility so that the performance is almost completely extemporaneous. Anglo-American vocal and instrumental folk musicians are often expected to create variants as they perform, and American jazz musicians are required to create new melodic or rhythmic musical material over specific chord progressions during particular parts of performances.

Creating in World Music Pedagogy

It may seem counterintuitive to ask children to create their own "world music," particularly when considering the emphasis of the previous WMP dimensions on replicating the sound of a recording or trying to emulate a culture-bearer by recreating music as close to the original as possible. However, many believe that musical exploration, improvisation, and composition are at the top of the cognitive ladder for music learners, and that using musical sources and inspirations from various music cultures should be part of the creative process in elementary music classrooms. Teachers who utilize World Music Pedagogy know that when children experience the sonic qualities of various musical cultures of the world through WMP listening experiences, they may be motivated or encouraged to express their understanding of musical meanings and structures through opportunities to create their own music using some of the sounds, structures, or skills of that musical culture.

According to Patricia Shehan Campbell (2016), "Composition, improvisation, songwriting, and even the act of extending a piece beyond the part of it that is represented on a recording are avenues of creative expression that are informed by attentive, engaged, and enactive levels of music listening" (p. 99). Music teachers can take advantage of children's natural tendency to play with sounds by adding some of the world's musical cultures to children's repertoire of familiar music, then encouraging them to connect in greater depth to the musical elements and meanings of these cultures through musical creativity. This creativity might include extending recorded musical pieces from WMP listening lessons, improvising or composing "in the style of" a certain culture's music, utilizing improvisational or compositional guidelines practiced by musicians of a particular culture, or writing songs in an attempt to illustrate similar meanings of songs within a particular musical tradition. Blends and fusions of various musical cultures surround children through television, video games, movies, and radio, so they may also be inspired to practice blending musical elements from two or more cultures as part of their creative music-making process.

Within the context of World Music Pedagogy, children might be asked to listen to and discuss the ways that musicians from a particular musical tradition improvise, compose, or arrange music, but elementary school-aged children would not necessarily be expected to be able to imitate these original creative practices. For example, children will not be able to improvise a Hindustani *khyal*, but they can discuss the structure and meaning of the *khyal* during Attentive and Engaged Listening activities, then learn to sing the *sargam solfège* system to learn a *raga*, and create their own vocal melodies using the learned pitches. Teachers of World Music Pedagogy consider the skills and knowledge of the children as they carefully select musical examples, then they present creative tasks that will allow the students to feel successful so that they will be motivated to learn more about the music and the culture.

Why Create World Music in Elementary School?

Activities that encourage musical creativity are very important in school curricula because children's creative music making may decline over time without encouragement, and because most societies value creating music as a skill that well-rounded musicians should attain. National and international organizations have put forth educational guidelines that support creativity for school children. In response to the question, "What do real musicians do in the world?" the designers of the National Core Arts Standards in the United States included "Creating" as one of the four main artistic processes. Similarly, Ireland's National Standards lists "Composing" as one of the three main content standards for music, and Singapore's Arts Standards names "Create and improvise music" as one of their six main objectives. Finland's Core Content standards include "Experimenting with one's own musical ideas by improvising, composing, and arranging, using sound, song, instruments, movement, and musical technology," (College Board, 2011, p. 41). Creativity and creative thinking also play prominent roles in the arts standards of many other countries, including Australia, Austria, Canada, China, Japan, the Netherlands, New Zealand, Scotland, Sweden, and the United Kingdom. Teachers everywhere realize that creative activities help children come to know music with greater depth and meaning. Therefore, Creating World Music encourages children to make a more meaningful connection to a particular music culture than they would if they only experienced the other dimensions of World Music Pedagogy, thus diminishing the distance between "us" and "them."

Elementary Music Classroom Culture

Elementary music classrooms have their own "cultures" in which particular behaviors, attitudes, and achievements become expectations or traditions. For example, children may know that the sixth graders put on a big performance at the end of the school year, that each time they leave music class they are expected to line up silently, or that there are children who take on roles such as leader, class clown, teacher's pet, and others. They might have learned that when they compose, they are expected to end melodies on tonic or to include some rhythmic material from the antecedent phrase when they compose a rhythmic consequent phrase. They may be in the practice of freely improvising in a pentatonic mode on the Orff xylophones using a piece of art or literature as an inspirational prompt. Some of these expectations, particularly those that have been previously set in relation to composition and improvisation, will certainly influence any music that is created in a school setting. Whenever music is performed in a music classroom, be it classical, pop, folk, or rock, there is inherently a fusion of classroom music culture into the music being performed and/or created. Because

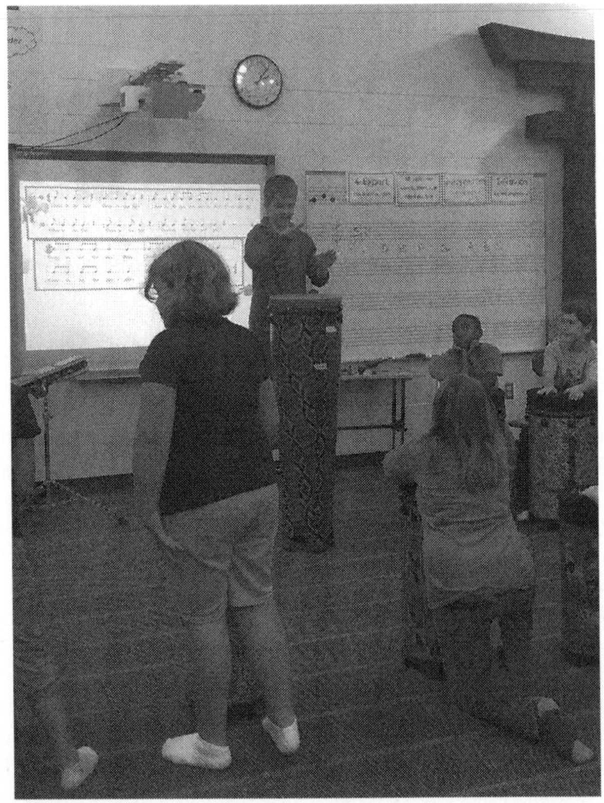

Figure 5.1 Children improvising on *tubano* drums

Photo courtesy of BethAnn Hepburn

all musical recordings capture a particular place and time, whenever a recording is reproduced in a music classroom, the music is reborn as a "new" music, in a sense. As music travels from place to place and across time, it always changes sound in some way, and therefore all music is "authentic" to the people who study and find meaning in the music. One of the unique aspects of World Music Pedagogy is that both the "older" (i.e. recording of Japanese *taiko* made in 1978) and the "newer" music (i.e. a class of ten- and eleven-year-old children creating a composition using the sounds and movements of Japanese *taiko* using available hand drums and mallets in their Canadian music classroom) can be considered "authentic."

Active Music-Making Methods as Models for Creating World Music

Teachers who utilize World Music Pedagogy attempt to respect the traditional transmission practices of the original culture when possible, but also understand that there are teaching and learning techniques that work best for elementary-aged children that may be removed from the original ways of giving and receiving music. If a particular teaching method allows children to have a more positive experience with the music, there is nothing wrong with using that method in conjunction with the components of WMP, as long as it does not cause confusion among the children or offend those who know the musical culture well.

Patricia Shehan Campbell points out that techniques of Orff Schulwerk, Kodály, and Dalcroze

> fit quite naturally the music from various places on the African continent; the Pacific Islands; parts of East, South, and Southeast Asia; Latin America . . . the old-style and mostly rural European traditions; and the many diverse communities of North America.
>
> (Campbell, 2016, p. 105)

Such active music-making approaches provide models for techniques that can be used to encourage children to improvise and compose their own music. Teachers who use Gordon's Music Learning Theory believe that children learn to improvise music similarly to the way they learn to speak, by internally hearing sound patterns (*audiation*) that can be put together to form sentences or musical phrases. Gordon practitioners present familiar or unfamiliar rhythmic or melodic patterns, and then ask children to respond by creating patterns of their own, first on neutral syllables, then later with rhythmic syllables or *solfège*. Children in Dalcroze-inspired classrooms spontaneously create movement and rhythmic patterns in response to musical cues and improvise vocal melodies using *solfège*.

The main goal of the Orff Schulwerk approach is for children to create their own music and movement, so children are guided through a process of imitation, exploration, and improvisation that eventually leads to composition through moving, rhythmic speaking, singing, and playing recorders, small percussion, or Orff instruments. Children in Kodály-based classrooms are sometimes encouraged to change particular parts of singing games and improvise or compose their own songs. Improvisation and composition is sometimes used by both Orff- and Kodály-trained teachers as a means for children to demonstrate mastery of particular rhythmic or melodic elements. These methodological approaches can contribute to the creative component of World Music Pedagogy by providing techniques that teachers can use to propel world music listening experiences to higher levels, in which children explore, expand, and invent new music that is informed by knowledge of various world music cultures.

If children are in the habit of making musical choices each time they come to music class (e.g. deciding on tempo or dynamic levels for a song they are practicing or choosing how to order four different 2-beat rhythmic building blocks to create an 8-beat rhythmic phrase), they will be more prepared when it comes time to exercise greater musical flexibility as they improvise and compose using musics of various world cultures as jumping-off points.

Planning for Creating World Music

Preparation

Children will be more successful in creating new music if they are highly familiar with the musical culture that will serve as a starting place for extension, exploration, improvisation, or composition. Extensive experience with Attentive and Engaged Listening to one or more examples from a particular world culture should precede Enactive Listening and Creating World Music. Without many previous experiences of Attentive and Engaged Listening to culturally representative examples, children might fall back on stereotypical and/or inaccurate sounds such as those portrayed by the media. For example, if fourth graders are given the task to create a group drumming piece while studying Sioux powwows, without much listening experience, they might begin accenting every fourth beat (**1**234) as they may have heard in portrayals of Native American drumming in television and movies, which is not typical of most drumming cultures of indigenous people of North American nations and would likely be considered offensive by knowledgeable listeners.

Creative music making requires adequate time to practice, plan, and revise. Even when improvising, children need time to learn and practice the musical material that will frame and/or provide rhythmic, melodic, or harmonic material for the improvisation. Lessons in musical creativity should not be rushed, and teachers should consider how to set appropriate boundaries and structural guidelines so that children know what is expected of them.

Selecting Listening Examples

Selecting musical listening examples from various cultural groups to serve as referents for children's creative music making involves acquaintance with children's skills and knowledge, consideration of available musical instruments, as well as awareness of the creative practices that exist in the musical culture(s) of the recording(s). Because creative activities need to be preceded by Attentive, Engaged, and sometimes also Enactive Listening experiences, teachers can refer to "selecting music" guidelines in Chapters 2 and 3 of this volume when considering musical examples that may be used as inspiration for children's exploratory creative impulses. There may be instances in which the recorded music is too difficult for children to perform through Enactive Listening, but they might still be able to utilize some of the sounds to create their own music (see Episode 5.3 for an example).

Musical models for improvisation and composition are best selected in consultation with a culture-bearer or visiting artist who might also instruct the teacher or children in techniques for improvising or composing. If a culture-bearer is not available for consultation regarding creative practices, teachers can research musical recordings by reading the liner notes downloaded from the Smithsonian Folkways Recordings and/or utilizing resources such as those listed at the end of this volume. The more that children are immersed in the creative practices of a musical culture, the more they will have an opportunity to successfully improvise or compose using the creative musical practices of that culture.

Musical traditions in which great musical flexibility is expected as part of the music-making process include drumming traditions that started in sub-Saharan Africa, classical music from India, and jazz that originated from the African diaspora in North America. Recordings, videos, or live performances from these musical traditions can serve as models for children's creative music making, offering examples of melodic, rhythmic, and structural improvisation. In the absence of a visiting artist who is a culture-bearer, recordings and videos of culture-bearers may also give clues as to performance, improvisational, and compositional techniques and practices. These recorded selections can also be utilized to build the musical skills and understanding within the music curriculum that are necessary for well-informed improvisation and composition.

Contextual Discussion

Children will benefit from discussions regarding context, including the ways that music can be influenced by time and place of creation and performance (also see Chapter 6). A discussion about context might be started by asking older elementary-aged children questions such as "If we make up our own song using the pitches in this *raga* from a North Indian classical music tradition, how will it be different from the recording of the classical Indian song that we have been listening to and talking about? How will it be the same? Do other musicians sometimes make up music that uses instruments or musical elements from this Indian classical music tradition, even if they aren't from that culture? Is this okay? Why? Why not?" Younger children might also be encouraged to answer questions such as "What are the differences and similarities between the recording of an English folk song made in 1969 and the same folk song that we are singing in class today? Who were the people who made up the music? Why did they make up this song? Why are we singing this song in class today and making our own 'version' of it?"

Examples of Six Ways to Create Using World Music Pedagogy

There are many ways to engage children in creative musical activities that fall within the purview of World Music Pedagogy. The following examples demonstrate some ideas for encouraging elementary-aged children to create music in six ways: (a) extend a culturally representative listening selection in order to perform it, (b) explore sounds and structures of a certain musical culture, (c) compose a new piece in the style of a musical genre or piece from a particular culture, (d) improvise within a structural format that is characteristic of a musical culture, (e) compose a piece that is a fusion of several musical styles, and (f) write a song in a particular style.

Extending Listening Examples

Creative activities may be precipitated when children gain appreciation for a listening selection to the point of wanting to perform it. If the listening selection is from one of the brief links provided in this text, teachers and children may want to extend the musical example for the purpose of performance. Children may also be inspired or encouraged to create new arrangements, add their own introductions or codas, and/or make interpretive decisions regarding dynamics, tempo, and phrasing, for example first graders adding an introductory hand-clapping pattern to a German counting game, third graders deciding how to arrange two Irish or Scottish folk tunes for a penny whistle performance, or fifth graders creating new verses to a South African freedom song.

Teachers can ask questions to encourage children to extend the recordings, such as (a) What could we add to this song or piece in order to perform it for an audience? (b) How should we begin and end the performance? (c) How can we make these changes or additions while still being respectful of the original musical tradition? (d) How is our creation similar to and different from the original musical tradition?

Episode 5.1 describes a learning sequence in which the teacher leads the children in extending a well-known Mexican song by making arrangement decisions for an upcoming performance. This *marimba* band recording used in this episode was made by Emory Cook in 1954 as part of a collection of *marimba* band pieces from Chiapas and Oaxaca, Mexico. Before participating in this episode, children have already learned to play the melody and the bass accompaniment part in ensemble on classroom *marimbas* or xylophones. They have also studied the history of the piece: a waltz that is known as the unofficial anthem of the Mexican state of Oaxaca that was composed by violinist, pianist, and songwriter Macedonio Alcalá in 1868. Alcalá wrote the song at the request of local indigenous people who wanted a song in honor of the Virgin Mary, who was the patron saint of their village. He wrote this during a time that he was unhappy because he couldn't make enough money as a musician to support his family. The original lyrics refer to the difficulties of life and that faith in God can ease the fear of death.

Episode 5.1: Mexico: "Dios Nunca Muere"

Specific Use: Upper Elementary General Music Class

Materials:

- "Dios Nunca Muere," performers unknown (from *Marimba Band*), Cook Records
- *Marimbas* and/or xylophones

Procedure:

(Creating)

1. Play track (0:00–0:30), as children enter the room.
2. Ask the children to make suggestions to the overall structure of their performance:
   a. Should there be a musical introduction?
   b. Should there be layered entrances?
   c. How many times should the melody be played?

   d. Is the tempo the same as the recording? Why or why not? Should it be?
   e. Should we add another section? What should be the same and different about it?

3. Play track as needed while discussing where additions should go and/or what should be changed.
4. Practice performing the piece according to student suggestions.
5. Decide as a class on changes for a final performance for the piece.
6. Practice as time permits in order to finalize the performance.
7. Discuss which historical information the audience should know about the piece and how to communicate this with the audience: written program notes, verbal introduction, other ideas?
8. Play track again and ask students to compare their performance to the recording.

   (**Transcription** below is an approximation.)

Figure 5.2 "Dios Nunca Muere" from Mexico

Episode 5.2 follows Learning Pathway #1 and provides an example of children extending the musical recording of the song *Maburu We* through creating movement. The teacher should give the students some historical knowledge about the children of the Bakgaladi tribal group that was gleaned from the liner notes provided on the website for Smithsonian Folkways Recordings.

Episode 5.2: Botswana: "Maburu We" (Learning Pathway #1)

Specific Use: Upper Elementary General Music Class

Materials:

- "Maburu We" (Oh, a Shoe, a Shoe), young children of the Bakgaladi culture group (from *Traditional Music of Botswana, Africa: A Journey with Tape Recorder along Southern Botswana from Mochudi to Kang*), Smithsonian Folkways Recordings
- Open space to play

Procedure:

(Attentive, Engaged, and Enactive)

1. Children have participated in the Attentive, Engaged, and Enactive experiences in chapters 2 and 3. They can sing the song without the recording.
2. To review, ask the children to sing the song with the recording.
   - Play track while children sing.
3. Sing again, without the recording. Check for accuracy of the children's performance.

(Integrating)

4. Inform the children that the singers are doing something while the performance is occurring. Ask them to listen to the recording again, attempting to determine what the performers are doing.
   a. Play track and field answers. (A: Playing a singing game.)
   b. If answers are incorrect, remind them that the singers are children, and say, "They are doing something that you sometimes do in music class, when we sing songs." Lead the children to understand that it is a game song or a singing game.
5. Inform the children that directions for the game are not provided on the liner notes to the album. However, game songs of children from the Bakgaladi culture group usually involve some sort of leg or foot movement, or a dance pattern performed by a small group in front of the singers.

(Creating)

6. Lead the class through a process where they create movement for the singing game to accompany the song, one that involves leg or foot movement:

e.g. (a) ask for volunteers to demonstrate movements that can be made by feet or legs, (b) decide on two to three movements that the entire class can do, (c) sing the song again, maybe replacing the claps with sounds made via the new movements with feet or legs, (d) decide how many times each movement should be done to make the singing game work with the song.

7. As an entire class, sing the song while playing the singing game that the class created.
8. If they are able to do this up to tempo, try it with the recording.
   - Play track.
9. If successful, divide the children into groups, asking them to work with their peers to repeat the activity, creating a new singing game.

Exploring Sounds and Structures

As children listen to a musical example from a particular world culture, they are often excited to try out the instruments they hear, to explore ways to make vocal sounds or movements that they observe, or freely play with rhythms, melodies, harmonies, or forms they identify from the example. For example, children in early elementary grades may explore "found sounds" to play with after listening to tracks from "Sounds of the Office" by Michael Siegel, or take turns blowing into panpipes after hearing a recording of the syrinx of Bolivia. Children in middle elementary grades might explore telling Hawaiian stories through movement after learning hula movements by watching an instructional video found online through a Hawaiian cultural center, or upper-elementary-aged children might try out various ways to perform Ghanaian call-and-response drumming patterns that they've learned from a visiting culture-bearer. In Episode 5.3, the teacher fosters exploration of scat sounds that early elementary children hear in the American jazz standard *Stompin' at the Savoy*, composed by Edgar Sampson in 1934 and recorded by Louis Armstrong and Ella Fitzgerald in 1956.

Episode 5.3: United States: "Stompin' at the Savoy"

Specific Use: Early Elementary Music Class

Materials:

- "Stompin' at the Savoy," Louis Armstrong and Ella Fitzgerald (from *Jazz: The Smithsonian Anthology*), Smithsonian Folkways Recordings

Procedure:

(Creating)

1. Play track (0:00–0:27) while reviewing the list of the scat syllables that they have heard before.
2. Imitate teacher chanting 8-beat rhythms using scat syllables.
3. Imitate 8-beat melodies using vocal scat syllables after teacher plays each brief melody (preferably on a trumpet, saxophone, or other common jazz band instrument).
4. Quietly explore or "play around with" different syllables to make up their own scat patterns (chanting or singing).
5. Volunteers share their ideas with the rest of the class; ask the class to listen for the syllables that the volunteer performer uses as he/she explores syllables.
   - Play track to compare their scatting with that on the recording.

Before participating in this lesson, the children should have learned that jazz originated in African American communities of New Orleans in the United States, perhaps by reading a picture book about Ella Fitzgerald (such as *Skit Scat, Raggedy Cat* by Roxane Orgill or *Ella Fitzgerald: The Tale of a Vocal Virtuosa* by Andrea Davis Pinkney) to learn that she is considered to be one of the greatest scat singers in jazz history. They should have also listened to the brief *Stompin' at the Savoy* example at least three times, utilizing Attentive and Engaged Listening techniques. The teacher should have helped the children define scat singing as a jazz singing technique, in which a soloist imitates a musical instrument by singing something other than lyrics, and assisted the children in making a list of the scat syllables that they hear in the example.

Creating Compositions

Composition in most elementary classrooms is usually organized in one of two ways: (1) individuals compose at the computer or using the instrument that they feel most comfortable with (this allows children to continue their process of composing outside of music class time), or (2) small cooperative groups work together to compose something to share with the rest of the class. Within the realm of World Music Pedagogy, it is more common for children to work in cooperative groups to compose a piece "in the style of" a particular world music genre that can be reproduced using classroom instruments that resemble the sounds of the original music (xylophones, metallophones, drums, small percussion, etc.). In addition to focusing on repeated listening to recordings of culture-bearers, World Music Pedagogy is largely aimed at human interactions and connections to music, so individual work on computers is not common. However, if the world music culture under study is a popular, dance, or film genre in which computerized sounds comprise most of the pieces of that musical culture, it might be appropriate for children to explore and compose music using computers or electronic instruments with an original popular, dance, or field piece as a model. Technology can also be a useful tool for Creating World Music if an elementary music classroom doesn't have instruments that would usually be played within a musical culture and the children can replicate the sounds of those instruments via apps, synthesizers, or computer programs.

Episode 5.4 is an example of groups of children working together to compose a performance in the style of "modern" *taiko* drumming, following the selection, *Suwa Onbashira Kiyari-Taiko* of Learning Pathway #3. Prior to this lesson, ideally the children have been working with a culture-bearer, attending *taiko* drumming concerts, and/or watching videos of *taiko* drumming. As part of Attentive Listening, they should have discussed the characteristics that make *taiko* unique: the instruments, the way the performers move, the way the rhythmic parts enter and exit, and the variation of tempo. They should have also completed Engaged Listening experiences such as moving to distinguish between high and low drum sounds and playing body percussion to demonstrate the change in tempo, as well as Enactive Listening by reproducing the piece with and without the recording.

Episode 5.4: Japan: "Suwa Onbashira Kiyari-Taiko" (Learning Pathway #3)

Specific Use: Any Age General Music Class (Small Group Work for Middle or Upper Only)

Materials:

- "Suwa Onbashira Kiyari-Taiko," Ensemble O-Suwa-Daiko (from *Japan: O-Suwa-Daiko Drums*), Smithsonian Folkways Recordings
- Tambourines or jingle bells
- *Taiko* or other drums that can be hit hard with felt mallets or drumsticks
- Visual Aid: 1. Form (repetition/contrast), 2. Instruments and Order, 3.Tempo, 4. Movement

Procedure:

1. Listen to the piece (3:15-4:11) and ask, "Where does repetition and contrast occur? Do you think there might be repetition and contrast in the performers' body movements as well?"
   - Play track (3:15–4:10) and field answers. (A: There are repeated rhythmic patterns played by particular instruments, parts that speed up and slow down, and different instruments play at different times. Answers will vary regarding body movements.)

2. Divide the class into small groups with about 5–6 children per group (make sure each group has at least one instrument from each category: high drum, low drum, clicking on drum rims, and jingling).
3. Small groups are given time to explore and to decide (use visual aid to remember tasks):
   a. on a form for the piece (how to begin, continue, and end; how to include repetition and contrast).
   b. which instruments should play in which order.
   c. when to increase or decrease the tempo.
   d. how players should move (safely) while performing.
4. Small groups are given time to practice for performance of their compositions (this may take several class periods).
5. Small groups perform for the class, and the listening children are asked to give verbal feedback about what made the piece sound like or unlike the *taiko* drumming they had been studying.
   - Play track (3:15–4:10) as needed for comparison to children's group compositions.

Implementing Improvisation

Musical improvisation requires a great deal of musical skill, knowledge, and flexibility, so previous Attentive, Engaged, and Enactive Listening activities should provide children with a solid understanding of the structures, musical material, and/or performance practices that they will be asked to utilize as they create their own music while they are performing. Children could add an improvised section to a recording, e.g. children take turns improvising a brief melodic introduction for a recording of a classic Bollywood song from a well-known film, such as *Hum Bhi Agar Bacche Hot* from the film *Door Ki Awaaz* (1964), or *Chakke Pe Chakka—Chakke Peh Gaadhi* from the film *Brahmachari* (1968). They might also improvise with similar structural parameters or performance practices that the musicians from a particular musical culture might utilize. For example, upper elementary children could take turns improvising a hythmic solo by creating new rhythmic patterns on a *djembe* over an ensemble of other drummers as the lead drummer would do while leading a community dance in Guinea. Children who feel comfortable improvising might be encouraged to do so as part of a performance for an audience in order to share their improvisational skills.

Not all creative activities with music of the world's cultures will require children to imitate specific cultural creative practices, such as improvising or composing within particular structural, melodic, or rhythmic guidelines. However, if children are able to improvise or compose using similar techniques that musicians of that culture would utilize, such as improvising a vocal melody utilizing a particular Arabic *maqam*, this type of interaction with a musical culture will help them come to know the music at a much deeper level. Some teachers, particularly those who work with upper elementary-aged children, might select a particular musical culture to study with the main goal of developing a keen awareness of the music through improvisation and/or composition.

Episode 5.5 describes the last in a series of lessons for Learning Pathway #2 for the El Salvadoran song *El Carnaval de mi Tierra*. Before this episode, the children should have participated in the Attentive, Engaged, and Enactive Listening experiences presented in Chapters 2–5. If this episode occurs at an earlier time of exposure and experience with the song, then further Engaged and Enactive Listening can serve to reacquaint students to the music. In such a case, the teacher plays the track at least three times for children to (a) review the overall form of the entire piece, (b) review the harmonic structure of the chorus and verse, and (c) learn the chord roots of the harmonic structure of the violin bridge by singing and playing the chord roots with and then without the recording: I-V-V-I; I-V-V-I and/or G-D-D-G; G-D-D-G.

Episode 5.5: El Salvador: "El Carnaval de mi Tierra" (Learning Pathway #2)

Specific Use: Upper Elementary General Music Class

Materials:

- "El Carnaval de mi Tierra," Los Hermanos Lovo (from *¡Soy Salvadoreño! Chanchona Music from Eastern El Salvador*), Smithsonian Folkways Recordings
- Form of the chords written on the board using Roman numerals and/or letter names
- Visual aid with harmonic structure of chorus, verse, and bridge
- Visual aid showing the chord pitches of a G major chord and the chord pitches of a D major chord
- *Marimbas* or xylophones with F removed, replaced by F#

Procedure:

Students have participated in Attentive, Engaged, and Enactive activities in previous lessons.

(Creating)

1. Play track (00:00–01:01) to review singing the chord roots of the song.
2. Using a visual aid that shows the chord pitches of a G major chord (I) and the chord pitches of a D major chord (V), practice playing and singing the note names for each chord.
   - Play track (01:19–1:27) to listen to the harmonic structure of the bridge.

3. Practice playing the harmonic structure of the violin bridge using a visual that shows the chord structure of the bridge for each measure in the meter of 2/4 (G-B-D, D-F#-A; D-F#-A, G-B-D). Once this is mastered, practice repeating this 8-beat pattern.
4. While children sing and play the chord roots on the downbeat of each measure, the teacher models a melodic improvisation in which she plays and sings the chord root on the downbeat of each measure, then chooses which notes of the appropriate chord she will play and sing on the other beats in order to create a new 8-beat melody.
5. Half of the children play and sing chord roots ("one" and "five") on the first beat of each measure, while the other half of the class practices improvising new melodies for 8 beats as the teacher points to the visual aid. Encourage children to try to play and sing at once. Switch parts.
6. Children try to remember each 8-beat melody that they improvise so that they can play it twice in a row for a total of 16 beats. If it is not exactly the same, that's okay.
    - Play track (00:00–02:00) to review the form of the entire song, then ask for volunteers to perform solos during each violin bridge (slowly, without the recording). If necessary, practice just the solo improvisations before performing without the recording.
7. Perform the entire song with half of the children accompanying on small percussion or playing chord roots on *marimbas*/xylophones, while others sing along for the verse and chorus with volunteer soloists improvising sections played during the verse or chorus of the song.
8. Extension: Children could improvise a vocal descant or harmony part for the chorus section by reviewing the harmonic structure for the chorus using a similar procedure.

Mixing and Fusing Musics

Many composers have been inspired by music, stories, and ideas from various cultures and have combined components of various cultures to create new musical pieces or genres. For example, Philip Glass's early compositions were shaped by Tibetan music and Zoltán Kodály's compositions were informed by Hungarian folk music. The rhythmic elements of the African diaspora helped to build many new musical styles including *samba*, *forró*, *maracatu*, and *coco* in Brazil, the *tumba francesa* and *festejo* in Afro-Cuban and Afro-Peruvian cultures, respectively, as well as the African American genres of *blues*, *jazz*, *rhythm and blues*, *funk*, *soul*, *reggae*, *hip hop*, and *rock and roll*. Composing music that includes musical instruments and stylistic elements of a particular musical culture may not require extensive knowledge about compositional processes of the musicians where the genre or style originated, but elementary-aged composers will benefit from repeated listening of a variety of pieces from the musical culture's specific style in order to get the music "in the ears" before using these sounds and structures in a new composition.

Fusions of various styles and genres are a common compositional technique utilized by musicians, DJs, and choreographers in many parts of the world. When planning lessons that include Creating World Music, teachers can find many examples of compositions that combine musical stylistic elements from various cultures that might serve as models for composing new music that includes two or more musical genres or styles. Examples of Western popular musicians who have incorporated sounds of various musical cultures include Rihanna's use of *gamelan* instruments in one of the recordings of her song *Diamond*, Harry Belafonte's *calypso* arrangements from Jamaica, George Harrison's inclusion of *sitar* and *ragas* from India, and the use of Arabic melodies by Led Zeppelin. Children may be interested to learn that the technical definition of "fusion music" is music that combines two or more genres, and there are many subcategories of fusion music such as gypsy jazz, Celtic fusion, and country rap. The band "Ancient Future" has posted a list of artists who have dedicated their careers to "World Music Fusion" online.[1]

Episode 5.6 illustrates learning activities in which children are encouraged to consider ways of mixing musical materials from different traditions. Preparation for this episode includes knowledge of characteristics of instrumental jazz music such as trumpet, saxophone, and drum set instrumentation, swing rhythms, and improvisatory nature of the genre. Children should also be familiar with Afro-Peruvian music through Attentive, Engaged, and Enactive Listening to the Afro-Peruvian song *Samba Malato*, recorded in 2007 by an Afro-Peruvian singer, Lucila Campos (1938–2016). The children should have learned that Afro-Peruvian music is a mix of Spanish elements (language and guitar) and African elements (call-and-response form, percussion instruments) that developed over a very long period, originating with slaves during the Spanish colonial era and revitalized in the 1950s. They should have learned how to clap the beat, sing the response part following each call, and to play the *cajón*, *quijada*, and cowbell parts. The children should also know that, according to the liner notes of the recording, "*Samba*" is the name of a traditional Kôngo dance and "*Malato*" is a deformation of the words "mala" and "eto," which is an archaic expression for "in our villages."

Episode 5.6: Peru and United States: "Samba Malato" (Afro-Peruvian) and "Junio y Garú" (Afro-Peruvian jazz)

Specific Use: Upper Elementary General Music Class

Materials:

- "Samba Malato," Lucila Campos (from *The Soul of Black Peru*)
- "Junio y Garúa" Gabriel Alegría Afro-Peruvian Sextet

Procedure:

(Creating)

1. Review the definition of "fusion music" as music that combines two or more genres.

- Play track "Samba Malato" to verbally review which musical characteristics could have been influenced by Spanish genres (A: guitar and Spanish language) and which musical traits might have been influenced by African genres (percussion instruments and call-and-response form).
- Play track "Samba Malato" while students write down African- and Spanish-influenced characteristics.

2. Review the history of Afro-Peruvian music as a blend, mix, or fusion of African and Spanish music that developed over a long period, as African slaves and Spanish explorers moved into Peru and mixed their musical ideas with those of indigenous Peruvian populations.
3. Add to the story: The original "Afro-Peruvian" music from the mid-19th century was lost until a scholar and several musicians revitalized the music in the mid-1950s by starting Afro-Peruvian theatrical companies that traveled around Peru. In the 1960s and 70s, as blacks tried to gain social opportunities and recognition, Afro-Peruvian music took on a political function as a music that represented the pride of black Peruvian heritage. Afro-Peruvian music traveled again in the 1990s when a famous American musician discovered it and invited the Afro-Peruvian musician, Susana Baca, to perform her music in the U.S. and Europe. As the music became more popular, jazz musicians from both the U.S. and Peru began to create their own fusion of music called "Afro-Peruvian jazz."
   - Play track Gabriel Alegría and the Afro-Peruvian Sextet performing "Junio y Garúa" and write down the elements of Afro-Peruvian music that they recognize, as well as the characteristics of jazz that they had previously studied.
   - Play track while children write down characteristics of "jazz" and characteristics of "Afro-Peruvian" music that they hear.
4. Children write down musical elements of one or more completely different musical cultures that they are familiar with: i.e. Irish folk songs, Mexican *marimba* music, etc.
5. Children create and perform a piece of music that uses at least two elements from each of the two musical genres that they chose.
6. After several class sessions with time to compose and practice, children perform compositions for each other and discuss the various musical characteristics of the genres that they have chosen.

Structuring Songs

Songwriting presents further opportunities for children to engage in Creating World Music, perhaps by writing songs in the style of a musical culture they have been studying and/or composing lyrics that express what the students have learned about a particular sociocultural concept through World Music Pedagogy experiences, such as discrimination or racism. Songwriting is a unique type of composition that can require a great deal of skill in melodic and harmonic structure, in addition to a command of language and song forms. It is also one of the most powerful ways for children to clearly express their own personal feelings through music, because the use of lyrics can tell a story or express specific sentiments.

For elementary-aged children, poetry or verse is often a good place to start when encouraging children to write songs, because it can provide a formal and rhythmic structure upon which to create melodies. *Haiku* is a very short form of Japanese poetry with a metric pattern of three lines with five, seven, and five (syllables in English). Middle or upper elementary children could write poems in *haiku* form, then add sound effects with Japanese small percussion instruments such as the *kokoriko*, the *kagurasuzu*, or the *den-den daiko*, and/or possibly add a melody to sing. Another musical structure that can be used to encourage songwriting is a ballad, which is a form of verse that is usually a story set to music. Ballads originated in the British Isles in the late medieval period, spread across Europe, and then through Australia, South Africa, and the Americas. A common form that children might use to compose a ballad is ABAB or ABCB repeated. The *corrido* is another form of ballad that is part of Mexican and Mexican American cultures, historically with topics that covered actual events, such as the death of someone who was fighting for justice or the adventures of a famous hero.

Topics of songs such as these can open the door for educators to invite children to discuss and perhaps create their own music to express perspectives about social justice issues that are related not only to geographic cultures, but also to ability, age, gender, and more. World Music Pedagogy can include any musical culture, and sharing more "local" music from underrepresented or minority groups is fair game when the aim is to bring awareness of social meaning of musical practices. A music teacher might develop a series of lessons in which sixth graders listen to and discuss music of Asian American immigrants, beginning with the Smithsonian Folkways magazine cover story, "A Grain of Sand: Music for the Struggle by Asians in America,"[2] culminating with children composing a song about the struggles of immigrants to America. Another teacher might create a unit of study in which upper elementary children are tasked with writing a song after exploring gender discrimination and segregation in music in a particular locale, or throughout the world. The Smithsonian Folkways Recording compendium includes several resources that could serve as a starting point for such a unit of study. One such resource is a "Soundscapes" web page called "Women Breaking Musical Barriers: She isn't supposed to play that."[3] Another is an archive of the *Fast Folk* magazine/record collection, which acted as a cooperative for North American folk songwriters and performers from 1982 to 1997 to get their music to the public at a time when recording equipment was prohibitively expensive for independent artists. The November 1982 issue of *Fast Folk* was focused on women's music, and reading the magazine that accompanies the recording reveals a great deal about the history of women's folk music at the time, including ongoing issues of social repression and abuse of women. Episode 5.7 is an example of using one of the songs from this collection as an inspiration for older elementary children to write and perform their own songs. Before participating in this lesson, children should have attentively listened to at least the first two verses of the song *All You Can Do* for instrumentation (guitar), form (verse-chorus), and harmonic structure (Chorus: I-V-IV-I, Verses: I-IV-iii-IV-iii-IV-ii). They should have sung the lyrics along with the recording (Engaged Listening) and worked to recreate

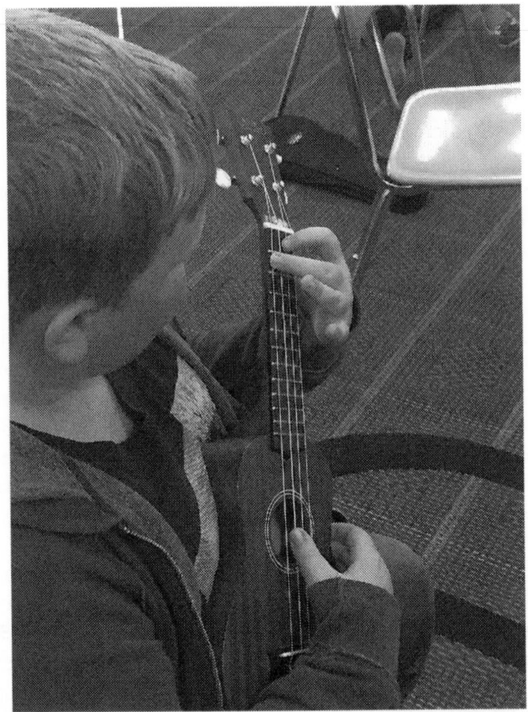

Figure 5.3 Writing a song accompanied by ukulele

Photo courtesy of BethAnn Hepburn

the harmonic structure of the song on keyboard, ukulele, or guitar through repeated listening (Enactive Listening). Perhaps with the help of their classroom teacher, they should have read the article, "The Women's Network for Music" by Gary Boehm included in the *Fast Folk* magazine accompanying this song and have discussed the feminist movement in the United States, including challenges for American female songwriters in the 1970s and 80s.

Episode 5.7: United States: "All You Can Do"

Specific Use: Upper Elementary General Music Class with piano, ukulele or guitar skills

Materials:

- "All You Can Do," Martha P. Hogan and Mark Dann (from *CooP—Fast Folk Musical Magazine [Vol. 1, No. 10] Women in Song*), Fast Folk Musical Magazine Recordings

- *Fast Folk* Magazine: http://folkwaysmedia.si.edu/ner_notes/fast_folk/FFSE110.pdf

Procedure:

1. Listen to the first two verses and the chorus of the song, "All You Can Do" again. "Write down what the lyrics mean to you. What do you think the songwriter meant to say in this song? What do these lyrics make you think about from your own life or experiences?"
   - Play track.
2. In small groups, briefly discuss what the lyrics might mean.
3. Review the structure of the song and tell the children that they will be writing their own song that uses the same form as the listening selection, as well as a similar harmonic structure. Tell them that they must be able to tell the rest of the class how their song relates to the recorded song.
4. Review performing the harmonic structure on the keyboard, ukulele, or guitar.
   - Play track and practice playing chord structure.
5. "Individually or with a partner, write down some ideas for song titles and some ideas for lyrics that are meaningful to you. Consider some of the social issues we have been discussing." Review social issues that are relevant to the children's community or school: Who gets to make decisions? Who doesn't feel like they have any power?
6. Individually or with a partner, play the harmonic structure of the chorus and try to sing some ideas for the chorus, either with or without lyrics. Use repetition and contrast.
7. When the chorus has been solidified, add at least one verse. When ready, write another verse for the same melody.
8. Practice each song until each child can sing and play the accompaniment at the same time, or pairs of children can perform with one child playing and the other child singing.
9. Perform the songs for each other and reflect upon how each song relates to the original listening material, "All You Can Do."
   - Play track as needed for comparison.

Let's Create!

The Italian physician and innovative educator Maria Montessori postulated, "Play is the work of the child." Children are naturally inclined to play with new objects in order to learn more about them. It is the same with music. As children's ears are opened to new sounds through listening, meeting culture-bearers, and watching live and video-recorded musical performances, they will likely want to play with these sounds, and their creative juices may be encouraged to flow freely by teachers who allow children to make music their own. Through exploration and expansion of world music examples, children can experiment with ways of organizing sounds and trying out instruments that are used by musicians who are from a far-away locale. Through improvisation, they can demonstrate their musical and cultural knowledge through using musical tools of musicians who may live in their city, but might have been previously unknown to children at the school. Through composition, children can find new ways to express themselves through creating something new out of sounds and structures from various groups of people. Music will be more meaningful to children who are encouraged to connect to it through creative music-making experiences, and teachers will learn a great deal about their students as they observe children in their creative processes and listen to their produced products.

Teacher Feature: Tim Fuchtman

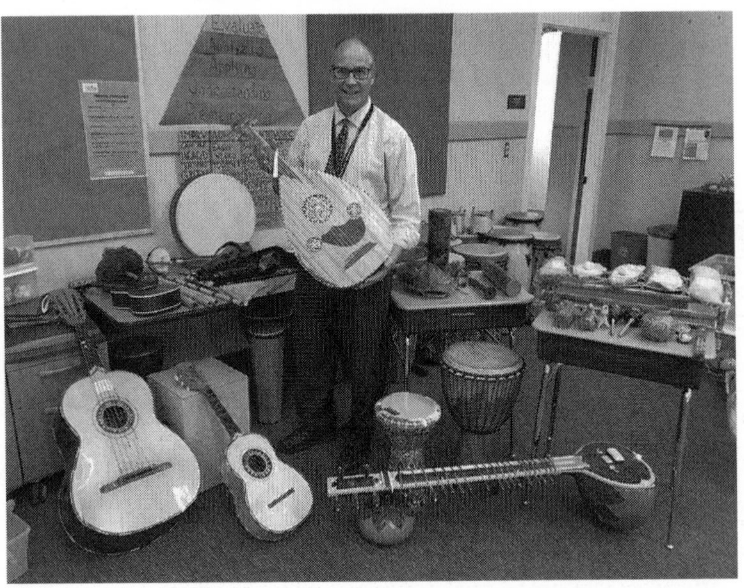

Tim Fuchtman, Elementary School Music Teacher

Tim Fuchtman has been teaching music for over 35 years. After 25 years of teaching band, he switched to elementary music. He currently teaches music to children in kindergarten through sixth grade in an urban public school where the population is 99% African American. He has a large collection of beautifully crafted instruments from Mexico, Guatemala, Ireland, Lebanon, India, Cuba, Hungary, Malaysia, Vietnam, and Mali in his classroom. Most were collected during his travels to these places. His travels are often to visit family, to conduct missionary work, or to vacation.

Q: Describe your philosophy of listening to music.
A: Sometimes I give them something to listen for and then sometimes I just want to get it in their ear. I might have a rhythm going, and turn on a tango and have little kids

stepping to the beat just to hear and experience it. Sometimes we do a folk dance so you have to listen to the music in that way.

Q: How do you encourage children to listen attentively to world music?
A: If we're talking specifically about world music, that's different! I use maps and speak a few words of the language. I have clothing from lots of countries that I have instruments from, and I have some for the kids, too. That starts to make the culture real. The kids come into music class and ask me, "Why are you wearing a dress?" and we talk about differences in cultures. That's what I want for them. They are different, and not right or wrong. It's natural to have that "weird reaction . . ." that's part of your culture, but then to understand it's a natural part of their culture and that doesn't make it bad. I also have money from around the world and they like to see that. When we are listening, many times I have that instrument. If they've got a *gambus* [a Malay short-necked lute], and they've felt it in their hands and vibrated against their chest, that makes in more tangible. They have a closer contact with that culture. That's the primary reason I do world music. In this day, it is crucial to have an understanding of other cultures. I have this idea that what you don't understand, you are afraid of.

Q: How do you encourage children to engage in world music?
A: Engaging kids in world music, I try to find something authentic from the culture that they can experience. Since I've been to those countries, I have instruments from there. Speaking the language helps, too. I show them videos so they can see somebody actually playing the instruments. I use YouTube and the Smithsonian Folkways website. When I was teaching in Dallas, there were big Indian and Iranian communities, and I knew people that could come into class. People who have a name that doesn't sound like John or Frank. If they just see a real guy or a real lady and they're just another human being, but their name is like Abrahim, it helps to familiarize the unfamiliar part of the culture.

Q: What world cultures are of interest to you and how do you incorporate listening examples from these cultures?
A: Hungary was the first place I ever went. There are quite a few elementary songs that we already use that have a Kodály influence. I sing some Hungarian to start with. I try to actually play it myself on an instrument from that country. After they've seen me playing familiar songs, they hold and play the instrument, then I'll show them Ravi Shankar in context. I play it in a not great way, so they watch a video to see how it's played by someone who's good. I also do a lot with Irish music. Guatemala, because I was there. Cuban music is very interesting. We're doing the Cha Cha right now. It's going to be a big thing this spring.

Q: Do you ever encourage children create their own music in the style of a particular world music?
A: Yes! That is especially important. The one we just did was from Malaysia. There is a tradition where there are some tunes, and everybody knows the tune, but they make up their own words. I made up my words first, then they each made up their own in groups.

When we did Arabic music, we used that scale that's got the flat two which has got such a great sound. They created a melody that incorporated that scale. For Indian music, we created our own *tala*.

Notes

1 Montfort, M. *Artists dedicating large portions of their careers to world fusion music.* www.ancient-future.com/links/artists.html
2 Kim, S. (2011). *A grain of sand: Music for the struggle by Asians in America.* https://folkways.si.edu/magazine-spring-2011-grain-sand-struggle-asians-america/protest-folk/music/article/smithsonian
3 Smithsonian Folkways Soundscapes. *Women breaking musical barriers.* https://folkways.si.edu/women-breaking-barriers-she-isnt-supposed-play-that/struggle-and-protest/music/article/smithsonian

References

Campbell, P. S. (2016). World music pedagogy: Where music meets culture in the classroom. In C. R. Abril & B. M. Gault (Eds.), *Teaching general music: Approaches, issues, and viewpoints* (pp. 89–111). New York: Oxford University Press.

The College Board. (August, 2011). *International arts education standards: A survey of the arts education standards and practices of fifteen countries and regions.* New York: The College Board.

Gluschankof, C. (2016). Public and secret musical worlds of children. In B. Ilari & S. Young (Eds.), *Children's home musical experiences across the world* (pp. 57–68). Bloomington, IN: Indiana University Press.

Wade, B. (2004). *Thinking musically: Experiencing music, expressing culture.* New York: Oxford University Press.

Recording List

"All You Can Do," Martha P. Hogan and Mark Dann (from *CooP—Fast Folk Musical Magazine [Vol. 1, No. 10] Women in Song*), Fast Folk Musical Magazine Recordings, www.folkways.si.edu/ martha-p-hogan-and-mark-dann/all-you-can-do/american-folk/music/track/smithsonian

"Dios Nunca Muere," performers unknown (from *Marimba Band*), Cook Records, www.folkways.si.edu/dios-nunca-muere/latin-world/music/track/smithsonian

"El Carnaval de mi Tierra," Los Hermanos Lovo (from *¡Soy Salvadoreño! Chanchona Music from Eastern El Salvador*), Smithsonian Folkways Recordings, www.folkways.si.edu/los-hermanos-lovo/el-carnaval-de-mi-tierra-the-carnival-of-my-land/latin/music/track/smithsonian

"Junio y Garúa," Gabriel Alegría Afro-Peruvian Sextet (permission to access via YouTube has been granted by Gabriel Alegría).

"Maburu We" (Oh, a Shoe, a Shoe), young children of the Bakgaladi culture group (from *Traditional Music of Botswana, Africa: A Journey with Tape Recorder along Southern Botswana from Mochudi to Kang*), Smithsonian Folkways Recordings, www.folkways.si.edu/young-school-children-of-the-bakgaladi-group/tribal-songs-of-batswana-oh-a-shoe-oh-a-shoe/world/music/track/smithsonian

Michael Siegel, *Sounds of the Office*, Smithsonian Folkways Recordings, www.folkways.si.edu/sounds-of-the-office/album/smithsonian

"Samba Malato," Lucila Campos (from *The Soul of Black Peru*), available on Spotify.

"Stompin' at the Savoy," Louis Armstrong and Ella Fitzgerald (from *Jazz: The Smithsonian Anthology*), Smithsonian Folkways Recordings, www.folkways.si.edu/louis-armstrong-and-ella-fitzgerald/stompin-at-the-savoy/jazz-ragtime/music/track/smithsonian

"Suwa Onbashira Kiyari-Taiko," Ensemble O-Suwa-Daiko (from *Japan: O-Suwa-Daiko Drums*), Smithsonian Folkways Recordings, www.folkways.si.edu/ensemble-o-suwa-daiko-under-the-direction-of-oguchi-daihachi/suwa-onbashira-kiyari-taiko/music/track/smithsonian

6

Integrating World Music

"I think you might recognize the instrument on this next recording," says Ms. Cedergreen to the first grade class seated quietly in front of her, "so when you hear it, you can just shout it out." A recording starts playing, and three seconds later, the children excitedly blurt, "The didjeridu!" Ms. Cedergreen smiles, knowing full well that the children have been studying Australia and the didjeridu in their homeroom class. She asks them to tell her what they know about the instrument. The ideas from the children fly out of the children's mouths, fast and furious:

- *"It's played by the Aboriginal people!"*
- *"They live in Australia!"*
- *"You blow into it, that's how you make a sound!!"*
- *"Casey's dad bought one when he was on vacation in Australia and he's going to bring it for show and tell!"*
- *"It has cool pictures on it sometimes."*

After a minute, Ms. Cedergreen puts up her hand for quiet, and remarks, "Wow, you sure know a lot about this instrument." Using the interactive whiteboard, she projects pictures that she has found on the internet. First, the children view three examples of a didjeridu, discussing the length of the instruments and the details of the artwork. Then she tells them to think about the differences between the two performers they are about to see. The children watch two 30-second videos that Ms. Cedergreen found online: first, of an Aboriginal man playing the didjeridu in a rural setting, and then of a Caucasian woman playing the instrument in a town square. Ms. Cedergreen asks the children to compare the two performers, and they quickly point out the fact that the man is Aboriginal and the woman is white. She tells them that some people think that only the Aboriginal people should be able to play this instrument, because they are the ones who created it. She asks them, "What do you think?" They sit quietly for a minute, and then have a surprisingly robust conversation about fairness and appropriation:

- *"If they created it, then maybe it should be theirs to share."*
- *"But everyone should get to do it, it's cool!"*
- *"What if so many white people played it that the Abo- Abori-Aboriginals couldn't play it anymore?"*
- *"I bet they could just make some more."*
- *"If white people are nice about it, I think it would be OK."*

Although different opinions are aired, the majority of these first graders ultimately believe that all people should be able to play this intriguing instrument—in keeping with their general attitude of fairness towards all. Glancing at her lesson plan, Ms. Cedergreen considers raising issues of gender; in traditional Aboriginal culture, the didjeridu was a considered an instrument that only males could play. She would like to probe the children's critical thinking about this topic, but the lesson has lasted 6 minutes so far. Ms. Cedergreen wants to move the children into participatory musicking, so decides to return to the issue of gender equity another day.

Life, Integrated

Musicking always occurs in context, in a specific time and place. These experiences are culture-specific; what is meaningful in some contexts will not be meaningful in others. When the song *Happy Birthday* is played on a piano, children in Kazakhstan or the Central African Republic may hear it as a simple melody that holds little interest, but children of the United States may instinctively join in and sing the well-known words with a smile creeping over their faces as they recall a recent birthday party. When *Himno Nacional Mexicano* is blares over loudspeakers mounted on a truck in Mexico City, Mexican children may swell with pride at the sound of their national anthem, while children hearing the same song in the Philippines may play on, paying no attention to the music. Even within a country or culture, music can hold different meanings for different children. When the home soccer team's theme song wafts over the speakers at a grocery store, soccer fans may envision their favorite player heading a ball into the net (thinking to themselves "gooooooaaalll!!!"), while non-fans may not make this connection at all. To be sure, the sonic properties of musical material produce melodies or chords that are pleasing to the ear or rhythms that compel people to dance, but the cultural milieu in which it occurs is a core aspect of the way that all people experience music—both children and adults.

It is this cultural context that gives music meaning. Although the dimension of "Integrating World Music" has been saved for the penultimate chapter, in many ways it is the starting point of the musical experience—without the culture, the music would not exist. In order to make learning experiences with World Music Pedagogy as meaningful as possible for children, integrating cultural aspects is essential, as context and meaning are woven throughout their experiences with the other four dimensions. One priority of WMP is to move children to understand and honor the variety of the human experience, both musical and human. Providing context about the music—the people, the culture, the sociocultural context of the music—contributes to this growth. Elementary children in particular tend to take things literally, and if the music remains as an isolated musical experience without connections to the lives of the people who make up the culture, the children will be much less prone to move towards the goal of intercultural understanding in which people honor difference, respect others, and celebrate the broad diversity of experiences of peoples throughout the world.

Integrating World Music in World Music Pedagogy

In the elementary music classroom, integration in the context of World Music Pedagogy can occur in three main ways. The first form of integration springs directly from the specific musical example or genre. This may include information about the performers, the way in which the music is taught or learned, or aspects of performance practice that are distinctive or significant. The second form of integration involves experiences that explore issues related to the culture more broadly, such as the geography of the area, the history of the region, or common cultural celebrations. The third form of integration emerges out of a conscious intent to coordinate the music curriculum with the discipline of another subject such as science, social studies, or literature. Most commonly, these forms of integration provide information that is factual in nature, but an initial investigation into specific topics can lead to broader discussions that allow children to engage in issues such as gender, race, class, and nationality.

Following a deeper exploration of each of these forms of integration, this chapter will address issues related to culture-bearers and other visiting artists. The term culture-bearers most commonly refers to people who were raised in a particular culture, and they offer a unique opportunity to provide integrative experiences that are particularly resonant and inspiring to children in elementary school. While some culture-bearers can also contribute experiences with Attentive, Engaged, and Enactive Listening, it is their potential to provide deep integrative experiences that makes them most distinctive. Relatedly, visiting artists may not have grown up in a particular culture but studied the music so extensively as to have developed a deep understanding of the culture as well as the music, and can also offer singular benefits for elementary students. The possibilities for incorporating the participation of culture-bearers and visiting artists will be explored in the last section.

In the episodes throughout the chapter, the words "play track" do not make as frequent an appearance in the description of the lesson as in previous chapters. All lessons of World Music Pedagogy must be grounded in the sounds of culture-bearers making music, but the specific dimension of Integrating World Music does not always require listening in the moment. However, an entire lesson would rarely be comprised solely of Integrating World Music, and all of the episodes suggest that other dimensions will be occurring either before or after the integrative content—or both. It is during those periods that the recording would be played.

The next section describes the range of content that a teacher can consider including when creating lessons that integrate cultural context, with attention to effective pedagogical approaches for Integrating World Music saved towards the end of the chapter. However, one pedagogical principle warrants a mention here: Elementary-aged children are often highly visual learners, and the adage "a picture is worth a thousand words" is perhaps more apt in this phase of WMP than any of the others. A detailed description by the teacher of the attire of a Peking opera singer will not have nearly the impact as an image in which the children identify what they see; a story of the Balinese puppet theater *wayang kulit* will be much less meaningful than watching a video while listening to the music which accompanies the performance; a report of dense foliage in the interior of Jamaica will not be nearly as interesting and engaging as a photo of a family living in their house in the midst of such greenery. In the following sections that focus on the types of integrative content that can lead to successful learning experiences, the ways in which the material can be presented to children will not be considered explicitly. When creating integrative content, however, teachers should always consider whether the information lends itself to visual representation.

Integration Inspired by the Music

Lessons of World Music Pedagogy almost always begin with the music sounding, for it is these rich musical expressions that stand as the primary focus of the lessons. When considering integrative material, teachers should start with the music as well, thinking about the various contextual aspects that may lead to deeper understanding of the musical culture and the people who created it. The most organic way to Integrate World Music is to think like a child. Before they reach elementary school age, young children often pepper their parents with the incessantly asked question: "Why?" While elementary school children have typically learned to edit that impulse, the question remains. The classic queries of who-what-where-when-why-how function as an effective starting point when considering ways to determine the cultural context that may be relevant to elementary school children and to the lesson itself.

Who Are the Musicians?

To children (and to adults as well), unfamiliar musical genres can elicit stereotypical ideas of people that are inspired by their previous experiences with media. A child in Rome, Italy, or Rome, New York, may hear a song that "sounds Hawaiian" and think of the animated movie *Moana*, envisioning the performers as impossibly thin young women in grass skirts and muscle-bound men covered in tattoos that dance to the music. Providing information about the performers can be the first step in demystifying this foreign music. Questions can include:

What are their names? Simply naming the performers allows them to be viewed as real people. Children can practice saying the names with the correct pronunciation, rolling the syllables around in their mouths.

What is their gender? In some musical traditions, particular musical genres are associated with gender. Historically, performances on many instruments were typically restricted to men, such as the *ney* in Egypt, the *shamisen* in Japan, and the *gaida* in Bulgaria. Other instruments have been historically viewed as the province of women, such as the *koto* of Japan. While many of these gender-specific associations with instruments are evolving in the 21st century (perhaps partly due to globalization), the traditional roles are intriguing for many elementary-aged children and can lead to discussions about gendered stereotypes in their lives.

How old are they? Elementary students are particularly interested in musicians who are also children. In *El Carnaval de mi Tierra* (Learning Pathway #2), for example, the band *Los Hermanos Lovo* is comprised of six men and one boy in upper elementary school. "How did he get to do that?" may be an envious query from a student of a culture in which such multi-aged musical participation is unusual.

What do they look like? Children can view pictures or videos of the performers and describe what is most notable to them. Race, ethnicity, attire, hairstyle, height, and weight are all topics that may elicit discussion on part of the children.

This list of questions about the performers serves as a starting point. For the teacher, there are multiple aspects of the musicians' lives that may be relevant to the music and/or interesting to the children in their classes, such as religion, job, social class, or family makeup, to name a few. The best factors to choose are those that highlight characteristics that may be unique to the culture or highlight contrasts to other musical genres. The Tanzanian female *muheme* drumming tradition is notable, because it is much more common to find drumming traditions in the world that are male. Aspects of the performer's personal lives that highlight differences from the children's experience can also evoke their interest—"That musician has 10 children? Wow!"

Where Does the Music Occur?

Simple information about the location and timing of the musical events can provide children with a broader image of how the music unfolds in the course of life in the culture. For example, music from the Western Classical tradition is generally performed indoors, ideally in spaces that maximize the opportunity for audiences to hear particular musical aspects of the performance. Yodeling, on the other hand, developed in many cultures as a way to communicate over vast distances. In some of those cultures, such as the Mbuti peoples from Central Africa, yodeling was then incorporated into their music that was performed under the open skies. In addition, music is sometimes associated with specific venues. While jazz has made its way into schools and other places, it originated in nightclubs and still carries that connotation for listeners familiar with the history of this musical culture. Similarly, *gagaku* court music of Japan was only performed in palaces of royalty until the 1950s.

When Does the Music Occur?

Much music in India is organized around a set of pitches called a *raga*, which is similar to the Western concept of a scale. Some of these *ragas* are associated with a specific time of day and season. For example, a piece that uses the *Bageshri rag* is typically performed at night and music in the *rag Basant* is restricted primarily to spring. Also, during the Zhou dynasty in ancient China, metal instruments were associated with autumn and bamboo instruments were associated with springtime. In northern Vietnam, during the time of year when rice fields would flood, farmers would produce performances that involved puppets acting out Vietnamese folk tales while being moved over water, while music reflected the story. All of these distinctive factors can arouse children's interest.

Deciding which information to include in the dimension of Integrating World Music can be challenging. Episode 6.1 offers an episode of *Suwa Onbashira*

Kiyari-Taiko (Learning Pathway #3) in which the twin principles of "think like a child" and "identify the most important factors relevant to the musical example" guided the planning of the lesson. In this case, the lesson includes characteristics of the Shinto ceremony, the activities that accompany the piece, and the time of year (and decade!) that the music occurs. While information about the specific performers is available on the liner notes of the album, the information is less pertinent to the musical experience and would be less intriguing for elementary children. In a multi-day experience of World Music Pedagogy that involved *Suwa Onbashira Kiyari-Taiko*, this integrative content could be presented at any time, before or after lessons with any of the other dimensions.

Episode 6.1: Japan: "Suwa Onbashira Kiyari-Taiko" (Learning Pathway #3)

Specific Use: Any Age General Music Class

Materials:

- "Suwa Onbashira Kiyari-Taiko," Ensemble O-Suwa Daiko (from *Japan: Onbashira Kiyari-Taiko*), Smithsonian Folkways Recordings
- *Taiko* or other drums that can be hit hard with felt mallets or drumsticks
- PowerPoint slides of images from the internet (per the procedure below)

Procedure:

(Attentive and Engaged Listening experiences have occurred in previous lessons)

1. "What holidays do you know?" Field answers.
2. As answers are provided, write answers in two columns (one set of holidays are religious in nature, the other is not). Ask students to determine the difference between the two columns. Field answers.
3. Once class arrives at the answer, explain that the *taiko* drum piece that they have been playing is part of the Shinto tradition in Japan called the "Festival of the Honorable Pillars," or "*Onbashira*" in Japanese. This festival occurs every six or seven years.
4. Report that this festival takes place in the Lake Suwa area, where the *taiko* piece that they have been playing is from. During the festival, four huge trees are found and cut down in the Yatsugatake Mountains that flank Lake Suwa. Brainstorm other types of huge trees. Field answers. (Possible A: Redwood trees, sequoia trees.)
5. Display images of trees in the Yatsugatake Mountains (available online). Compare to the tree types suggested by the students.

6. Explain that the trees are brought down to the town of Suwa. The word "*Kiyari*" in the song's title means "woodcutter," and this piece is played while the trees are cut down. Ask the children if they know any songs that are sung during work time. Field answers.
7. Note that after the trees are felled, they are slid down the mountain. Some festival participants actually ride a top the trees as they make their way to the bottom, an endeavor that can be very dangerous. Ask the children to make comparisons to other similar rides that they might know about. (Possible A: Log flumes at amusement parks; downhill skiing; some students may have heard of "running with the bulls" in Spain.)
8. Show pictures (available online) of various points of the ceremony.

(Depending on the skill of the students, some students can move into Enactive Listening, playing the drum piece, while other students "act out" the process of riding down the mountain on a log.)

The Korean song *Arirang* is well-known among music educators in North America and can be found in some elementary series textbooks and in choral octavos (on the recording linked here, the word is spelled *Ah-Rirang*). The song holds great importance in the minds and hearts of many Koreans, and the following Episode 6.2 addresses the nationalist sentiment that the tune often inspires. The recording selected is not a sung version of the song (although those abound), but an instrumental one that allows the children to hear an unfamiliar timbre. Replicating this particular recording would be very challenging for most students in lower and middle elementary, so the WMP dimensions that would be incorporated into fuller lesson planning with this recording would likely be restricted to Attentive Listening, some Engaged Listening, and Integrating World Music.

Episode 6.2: Korea: "Ah-Rirang"

Specific Use: Lower or Middle Elementary General Music Class

Materials:

- "Ah-Rirang," Kim Ok-sim (from *Korea: Vocal and Instrumental Music*), Smithsonian Folkways Recordings

Procedure:

1. Inform the students that *Ah-Rirang* (or *Arirang*—the song has different spellings) is considered a national song of Korea.

2. Brainstorm a list of nationalist songs that represent the country of the students. (A: Varies; in the United States, it might include *Star-Spangled Banner, This Land Is Your Land, America the Beautiful*, and others.)
3. Inform the students that the *aak* musical tradition was court music, intended to be performed at specific ceremonies. (Optional: Show images of *aak* instruments, and listen to a recording of one of the few existent *aak* melodies, available online.) *Ah-Rirang*, by contrast, has always been seen as a song of the people.
4. Note that there are many versions of the song, and that the version that is thought to be the original is called *Jeongseong Arirang* and is more than 600 years old. Remark that the different versions hold widely varying texts, with different meanings. One common version mentions "Ah-Rirang pass," a natural route between two mountains.
5. Show images of mountain passes in Korea, and invite children to compare the images to mountain passes that they know.
6. Inform the students that there used to be one country of Korea, but that war led it to split into two countries, North Korea and South Korea. The countries have different governments, and people from one country cannot easily visit people in the other. Discuss how it would feel if you had friends or family in the other country.
7. Report that the song has remained an important marker of Korean cultural identity in both countries.
8. (Optional extension: Research other versions of *Ah-Rirang*.)

(3–4 minutes of Engaged and Enactive Listening)

What Else Characterizes the Performance?

Many of the basic "what" questions (such as "What are you hearing?") are included in Attentive Listening activities of WMP. However, when thinking about ways to Integrate World Music, teachers can explore broader issues, essentially asking, "What else is going on here?" Possible questions include:

What do musicians and dancers wear? Children are intrigued by the idea of outfits and costumes; think of the dress-up parties and holidays such as Halloween where children don particular garb to pretend to be a character and go door-to-door collecting food or candy. In performances of the world's musical cultures, there may be specific clothes that performers wear, and displaying images of those can serve to pique children's interest and provide a hook that allows them to remember the music for a longer period of time once the unit has been completed. The traditional attire worn by the Lakota Native Americans in the United States at celebratory powwows, for example, will invariably draw children's attention.

Why does the music occur in this culture? Music often has significant extramusical meaning. Japanese *gagaku* music, for example, is known for its association as court music of the royal family, *Gregorian chant* was created to be performed in medieval cathedrals in Catholic Europe as a part of worship, and the *woi-mene-pele* genre from the Kpelle people of Liberia, West Africa is an epic story that tells a tale about a hero named Woi. These three examples are related briefly, but the cultural significance of each of them fills entire books. When a genre of music has a deep history or significant cultural relevance, it is often worth more than a cursory mention in class; information about *gagaku*, for example, would warrant more extensive research on part of the teacher and more significant curricular integration.

What else accompanies this piece of music? In Brazil, the *capoeira* tradition consists a stylized martial art that incorporates dance-like movements along with the music; in Java and Bali, the *wayang kulit* tradition consists of a shadow puppet play that is performed along with *gamelan* music; and throughout the world, dance accompanies a wide variety of instrumental and vocal traditions. When dance or drama is involved, videos are a particularly effective means by which children can develop a sense of the genre.

What is the role of an audience? In some Hindustani performances in India, the audience participates in the performance and can influence its outcome. When an audience member exclaims "Wah! Wah!" it is seen as a form of encouragement, and the performers may repeat the specific musical idea that was just presented or modify it in some way. In Western Classical performances, on the other hand, the audience is expected to sit quietly, clapping only at specified points in the performance. To applaud at a socially unexpected time can earn disapproving glances from fellow audience members. In the *fandango* performance of *son jarocho* music from Veracruz, Mexico, there is rarely an audience in the typical sense of the word, as all attendees participate in the musical expression.

What aspect(s) highlight unique characteristics of the musical culture? At times, a teacher knows that the particular piece of world music that has been selected demonstrates a defining aspect of the musical culture. The song *Ndandihleli* from South Africa, for example, highlights the multi-part homophonic choral pieces that are common throughout this region. At other times, a series of lessons will feature three or four selections from a region, but those pieces may be chosen to reflect a diversity of musical genres within the culture group. In either of these situations, it behooves a teacher to determine whether the piece comes from a particular musical genre, and if so, how that piece reflects (or does not reflect) the genre as a whole. For example, a piece of *rhumba* music from Cuba will likely contain the familiar *clave* rhythm that grounds the piece in a classic sound. This rhythmic pattern is common not only in *rhumba* but also in a variety of Afro-Cuban musical genres such as *mambo* and *salsa*, as well as other genres throughout Latin America.

How Is the Music Learned?

Musical knowledge can be transmitted in a variety of ways. In an elementary music class, students may learn a piece of music by echoing the teacher, by watching a video, or by decoding Western notation. Different cultures have different ways of learning music, a fact that can be worthy of attention.

Does learning occur primarily through oral or visual means? Visual representation of music through staff notation has stood at the center of musical education in the West. But in most of the world's cultures, music is taught and learned aurally and orally, with learners relying on their musical memory to replicate the sound. Balinese *gamelan* music is primarily taught by oral means, as is panpipe music in Peru, Wolof drumming in Senegal, and old-time fiddle music in the United States.

If musical notation is included, what does it look like? In addition to the five lines and four spaces that comprise the Western staff tradition, other forms of notation exist in other cultures. Indonesian *angklung* instruments typically rely on cipher-type notation, and most traditional Chinese instruments use *jianpu* notation today. In the image of *jianpu* notation in Figure 6.1 below, the notes are given numbers that generally correspond to the Western scale (i.e. 1 = the tonic). Measure lines may be familiar, but the dots, dashes, and underlines are likely to be less well known. The meaning of the marks is as follows:

Line below two numbers	=	Two eighth notes
Dot above a number	=	The upper octave
Double line under four numbers	=	Four 16th notes
Dash after a number	=	Half note

Students can be challenged to decode the pattern of the notation, using a known song written in *jianpu* notation.

Are mnemonic devices utilized in learning? Mnemonic devices are short words or syllables that are used to help learners learn and retain a specific sound. In the West, *solfège* is the most common representation of melodic notes, using the syllables *do*, *re*, *mi*, *fa*, *so*, *la*, *ti*, and *do*. Indian music also has a *solfège* tradition, but the syllables differ (*sa*, *re*, *ga*, *ma*, *pa*, *dha*, *ni*, and *sa*). Elementary music classrooms often rely upon rhythm syllables to represent durations (e.g. *ta* for a quarter note and *ti-ti* for two eighth notes), but different syllabic systems exist for drumming traditions in India and Ghana, among other locales.

Is the music taught through direct instruction or enculturation? In Hindustani classical music of North India, the *guru* is a crucial figure in the teaching and learning of Hindustani music, but in children's singing games throughout the world, children almost invariably learn by watching their peers, without explicit instruction.

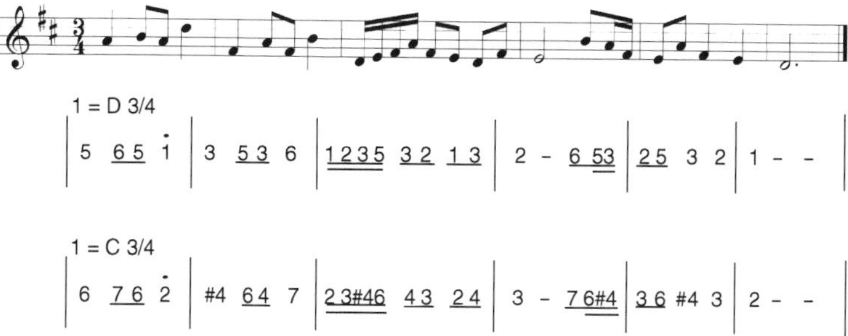

Figure 6.1 JianPu Chinese notation

Courtesy of Aik Khai Pung

Figure 6.2 Elementary children in traditional attire for Chinese New Year celebration

Photo courtesy of Julie Froude

When searching for integrative content, a teacher can:

- Consult liner notes from albums
- Consult library resources (including librarians)
- Consult the internet
- Consult members of the culture in the community
- Consult members of the culture internationally (via the internet)
- Consult an ethnomusicologist (or folklorist)

Integration Inspired by the Culture

In addition to integration that arises from the specifics of the musical example and the performers, integration can also spring from additional information about the culture at large. The range of information that a teacher can choose from is seemingly endless, from weather patterns to historical context to clothing. For elementary children, three areas serve as initial starting points when considering the wide array of topics for integration: the experiences of children in the society, the geographic features of the location, and traditional stories from the culture. All three of these topics can elicit interest and provide integrative material that is meaningful to the children and deepens their understanding of the musical culture. This section will begin by addressing each of these three areas of integration, and then list some additional areas of integrative experiences.

The Lives of Children

When teaching students, it is essential to consider what may be of interest to them. If children find a topic interesting, they are more likely to retain the material being presented. Children hold a particular curiosity towards their same-aged peers in other parts of the world, and determining the ways that their lives are similar to and different from those in other locales can illuminate and intrigue their young minds. Possible questions to ask about the lives of children within a selected musical culture include:

- Children at school:
  - How long is their school day?
  - Do they wear uniforms?
  - Is school compulsory, and if so, for how long?
  - Do girls and boys both go to school?
  - If the country is linguistically diverse, is the language that they speak at home the same language that they use in school?
  - How big are class sizes?
  - What time of year do they go to school?
  - How long is their school day?
  - What subjects do they take?
  - Do they have their own desks, share desks, or sit on the ground?
  - Do they have homework?
  - Do they walk to school?

- Children at home:
  - How many children are typically in a family?
  - Do children in the culture typically have chores?
  - When do children commonly move out of their parents' home?
  - Do children share a room with others?
  - Do children have time to play?

Geography

At a most basic level, the music that children learn as a part of World Music Pedagogy almost always comes from a place that is distant from the schools in which the learners are learning. Providing the children with information about various aspects of geography can help them ground their understanding of the musical culture in an actual place.

Maps are the logical place to start. A series of maps can be presented sequentially, in some ways like traditional Russian nesting dolls: first, begin with the continent highlighted as part of the entire world, then with the country highlighted on a map of the continent, and finally with a more in-depth map of the country itself. On the country map, the particular region or city can be highlighted, if that information is available.

Maps are an important first step for understanding the origins of a musical genre but they are abstract representations of a location, and elementary children may have difficulty deriving meaning out of this information. In order to make it memorable, find ways to provide some relevant information that is more literal and meaningful. With *Maburu We* (Learning Pathway #1), for example, a teacher in Kansas City could tell the students that the fastest way to get from their hometown to the capital of Botswana might require four different flights and over 24 hours, or that if someone tried to walk there, it would take 123 days ("with no sleeping, and walking on top of the ocean!").

Children want to know what the country looks like, with images being particularly effective. Questions to consider addressing include: Is the area mountainous or flat? Is it mostly urban or rural? Is there an ocean or another major body of water nearby, or is it landlocked? Are there distinctive physical features such as a jungle, rain forest, or desert? Are there famous geological highlights, such as volcanoes, waterfalls, or canyons? It is important to recognize that countries can have a wide array of distinctive geographic features, and a lesson should consider the location of the specific piece of music. For example, Italy is well known for its ocean playgrounds in the south, but if teaching a mountain song from the Alps region in the north, images of sun-kissed beaches will be irrelevant.

Picture Books

Elementary music teachers often include picture books in their lessons. Most commonly, these consist of illustrated versions of folk songs in which children watch the pictures go by as they sing along. Other stories or poems with accompanying books may be included in a lesson and serve as an inspiration for a sound exploration or compositional experience. When thinking of World Music Pedagogy, teachers can search for picture books that relate to the culture under study. These may consist of classic folk tales, portrayals of important historical events, or factual stories about particular experiences of children or adults in the culture. (See below for possible book resources for each of the Learning Pathways.)

Book Suggestions for Learning Pathways

Botswana (Learning Pathway #1)

Nelson, M., & San Artists of the Kuru Art Project. (2012). *Ostrich and lark*. Honesdale, PA: Boyds Mills Press.

Smith, A. M. (2012). *The great cake mystery*. New York: Anchor Books.

El Salvador (Learning Pathway #2)

Argueta, J. (2001). *A movie in my pillow/Una Pelicula en mi almohada*. San Francisco, CA: Children's Book Press.

Argueta, J., & Ruano, A. (2016). *Somos como las nubes/We are like the clouds*. Toronto, Canada: Groundwood Books.

Japan (Learning Pathway #3)

Sakade, F., & Kurosaki, Y. (2005). *Japanese children's favorite stories*. Tokyo, Japan: Tuttle Publishing.

Sakurai, G. (1997). *Peach boy: A Japanese legend*. Mahwah, NJ: Troll Communications.

Yasuda, Y. (1956). *Old tales from Japan*. Tokyo: Tuttle Company.

There is much more information that may be of interest to children and provide them with a deeper understanding of the culture. It may be pertinent to provide information about issues such as housing, weather patterns, clothing, jobs, and leisure-time activities, to name just a few. Topics for contemplation and some initial questions to consider for integration inspired by the culture include:

Housing

- What does housing look like?
- What is the housing made of?
- Do houses have heat and/or air conditioning?
- How many people usually live in one house?
- Do multiple generations usually live in the same house?
- Do people move very often, or do they stay in the same house or town/village/city?

Clothing

- What do people usually wear?
- Do men and women wear different clothes?
- What do children wear?
- Is there traditional attire that is different from contemporary attire?
- Do people get "dressed up?" If so, how does that look different from what they normally wear? When do they wear special clothing?

Weather

- What is the average temperature?
- Is it typically rainy or dry?

- Does the weather change a great deal with the seasons?
- Are there ever weather-related disasters, such as hurricanes, typhoons, or tsunamis?

Leisure-time activities

- What sports are common?
- What games do they play?
- Is music used for leisure?

Professions

- What are common jobs for adults?
- Are jobs different for men than for women?
- What is the unemployment rate?
- How long is the typical work day?
- How old are people when they usually get their first jobs?

Religion

- What are common religion(s)?
- How often are typical religious services?
- Are there any special days that are particularly interesting?

Animals

- What animals are found in the country?
- Do people have pets at home?

History and Government

- Who is the leader of the country?
- What is the form of the government?
- Are there important historical factors that have influenced the evolution of the culture?

Contemporary Events

- What contemporary events are in the newspapers of today?

The following plan (Episode 6.3) highlights the integrative material that can be included in a series of lessons on panpipe music from Peru. Panpipe music among the

Aymara people is often performed in groups in which the melody is split between two different performers, with each performer responsible for different notes in the melody (a skill that students can try as a part of Creating World Music). The integrative content in this episode focuses on the mountainous geography, traditional clothing, and the historical context for the attire.

Episode 6.3: Peru: "Los Jilacatas: Panpipes from Chimo"

Specific Use: Middle or Upper Elementary General Music Class

Materials:

- "Los Jilacatas: Panpipes from Chimo," N/A (from *Mountain Music of Peru, Vol. 2*), Smithsonian Folkways Recordings
- PowerPoint slides of images from the internet (per the procedure below)

Procedure:

(2–3 minutes of Attentive and Engaged Listening)

1. From previous class, ask children to recall that the tune is from Peru, and that the mountain range is called the Andes.
2. Project an image of the northern half of South America. Ask one student to point out Peru.
3. Inform the children that the people performing on this recording are the *Aymara* people, and that they live not only in Peru but also in Bolivia and Chile. Discuss similar indigenous peoples in countries with which the children are familiar, such as Native Americans and First Nations peoples who live in the United States and Canada, or Aborigines in Australia.
4. Display two images of Aymaran women, found online, and invite students to describe their attire. Ensure that the students note the colorful dress and bowler-style hats.
5. Inform the students that Peru is an independent country, but that it was once a Spanish colony. After making connections to independence in the children's country (e.g. the United States was once a British colony), tell the students that the dress of the Aymara partly reflects their Spanish history, with the colorful attire.
6. Note that bowler hats are traditionally English. The English did not colonize Peru, but the bowler hats were introduced to Peru in the early 1900s, when British railway workers came to Peru to build railroads.

(3–4 minutes of Engaged and Enactive Listening)

Integration Inspired by Other Classes

When elementary music teachers consider the concept of integration broadly, they often envision working with other teachers in an effort to coordinate curricula and instruction across disciplines. World Music Pedagogy can easily occur in conjunction with other classes, from language arts and social studies to physical education and art. When the music teacher integrates content with other teachers, the material learned may become more deeply embedded in children's knowledge structures. Additionally, it can be an effective means by which musical expression can become a central focus in the children's developing understanding of how lives are created and lived. The following suggestions provide a starting point for thinking about ways to integrate with other disciplines.

Social studies is perhaps the most natural connection to make. Partly, this is due to the nature of the discipline; the National Council for Social Studies in the United States, for example, stated that integration was one of the five pillars of effective social studies teaching in the elementary grades. The musical culture that the music teacher selects for a WMP unit can be chosen to coordinate with a curriculum that explores issues related to a particular country or region. Some social studies classes may focus on particular topics, such as immigration, labor movements, transportation, the environment, or agriculture. For example, if immigration is a curricular focus in their classroom, the music teacher can select different songs about immigration from a range of countries, using the dimensions of World Music Pedagogy to complement the classroom curriculum while also increasing their musical knowledge and skill.

Common topics from the language arts curriculum can also be connected to World Music Pedagogy lessons. In addition to folk tales and picture books referenced earlier, elementary students often learn about rhyme schemes for particular types of poetry. Patterns of rhyming are also important in many song traditions, such as the *corrido* musical tradition of Mexico, which most commonly has an ABCBDB rhyme scheme. Virtually any song that contains text, from American hip hop to Portuguese *fado*, can be analyzed for patterns of rhymes. Even if rhyming does not exist, it can be a distinctive counterexample to the music that the children typically experience in class.

When the science curriculum addresses the properties of sound, examples of world music can be incorporated in the music class to demonstrate particular principles. For example, some middle elementary classrooms will address frequency, with students gaining an understanding of the way that vibration leads to sound. In Balinese *gamelan* ensembles, two metallophones are tuned to slightly different frequencies, leading to the shimmering effect of the sound. This connection can be made for the students as they engage in a WMP unit on *gamelan* music of Bali, and then connect back to what they have learned in their science class.

For schools fortunate enough to have teachers in art as well as music, the music teacher can team up with the art teacher to study the arts of a particular society. Similarly, music teachers can also join forces with a teacher of physical education to collaboratively teach a unit on dance or singing games of a specific society.

Pedagogical Strategies for Integrating World Music

It is not only the content that contributes to a successful integrative learning experience, but also the instructional design. If Ms. Cedergreen spends 10 minutes "teaching" her first grade students about the history of Australia but they do not remember any of it, little "learning" has actually transpired. Giving careful thought to the ways in which this phase of World Music Pedagogy is implemented is imperative.

Whether the integrative material is inspired by the music or the culture, it is often factual in nature. In these cases, the instinctive way for the teacher to present information to elementary children is to simply report the desired content. Although this can be concise, providing children with isolated bits of information through direct instruction does not always lead to a high degree of retention on part of the students. To maximize student learning when teaching factual information, teachers can keep the following ideas in mind.

Keep It Concise, Spread It Out, and Revisit Previously Learned Context

When it is most efficient to report information to the students, limit the length of time allotted to such experiences. Particularly in elementary music class, where children are used to active musical engagement, restrict the amount of "teacher telling" to 2–3 minutes. However, a few minutes may not be nearly enough to provide students with the cultural context that the teacher believes is important. One way to respond to this dilemma is to spread the information out over several classes. If teaching a song from Mongolia, for example, the first class period can highlight map-related information, the second class can end with a picture book that tells a tale from the culture, and PowerPoint slides on the third day can provide historical context about the political nature of the country. After each of these short activities, the teacher can move into the other dimensions of World Music Pedagogy that will likely comprise the main portion of the lesson. If the information is spread out over multiple days, review the previous day's learning before moving onto new material.

Choose the Most Interesting and Relevant Information

Teachers know their students and will have a sense of what they may find interesting. If the children do not find it interesting, they are less likely to retain the information. However, it is also important to select cultural context that relates to an aspect of the musical selection. For example, in creating an episode for *Maburu We* (Learning Pathway #1), it might be interesting to students to learn that the most popular sports in Botswana are football (aka soccer in the United States), cricket, and rugby. Athletics are not directly relevant to *Maburu We*, and an explanation of cricket and rugby could conceivably take a long time for students who do not know the sports at all. On the other hand, the text of the song indirectly refers to the apartheid political regime in neighboring South Africa. Although the song is from Botswana, the fact that the lyrics mention white South Africans renders a discussion about the politics in the region relevant. This would not necessarily be the case in other songs from Botswana. This episode (Episode 6.4) also provides a model for the way that context can be parsed out to students over multiple classes and includes material that would be broadly applicable to any piece from Botswana, such as images of food, geography, and housing.

Episode 6.4: Botswana: "Maburu We" (Learning Pathway #1)

Specific Use: Middle or Upper Elementary General Music Class

Materials:

- "Maburu We" (Oh, a Shoe, a Shoe), young children of the Bakgaladi culture group (from *Traditional Music of Botswana, Africa: A Journey with Tape Recorder along Southern Botswana from Mochudi to Kang*), Smithsonian Folkways Recordings
- PowerPoint slides of images from the internet (per the procedure below)

Procedure (Class 1):

(Attentive)

1. After the children have identified that the song is from Botswana, show images of Gaborone, the capital city of the country, then the town of Letlhakeng in the Kalahari Desert, where the song was recorded.
2. Ask children to note similarities and differences between the locations.
3. Provide historical context about South Africa, which is just over the border from Letlhakeng. Inform the children about the role of Europeans in Southern Africa and the nature of the apartheid political regime, then give the translation for the text:
   - *Maburu We*: the Boers (i.e. white South Africans)
   - *Ijoo*: (a sound indicating pain, somewhat like "ouch")
   - *Dichankananna*: prisons
   - *Setlhako we*: a shoe
   - *Komorago we*: from the back
4. Discuss the song's meaning, in light of the textual translation and the history of apartheid in the region.

Procedure (Class 2):

(Attentive and Engaged)

1. Inform the children that the song is from the Bakgaladi people, one of the different culture groups within Botswana. Show images of the typical houses of the Bakgaladi, often circular structures made of clay.
2. Compare the housing structures to those familiar to the students.

3. Show images of typical food in Botswana, such as *seswaa*, a thick meat stew and maize porridge that resembles polenta, and *morogo*, greens that are commonly served with *seswaa*.
4. Compare the food to that which is eaten in the students' cultures.

(Lesson continues with Engaged and Enactive Listening)

Lead Interactive Discussions Related to Children's Experiences

One way to make the novel information interesting is to compare it to the children's own experience. For example, before telling the students that the singers in *Maburu We* live near the desert, ask the children if they have ever been to the desert and to describe their experiences. Rather than reporting information to the students, ask them to describe what they can deduce from the information or images that have been supplied to them.

Incorporate Visual Imagery or Tactile Experiences

Children are visually oriented beings. Most elementary music classes are characterized by aural and oral approaches to learning, and the inclusion of visual representations of new knowledge can draw their attention—specifically because it is a less commonly utilized pedagogical approach. Whenever possible, show them. Children are also predisposed to tactile experiences. They like to touch, exploring items such as instruments and toys. If possible, borrow various materials from cultural insiders in order for children to experience the artifacts with their hands as well as their eyes and ears.

Invite Older Students to Conduct Research

School children in the upper elementary grades are often learning basic research skills on the computer. Although music educators will typically not want to invest their class time to send children to research particular topics that are not directly musical, they may be able to work with the classroom teachers or librarians to have children address these skills during those class times. If a school is studying a musical genre of a people who are well represented in the community, children can also conduct oral history projects or collect songs from culture-bearers.

Consider Starting a World Music Pedagogy Unit with Integrative Material

Most lessons that employ World Music Pedagogy begin with Attentive Listening activities. At times, however, it can be effective to begin with Integrating World Music to provide a hook for the students and connect to knowledge that they already have.

The following episode (Episode 6.5) provides an example of a lesson that incorporates the previous experience of the students with music from Zimbabwe. After reviewing their understanding about the importance of the *marimba* in Zimbabwean music, the episode transitions into information about the *mbira*, another key instrument in the musical culture of the Shona people of Zimbabwe. It also asks students to make connections between the new musical culture and other knowledge or opinions they may have about issues such as the national musical heritage.

Episode 6.5: Zimbabwe: "Kari Muchipfuwa Kanaziwa ne Mwene Wako"

Specific Use: Any Age Elementary General Music Class

Materials:

- "Kari Muchipfuwa Kanaziwa Ne Mwene Wako," by S. Murira with group (from *Songs for Ritual, Entertainment, and Dance from the Sena-Speaking Tonga of Zimbabwe*), International Library of African Music
- PowerPoint slides of images from the internet (per the procedure below)

Procedure:

1. Identify the instruments that come to mind when considering Zimbabwe. (In some schools, Zimbabwean-style *marimba* is a core component of the curriculum, sometimes played on xylophones. If this is not the case, inform the children that the *marimba* is common in Zimbabwe.)
2. "Can you hear the *marimba* on this recording?" (A: No.)
   a. Play track (0:00–0:30), then field answers.
3. Show an image or short video of an *mbira*, also known as a thumb piano. Compare the image of the *mbira* with a piano, noting similarities (e.g. multiple keys) and differences (e.g. size, timbre, *mbira* has metal keys).
4. Inform the children that although many people in the United States think of the *marimba* as the principal instrument in Zimbabwe, the *mbira* has a longer history as the representative instrument, and that it is still common today. Brainstorm a list of instruments that might be considered national instruments in the country of the students.
5. Report that the *mbira* has historically been associated with religious traditions of the Shona people of Zimbabwe. Brainstorm a list of instruments that might be associated with religions that they know.
6. The Shona have great reverence for their ancestors, and the special *mbira* songs are often played in Bira ceremonies that pay homage to family members who have died.

(Lesson continues with Attentive Listening)

Discussions of Difference

When learning about cultures that are different from our own, the instinctive response is often to notice the ways in which lives and experiences are similar and different. From an intellectual perspective, such compare and contrast can be an effective technique for children to identify the aspects of a culture that are unique. However, when this occurs, issues may arise that can appear difficult to discuss. One of the principles of World Music Pedagogy is that the world is filled with a multitude of ways in which people make music, and that this variety of musical expression is to be celebrated. The endless array of unique musical cultures illustrates the power that music holds for people. To be sure, we all have affective responses when we hear particular music or learn about something cultural that seems odd because it is so unusual, but as an approach, WMP works to celebrate the differences between our musical expressions. This also applies to the way that people live their lives.

Often, the students in schools that are able to have music teachers are relatively affluent when compared to the majority of the world's peoples. When integrating context, children may focus on the difference from a deficit perspective, with comments such as "They are so poor! They don't have shoes!" While in some situations this may be true, it can also lead to a discussion about why this may be the case, and depending on the maturity of the children, the class can either discuss the average temperature that may mean that shoes are not that important, or the geopolitical forces that have led to a high degree of poverty in a particular region of the world. In either case, it is incumbent upon the teacher to note the differences that are more likely to be viewed positively by the children—perhaps the families spend much more time together than the typical family in the teacher's school, or perhaps the children live by the beach and can go swimming every day after school lets out. Differences exist between cultures, and with careful leadership by the teacher, the children can learn to marvel at these differences, viewing them as a source of fascination and worthy of celebration.

Integrating Larger Societal Issues

The examples of Integrating World Music in the prior sections have been primarily factual in nature. There are certain aspects about the performers, the music, or the culture that can lead to a deeper understanding of the musical culture when children learn about them. In addition to factual information, there can also be broader issues that emerge organically through integrative aspects of World Music Pedagogy. These interactions can lead to powerful conversations in which elementary children are able to wrestle with bigger-picture issues that directly spring from the intersection of music and culture.

For example, in some cultures, specific musical genres have traditionally been the province of males or females. In Scotland, *waulking songs* were work songs sung by women to coordinate the act of beating new cloth in order to shrink and soften it. In Bulgaria, instruments have historically been played by men, and although both men and women have been involved in Bulgarian choral music, the Bulgarian choir phenomenon that enthralled many parts of the world in the 1960s led to the impression that choral singing was primarily in a women's musical genre. In the Andes region of South America, too, women have been more apt to be singers and men more apt to be instrumentalists.

Throughout elementary school, many children have an evolving view in which their understanding of their own gender becomes increasingly important to them. In the early grades, most children place limited importance on whether they are boys or girls, and cross-gender friendship groups are common. As they age, children are more likely to separate into gendered friendships, as they increasingly seek to identify "what they are" and "what they aren't." Alongside this traditional pattern of development, some elementary children are challenging contemporary conceptions of gender. This manifests itself both in children who choose to disregard traditional norms, and also in children who identify as transgender, those who see their biological sex as different from their understandings of themselves. For children, gender is an increasingly intriguing topic, one that is often worthy of discussion.

In the context of lessons of World Music Pedagogy, discussions about gender can arise organically. When teaching a unit on the music from Bulgaria, the teacher may lead the children through WMP lessons of the music of the *gaida*, informing the students that this bagpipe instrument has traditionally been played by men. In his book *Music in Bulgaria*, Timothy Rice (2004) noted that men usually worked in the fields and forests, tending to animals and building houses, while women were more commonly at home, engaging in domestic duties like cooking meals and making clothes for the family. Patterns of music making emerged from these traditional roles. Women's tasks often required the use of their hands, rendering instrument playing difficult, and so they grew to sing while they worked. Men's outdoor work, on the other hand, included constant contact with wood and animal skins, and therefore they had greater access to the materials with which they could make instruments. In an elementary classroom, the children can be led through a discussion about this issue: What do they think about the ways that these roles have played out? If the children were to perform this music, do they think that the boys should be the instrumentalists and the girls should be the singers? That is, should they follow the traditional patterns of gendered musicking or not?

Similar matters can arise concerning a range of issues, ones that emerge naturally from the music or the culture:

- *Social class:* Some music was traditionally performed for royalty or those in upper classes, such as the *pinpeat* from Cambodia. Other musical genres are associated with those with fewer financial resources or power, such as the *bomba* and *plena* working-class traditions from Puerto Rico. In some cases, there may be specific reasons that the class distinctions emerged, such as the cost of instruments. Elementary children can reflect on different activities in their contemporary lives that may be associated with people of different social class—both musical traditions and other activities.
- *Song ownership:* Some music of the First Nations in North America is not to be performed by those outside the tribe. After having broad discussions about ownership in their lives ("Do you own your own clothes? How would you feel if someone borrowed them without asking?"), they can ponder the idea of the proprietorship of songs.
- *Musical fusion:* Many traditional musical genres are becoming hybridized, influenced in particular by Western popular music styles that pervade many corners of the world. Some argue that this represents a natural process that

> allows musical traditions to evolve, while others believe that it leads to a loss of culture and highlights the insidious dominance of the Western paradigm that contributes to the decline of musical diversity.

The teacher can structure these discussions in a variety of ways. Most commonly, teachers lead the class through a group discussion on the topic at hand. Alternatively, students can be equipped with pen and paper and asked to brainstorm the pros and cons for each side of the issue, and then discuss their ideas with a partner. A third option is for the teacher to present the issue and then divide the class into two factions, each of which has to come up with arguments to support their side's stance. A debate can ensue.

The following episode (Episode 6.6) provides an example in which the text of an English folk song can lead to discussions about discrimination. The episode begins by eliciting the children's preconceived ideas about the word "gypsy," then moves into cultural and historical information about the Roma people of Europe. The episode also serves an example of the ways in which the approaches of World Music Pedagogy can be utilized with musical cultures that may not be as unfamiliar to most students.

Episode 6.6: England: "The Whistling Gypsy"

Specific Use: Upper Elementary General Music Class

Materials:

- "The Whistling Gypsy," by Jill Trinka (from *My Little Rooster*), Folk Music Works

Procedure:

1. "What do you know about gypsies?" (A: Varies, but the students will likely have visions of flowing skirts and turbans, fortune-tellers with crystal balls, and some may have a vague sense that gypsies are robbers.)
2. Inform the children that the groups of people who have typically been called "gypsies" are often members of a particular culture group commonly called the Roma people. Historically, the Roma people did not settle in one place for long periods of time, but were more nomadic (in fact, they have sometimes been referred to as "travelers"). Ask children to discuss what they think it would be like to move from place to place.
3. Tell the children that while today there is a wide range of occupations held by the Roma, historically, common jobs included selling and trading small goods, fortune-telling, and working in specialized trades such as making instruments. Due to their nomadic lifestyle, many gypsies did not own land or property, and over time high rates of poverty became common among the Roma.

4. For hundreds of years, the Roma people have faced significant discrimination in housing, employment, and education, and their migratory camps are often vandalized by others and bulldozed by the police. (If appropriate, inform the students that many Roma were killed during the Holocaust of the Second World War.) Relate a recent discriminatory act against the Roma, such as the 2014 event when the police destroyed the camp of 15 families who were set up in the woods outside of Paris. Ask the children to think of other acts of discrimination that they know of, either in their own country or in other countries.
5. Inform the children that the word "gypsy" is controversial today. Some Roma detest being called a gypsy, while others find it to be a marker of pride. If appropriate for the group, ask the children about other terms that they know that are derogatory towards a group of people.
6. Tell the children that the song *The Whistling Gypsy* is an old-fashioned tale about a "lady" (i.e. a wealthy woman) who falls in love with a gypsy man, and decides to be with him despite the opposition of others.
7. "See if you can figure out what happens in the story."
   a. Play track (entire song).
8. After listening to the song, discuss the tale, which can be interpreted in various ways.

Episode 6.7 offers a plan for *El Carnaval de mi Tierra* (Learning Pathway #2) that incorporates many of the issues raised to this point. The episode is designed so that contextual information is woven within three consecutive lessons. The integrative content within each lesson segment is kept relatively brief and addresses three distinct topics: the location of the musical culture, the history of Civil War in El Salvador and its impact on the performers, and the mode of teaching and learning through enculturation. Throughout it all, the children's perspectives and opinions are solicited, and other dimensions of World Music Pedagogy are suggested at specific times.

Episode 6.7: El Salvador: "El Carnaval de mi Tierra" (Learning Pathway #2)

Specific Use: Middle or Upper Elementary General Music Class

Materials:

- "El Carnaval de mi Tierra," Los Hermanos Lovo (from *¡Soy Salvadoreño! Chanchona Music from Eastern El Salvador*), Smithsonian Folkways Recordings
- PowerPoint slides, per the procedure below

Procedure (Class 1):

1. Display a slide with an image of the globe, and the heading "Where in the World?" Ask where they think the next song may be from, and why.
   a. Play track (0:00–0:26), then field responses. Lead discussion so that children discover it is from Central America.
2. Display a slide with an image of Central America, and the text "Name countries you know in Central America."
   a. Field responses, inform that the song is from El Salvador.
3. Display a slide with an image of Central America with El Salvador highlighted.
4. Note that this song is from the Morazán region of Eastern El Salvador. Display images of the region, asking students to describe the rural, hilly pictures they see.

(Move into Attentive Listening that focuses on instrumentation, and Engaged Listening in which the children pat the beat and then perform the rhythm of the shaker.)

Procedure (Class 2):

1. Play track (0:00–1:01). As recording sounds at low volume, pose review questions based on previous lesson.
2. Quickly display maps of Central America and El Salvador, from the previous lesson.
3. Display a slide on which the words "Civil War" are written, and ask the children to identify its meaning. Discuss.
4. After discussion, inform the children that El Salvador had a civil war in the 1980s, and that some people from El Salvador came to the United States in search of a better life. Most of the performers from *Los Hermanos Lovo*, the group on this recording, came to the United States during this time and settled in the Washington DC area, along with many other immigrants from El Salvador. Like many immigrants, they wanted to retain some of their own culture in this new country, and this *chanchona* music was important to them. Read one of the group member's words from the liner notes of the album:
   a. "We come from sadness, from war, which doesn't make us want to dance or rejoice. Here in the United States, after seeing that all one has is work, we sort of came up with the idea of bringing music into an afternoon family get-together to play whatever we felt like playing. When you get into playing music, you forget your problems for a little while."
5. "What are the different things that you like to do to forget your problems?" Discuss.

(Move into Engaged and Enactive experiences, learning the words of the chorus and beginning to put the song, shaker rhythm, and beat together.)

Procedure (Class 3):

(Through Engaged and Enactive Listening, continue to work on performing the song, shaker, and beat together, sounding as much like the recording as possible.)

1. Pose review questions about the civil war in El Salvador, and the immigration of the members of *Los Hermanos Lovo*.
2. Ask the children how old they think the performers are. Field answers.
3. Observe a video of *Los Hermanos Lovo* discussing their music, available on Smithsonian Folkways website, noting the age of the performers. "How do you think the boy that is a member of the group learned the music?"
4. Lead a discussion about learning music through enculturation, asking students to make connections to their own experiences.

(Return to Enactive Listening.)

Integrating World Music: Strategies for Success

Remember the Learning Goals

With the extensive array of possible integrative ideas, it is important to keep the main learning goal in mind. Ultimately, the principal aim of World Music Pedagogy is for children to become deeply connected to musical expressions of a given culture, and integrative experiences such as those described above must be selected with an eye on this overarching objective. Children may find it enjoyable to learn a non-musical playground game common among Indian children in New Delhi, but if it takes a full class period to teach and then play the game and the children fail to learn anything about the Hindustani music that is the focus of the unit, it will not serve the core purpose of World Music Pedagogy. In order to be effective, children must find integrative experiences interesting or fun, but just because they find them interesting or fun does not mean that the integration necessarily leads to greater learning on part of the students! Of the many options listed here, teachers must choose the ones that will contribute most directly to the children's learning.

This may be an issue that arises when integrating with the other teachers. The music curriculum cannot solely serve to support classroom learning, but must contribute to children's growth so that they can become skilled and knowledgeable musicians. At times, a teacher may be asked to supplement a particular curriculum, but the musical content is so far afield from the students' skills that it would not lead to musical growth. For example, a second grade classroom teacher teaching a unit on Mexico might have learned a song written by a European American intended to help children memorize the names of common food and drink in Mexico—clearly not a song from a culture-bearer. In these cases, the music teacher should stand her ground by explaining the music objectives. Then, the music teacher can suggest a specific song that comes from Mexico, one that holds musical characteristics that will make it more likely for the students to succeed in learning and performing the piece.

Consider the Length of Integrative Experiences

Discussions, particularly those that ask children to work in whole-group settings to brainstorm ideas or share their opinions, can grow lengthy as many children wish to share their ideas. Similar to the experiences in Attentive Listening, the teacher must carefully select the most relevant context, and make decisions about the amount of time he wishes to spend on contextual information.

Incorporating Culture-Bearers

When learning the music of an unfamiliar culture, one of the most powerful experiences for students is to work with *culture-bearers* from local communities (or who may be accessible via internet from across the world). The term culture-bearers refers to people who grew up in the culture of study, with the full knowledge of cultural context that only one who has spent much of a life enmeshed in that culture can possess. Two main types of culture-bearers can be incorporated into classes of World Music Pedagogy. Some culture-bearers share aspects of their life story and tell about their experiences with a range of topics that relate to the study at hand. Other culture-bearers will have an extensive musical background as well, which enables them to perform or teach the music to the children while also providing information about the culture at large.

Beyond culture-bearers, two other types of people may be potential classroom guests. Some people may not have grown up in the culture under study but lived in it for long periods of time, developing a deep understanding about the music and the culture. These "visiting artists" can share their knowledge about musical and non-musical aspects of the culture, performing music for the elementary children. Additionally, there may be people in a school community who are not culture-bearers but have visited the region on a study abroad program, on vacation, or as part of a trip with their church or community group. They can enter the classroom and describe their adventures and insights. These experiences are less meaningful than culture-bearers or visiting artists, but interacting with a person that the children know can make the foreign culture seem less alien and exotic.

When culture-bearing musicians or visiting artists are welcomed into the classroom, they can potentially lead the children through all of the dimensions of World Music Pedagogy, from Attentive Listening to Engaged Listening and on into Enactive Listening, in some cases culminating in a Creating World Music experience. When the culture-bearers are not practicing musicians, their contributions are usually limited to sharing cultural insights, so their unique contributions have been saved for this chapter.

Pedagogical Strategies for Incorporating Culture-Bearers

Elementary children often find visits from culture-bearers to be among the most satisfying aspects of units of World Music Pedagogy. Typically, the music teacher's knowledge of the musical culture is limited, and to the children a culture-bearer can be seen as one who has all the answers—who really knows the culture. Additionally, there is the novelty factor, which often means that children sit rapt, attending to every word of the visitor. However, as with all guests in a classroom, there are strategies to consider when planning for a culture-bearer that can help contribute to the success of the experience.

PLAN AHEAD

Teachers should hold conversations with the culture-bearer before the visit. Explain what has been accomplished in the class up to this point, informing him or her what the children will know about the music and life in the culture. Conversations can ensue about the best way to use the class time. Topical questions include: What is the culture-bearer's greatest area of expertise? How does that relate to the students' knowledge and skill? What would the culture-bearer like to do? Pedagogical questions include: Should the children come to class with questions to ask? Will the children be participating musically in the class period in any way? What sort of support does the culture-bearer need from the teacher?

While it is generally preferable to defer to the ideas of the culture-bearer regarding the best way to use class time, it is also appropriate to discuss the curricular goals of the unit. In some cases, the teacher may wish the culture-bearer to address a particular topic that has arisen in class or demonstrate a specific skill. After a discussion, the music teacher and culture-bearer can work together to create a general sense of how the time period will unfold.

PREPARE THE CHILDREN

After creating the plan for the activities of the culture-bearer, the teacher should consider whether the children need to be prepared in specific ways. For example, if a culture-bearer from Trinidad will be bringing a steel pan and the children have not previously seen the instrument, it can be helpful to give the children some basic information ahead of time. Teachers can show them a photograph, describe how it is made, and give an introductory explanation of playing technique. The children should be informed of the upcoming visitor, emphasizing that the class is likely to be different from their typical music classes. The culture-bearer can then skip some of the basic explanations and immediately start in on playing technique once he or she is in the class. Children can also generate questions before the visit, so that they are ready once the culture-bearer arrives. For the teacher, hearing the students' queries also provides a window into their interests on the particular topic. Further, the teacher can edit the questions to be asked, ensuring that the lesson stays on track in the case of limited time.

CONSIDER THE TEACHER'S LEVEL OF INVOLVEMENT

When guests from any culture visit a classroom to work with students, they always come with a less developed sense of how to work with children than teachers who interact with the children on a daily basis. This is true of a math-loving mother who volunteers to work with high-achieving third grade mathematicians or a stay-at-home father who comes to read aloud to first graders. It is impossible for visitors to have as sophisticated an understanding of the classroom climate as the teacher possesses. With culture-bearers, this is as true as with anyone else—and may be more so, if they attended school in another country where the expectations of teachers and students were different. Although pre-visit conversations will help set the stage for the culture-bearer to be successful, the teachers should also be prepared to support the culture-bearer during the class. Some issues to consider:

- Teachers know the behavioral expectations of the class, and should be ready to step in and remind children of expectations of behavior should issues arise. Additionally, teachers who work with classes every day are familiar with the issues of children with special needs. They can both alert the visitor ahead of time about particular children, and also respond to any issues regarding those children as they emerge.
- Teachers understand basic protocols within the class surrounding practical issues such as passing out instruments or papers, moving within the classroom, and sharing instruments. Teachers can be proactive at those times, stepping in to supply some quick directions that will help the class run more smoothly.
- Finally, teachers should use their knowledge of the learning processes of the students to ensure that the experience leads to student growth. If the visitor is talking a great deal and the students are growing restless, teachers can redirect their attention with a focusing question for the students (e.g. "Think about what other instruments you know that are like this one."). It can be effective to make connections to the children's knowledge base or skills. When any visitor comes to class, it can seem like a stand-alone lesson that holds little bearing on the curriculum (or little long-term benefit in terms of skills and knowledge of the students), and to make it as productive as possible, the teacher should appropriately intervene from time to time to make connections for the students. If the culture-bearer is advised of this ahead of time, it minimizes the chance that such interruptions will come across as rude.

Alternative Methods for Incorporating Culture-Bearers

In some cases, it may prove difficult to identify culture-bearers to invite to the classroom, or there may be scheduling issues with a live presentation. In such situations, other options for the inclusion of culture-bearers remain.

LIVE-STREAMED CONVERSATIONS

If a culture-bearer from the particular culture of study cannot be found locally, meetings can be arranged virtually. Armed with an interactive whiteboard and a computer with a video camera, teachers can set up an interaction with a culture-bearer from anywhere in the world. If the culture-bearer is currently living in his or her home country and if the time zones don't pose an overwhelming challenge, such an exchange can allow the students to see the culture-bearer in his or her environment—an experience which in many ways may be more impactful for the children.

RECORDED CONVERSATIONS

In some cases, a live internet-based conversation or demonstration may not be possible. However, if a teacher makes a connection with a culture-bearer in another part of the world, the teacher can elicit questions from the children and then send them on to the expert. The culture-bearer can reply through an online recording or e-mail, and the answers can be shared with the children in a future class. This sort of encounter allows the children to feel a sense of control over their learning as well, to have a voice in the types of information that they are able to obtain from the culture-bearer.

Finding Culture-Bearers

The idea of identifying a culture-bearer can appear daunting, but it is often a much easier task than it initially seems. When immigrants move to a new country, they are rarely asked about the experiences from their home country, and providing an opportunity for them to share their knowledge and skill (whether musical or not) can be a gratifying experience. The issue still arises: How can one identify and connect with potential culture-bearers for the classroom?

CONSULT PARENTS AND SCHOOL PERSONNEL

The first step is to check with the community of students at the school. The principal, classroom teachers, counselors, and office staff will often know more about the cultural heritage of the students than the music teachers will, and can identify students whose families might be of assistance. Many immigrant families feel disconnected from the school community, and inviting them to share their stories and experiences in the classroom can change that dynamic. Children in lower and middle elementary grades will almost always be incredibly proud to have their parents attend class to discuss their backgrounds. Some upper elementary students start to develop some self-consciousness around the ways in which they are different from other children in the school, and while this is rare, it should still be taken into consideration. Finally, there may be teachers or staff from within the school who are immigrants and can contribute contextual information about their culture. In particular, support positions such as custodians or lunchroom workers are more likely to be immigrants.

CONSULT THE LOCAL UNIVERSITY OR NEIGHBORHOOD GROUPS

If there is a college or university in town, the music department will often know of musicians from diverse cultures in the area. In particular, members of ethnomusicology departments will often be able to suggest potential contacts. Groups of expatriate immigrants are more prevalent than teachers may realize. For a teacher in Southern California who is teaching a unit on music of the Philippines, there are multiple associations that can generate leads of possible guests. A teacher in rural Iowa may feel like there is a smaller likelihood of finding an appropriate community group, but a recent internet search of "Filipino community groups in Iowa" found two organizations—a student group at Iowa State University and the Filipino-American Association of Iowa. If a teacher cannot find a culture-specific community group within their geographic area, it is still possible to reach out to groups in other localities. Often, leaders in one area have some knowledge of leaders in another region, and networking can lead a teacher to find potential visitors.

CONSULT SOCIAL MEDIA

For teachers who engage with social media, a general request ("Does anyone know any musicians from the Philippines?") can provide successful leads.

For elementary children, a visit from a culture-bearer can be among the most exciting and memorable experiences of a series of lessons incorporating World Music Pedagogy. Such visits take the sound-based lessons typical of most lessons of World Music Pedagogy and bring the culture to life in a way that the music teacher cannot. Here, in front of the children, stands a real live person who has lived through the musical and cultural experiences that have been discussed in class, a person who may dress or talk differently than the students but breathes and laughs and lives his life fully, just like they do. While the inclusion of culture-bearers is not essential for World Music Pedagogy, their presence brings the musical culture to life in a way that cannot be paralleled.

Let's Integrate!

Imagine if music was presented, voided of its cultural context. If children in South Korea learned the song *Here Comes the Bride* from the United States in their music class, they would be missing crucial aspects of the tune if they did not understand that it is typically played at a wedding, and that hearing it inspires the massed congregation to stand, turn their eyes to the back of the room, and grab tissues in order to dab at the impending tears. Similarly, if children in the United States learned *Ah-rirang* from South Korea, they would be missing out on a core aspect if they did not learn it is by far the most famous folk song of the nation, and hearing it instills pride in the hearts of its citizens. In these cases, the children's knowledge would be restricted to the simple sonic experience, and while sonic structures form the "ground floor" of WMP, the integrative experiences are essential. The more substantial knowledge that results from framing musical learning in a broader social and cultural context can lead children towards greater intercultural consciousness and a more profound understanding of the vast diversity of our world.

Julie Froude, Elementary School Music Teacher and Specialist in Japanese Culture

Julie Froude has taught in both public and private schools in the United States and in Japan. She currently teaches elementary music to children ages five through twelve in Hamilton, Ohio. Most of her 31-year teaching career has been at the elementary level, although she has also taught band, choir, and strings to older students. She is fully certified in Kodály and Orff approaches of music education, as well as Japanese language PreK–12. Julie is also a member of the Miami University Taiko Group.

Q. What world cultures are of interest to you and how do you incorporate listening examples from these cultures?
A. I am interested in music from all over the world, but particularly Japan and other parts of Asia, Latin America, Oceania and the South Pacific, Africa, and Europe. With young children, it helps a lot if the music will lead to drumming, dancing, games, or instrument playing. I teach geography, history, and cultural elements as appropriate. These details help to draw children in and make it more relevant to them. I try to keep it aural at first, because I want children to utilize their imaginations as much as possible. They are very visual, so if and when appropriate, I might incorporate a video that shows people singing or playing the music in their own cultures.

Q. Would you share a listening or world music activity?
A. In this activity, I find that it works best if the music comes in toward the end of the activity. My students in grades 5 and 6 enjoy learning an Indian stick game, five-step *Dandiya Ras* (or *Raj* in Sanna Longden's collection). We find India on a map, and the Gujarat region. We discuss how stick games are often mixers in social settings, and I introduce the 5-beat pattern with hands and aural cues only. Once the students can put the foot pattern with the hand pattern, we add the sticks. I used to work with an Indian woman in Cincinnati who told me that all sorts of music can be used when teaching the *Ras*. She said a lot of people use disco music in the beginning, as it has a very slow, but distinct beat. A great discussion point with upper elementary students is how it feels (as a Westerner) to put a pattern with five beats with music that is clearly in a meter of four beats. Once the students have mastered this, we try with partners, then in the rotating double line pattern of the full activity. As the students gain competency, I start changing the music. Slow disco to faster disco, to different Indian music.

Q. How did you develop an interest in Japanese culture and music?
A. I was raised in Japan, and moved there when I was three months old. I attended Japanese preschool and kindergarten, and part of second grade. The rest of my schooling was taught in English. I went to university and graduate school in the United States, but returned to teach music in an international school for six years. My parents and I traveled all over Japan and attended many cultural events and festivals. My fluency in Japanese is also helpful.

Q. How did you decide to translate this interest into pedagogical approaches and materials?
A. As I read, attend conferences, and travel, I am constantly gathering materials for use with my students. My school can't afford real *taiko* drums, but I have incorporated

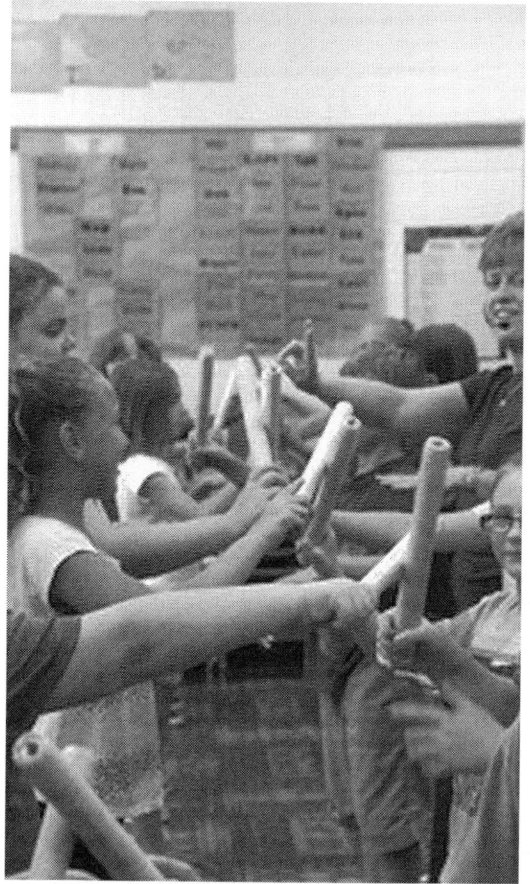

Figure 6.4 Children playing Polynesian stick game

Photo courtesy of Julie Froude

taiko pieces for bucket drums and taught them to my students. I believe it is important for our children to be informed and interested in the rest of the world.

Q. How do you get children involved in the singing/dancing/doing of Japanese music?
A. It is important to introduce the song or activity properly, in a way that sparks their interest. I put a lot of thought into whether a song or activity will be interesting for my students and at what grade level, and then carefully consider how I plan to demonstrate or introduce the material. Perhaps I introduce the activity through a picture book (such as *The Drums of Noto Hanto*, by J. Alison James). Making sounds in Japanese is not so difficult, as the sounds are very similar to Spanish. I have taught Japanese *Bon-Odori* which is no different than teaching a folk dance. If the motions have a meaning, we talk about them and what they represent. Learning music in context gives it meaning, and holds the interest of the children.

Q. What should music teachers of children in grades 1–6 know about bringing Japanese music into the classroom?

A. Japanese music often has historical or cultural context, or seasonal activities that accompany the music. It's important to research these a bit before introducing the music to the children. If possible, consult an "expert," who may be a parent, a student, or a friend who might visit your classroom. Game songs are always a wonderful way to introduce the music to children, because they are repetitive and quicker to learn. Lullabies, children's songs, seasonal songs, and folk songs are also accessible. *Shakuhachi*, *taiko* drums, *koto*, and *shamisen* would be very interesting for listening examples. I would recommend watching these with a video, *taiko* in particular.

Reference

Rice, T. (2004). *Music in Bulgaria: Experiencing music, expressing culture*. New York: Oxford University Press.

Recording List

"Ah-Rirang," Kim Ok-sim (from *Korea: Vocal and Instrumental Music*), Smithsonian Folkways Recordings, https://folkways.si.edu/kim-ok-sim/ah-rirang/world/music/track/smithsonian

"El Carnaval de mi Tierra," Los Hermanos Lovo (from *¡Soy Salvadoreño! Chanchona Music from Eastern El Salvador*), Smithsonian Folkways Recordings, www.folkways.si.edu/los-hermanos-lovo/el-carnaval-de-mi-tierra-the-carnival-of-my-land/latin/music/track/smithsonian

"Kari Muchipfuwa Kanaziwa Ne Mwene Wako," S. Murira with group (from *Songs for Ritual, Entertainment, and Dance from the Sena-Speaking Tonga of Zimbabwe*), International Library of African Music, www.folkways.si.edu/s-murira-with-group-playing-matebe-dza-mondoro-mbiras-and-murumbi-drum/kari-muchipfuwa-kanaziwa-ne-mwene-wako/track/smithsonian

"Los Jilacatas: Panpipes from Chimo," N/A (from *Mountain Music of Peru, Vol. 2*), Smithsonian Folkways Recordings, www.folkways.si.edu/los-jilacatas-panpipes-from-chimo/american-indian-world/music/track/smithsonian

"Maburu We" (Oh, a Shoe, a Shoe), young children of the Bakgaladi culture group (from *Traditional Music of Botswana, Africa: A Journey with Tape Recorder along Southern Botswana from Mochudi to Kang*), Smithsonian Folkways Recordings, www.folkways.si.edu/young-school-children-of-the-bakgaladi-group/tribal-songs-of-batswana-oh-a-shoe-oh-a-shoe/world/music/track/smithsonian

"Suwa Onbashira Kiyari-Taiko," Ensemble O-Suwa-Daiko (from *Japan: O-Suwa-Daiko Drums*), Smithsonian Folkways Recordings, www.folkways.si.edu/ensemble-o-suwa-daiko-under-the-direction-of-oguchi-daihachi/suwa-onbashira-kiyari-taiko/music/track/smithsonian

"The Whistling Gypsy," Jill Trinka (from *My Little Rooster*), Folk Music Works, available on iTunes and Spotify.

7

Surmountable Challenges and Worthy Outcomes

Cultural Competence and World Music Pedagogy

The goals of World Music Pedagogy fall into two categories: children's musical growth and children's *cultural competence*, or the ability to appreciate, understand, and interact with people from cultures different from one's own. These goals can be met when diverse musical cultures are introduced to children by dedicated and knowledgeable music teachers with a focus on developing the whole musician through extensive listening and creative musical experiences, while integrating cultural knowledge and encouraging acceptance along the way. Each musical culture in World Music Pedagogy is viewed through a praxial lens, as the human "doing" of all things musical, not just as recordings or pieces of musical repertoire.

The reasons for selecting specific musical cultures and the ways of organizing WMP lessons will vary from situation to situation and from teacher to teacher. As revealed in the Teacher Feature at the end of each chapter in this volume, it is becoming more common for elementary school teachers to thoughtfully consider an organization of their overall music curricula so that the Western European classical perspective is not in the center or at the top of the curricular map, but simply one of many cultures that inform music selection and transmission practices of the music curriculum. This is a model in which World Music Pedagogy is at the center of the curriculum, not as an "add on" of special units of study.

Even if teachers (or the larger curricular decision-makers of the school system) are not ready to adopt such a model of an entire curriculum focused completely on musical cultures through World Music Pedagogy, WMP techniques and episodes can be included in any music curriculum. The following vignette illustrates situations in which two elementary school teachers responded to current events through incorporating WMP lessons as a way to ease political tension within their teaching contexts.

On a sunny fall day, Mr. Jackson considers the election that occurred the night before. In a surprise, the winning candidate is a man who ran on a strong anti-immigrant platform, declaring that he planned to use his new power to root out undocumented immigrants and return them to their country of origin. Mr. Jackson thinks about his students, many of whom have Salvadoran heritage. While he does not know the immigration status of his students, he wonders if some of them do not have documentation papers or may have friends or family members in that situation. Thinking of his ultimate objective as a teacher—to ensure that all students feel safe and supported and that learning occurs—he imagines how scared they must feel on a day such as this.

As Mr. Jackson drives to school, he makes a last-minute decision to change his lesson plan. During the previous summer, he created a series of lessons for his third graders on the music of El Salvador, a unit that he intended to present in January after the winter break. But as he thinks about his students and the current situation, he knows that today is the day that he must begin teaching these lessons. He arrives early at school, finds the PowerPoint on the computer, and readies himself for the rest of the day.

When the third graders enter the music classroom at their assigned 9:45 music time, they are accompanied by a fretful air, and more students than usual are absent. As the class settles, Mr. Jackson smiles at his students and says, "Raise your hand if you think you know where this might be from." He presses play and the rollicking sounds of El Carnaval de mi Tierra *begin to resound throughout the space. Immediately, many of the children with Salvadoran heritage surreptitiously glance at each other, and a few children slowly raise their hands. When called upon, Fernando, a small-boned boy with a bright smile, quietly says, "El Salvador?" Mr. Jackson nods decisively and emphatically states, "Yes. El Salvador. This music is from El Salvador, and we have a lot of people in our area that used to live there but now live in the U.S. But I have never been there! What are the best things about El Salvador?" Many children share what they know about food, language, and holidays. After 2 minutes, Mr. Jackson decides to move from this integrating experience back into Attentive Listening, so that they can make sure to move into Engaged Listening during this first lesson. As the next 10 minutes unfold and children begin to move and clap with the music, the tense quality about the students slowly diminishes, as they joyfully participate in this musical experience. "This," thinks Mr. Jackson to himself, "is why I teach using World Music Pedagogy."*

***

On that same sunny fall day, Ms. Chen also considers the election that occurred the night before, and she too thinks of her students. She teaches in the same district as Mr. Jackson, but most of her students come from families that have been in the country for generations. Still, she knows that every school has more diversity than it sometimes appears, and imagines that there may be some students who are feeling immense anxiety about the election the night before. Additionally, she believes that all students must understand about the reality of diversity in her country.

As Ms. Chen drives to school, she too makes a last-minute decision to change her lesson plan to the unit of music from El Salvador that she had intended to teach later in the year. When her third graders enter the music classroom at their assigned 9:45 music time, they jostle each other jokingly, with none of the fretfulness of Mr.

Jackson's class. As the class settles, Ms. Chen smiles at her students and says, "Raise your hand if you think you know where this might be from." She presses play and the rollicking sounds of El Carnaval de mi Tierra *begin to resound throughout the space. The children listen, but their hands stay at their sides for a longer period than the students in Mr. Jackson's class. When the Spanish language starts after 26 seconds, a few children slowly raise their hands. When called upon, Parker, a small-boned boy with a bright smile, quietly says, "Mexico?" Ms. Chen replies, "Well, that's a great guess, because the lyrics are in Spanish. You're close; does anyone know another country in Central America that starts with 'El?'" Parker's eyes light up and he triumphantly states, "El Salvador!" Ms. Chen nods decisively and emphatically states, "Yes. El Salvador. This music is from El Salvador, and in our area we have many immigrants from El Salvador. I can't stop listening to this piece!" The class proceeds, incorporating aspects of Attentive Listening, Engaged Listening, and Integrating World Music as the students joyfully participate in this musical experience. "This," thinks Ms. Chen to herself, "is why I teach using World Music Pedagogy."*

Teachers might select musical cultures for WMP lessons with the express intent of connecting in some way to particular students in the class. As Mr. Jackson's experience demonstrates, WMP lessons can be used to allow those students whose cultures are typically underrepresented in music education curricula to see themselves and be recognized by others. As children enter elementary school after time at home, they are often unaware of the ways in which they may be different from others around them. As they grow from ages six through twelve, they begin to understand more concretely their place in the wider culture. Immigrant children, in addition to dealing with frequent residential moves and the loss of family and community connections from their original homeland, may begin to feel as if their lives and experiences are viewed as "less than" the dominant culture in their new home. Other children who are members of minority groups may also develop an understanding that their lives are seen as "other" by some people in the majority. In her book, *Culturally Responsive Teaching: Theory, Research, and Practice* (2010), Geneva Gay highlights the importance of immigrant and minority students seeing their cultures represented in the curriculum. This refers to all parts of the curriculum, including music class. World Music Pedagogy can be employed effectively to bridge the divide between the cultures of the children in the class and the typical content of music classes, which has tended to be dominated by music from the European and European American traditions.

In the vignette above, Ms. Chen's classroom offers a separate but related rationale for deciding to teach the music of El Salvador. In her class, most of the students come from the dominant culture, and as such rarely question their position of relative power. Leading them through lessons in which they learn about the music of a marginalized group of people can allow them to develop a sense that there are children with experiences that may be different from their own. Elementary school children are at the perfect age for learning experiences designed to facilitate their understanding of their place in the broader world. The self-focus that is typical when they enter traditional schooling changes as they age through the elementary years, with an increased awareness that other people hold different perspectives and experiences and that these can be a source of great interest and value. Additionally, a highly developed sense of right and wrong emerges over the elementary years, making this age an ideal time to introduce issues of privilege. In Ms. Chen's class, there may be students of the dominant culture who are hearing hateful rhetoric about immigrants in other parts of their lives. The process of learning about the music, history, and culture of a particular immigrant group can provide them with a more nuanced understanding of diverse peoples' varied experiences. Geneva Gay (2010) points out the importance of teaching *relational competencies* in school, "If we are to avoid intergroup strife and if individuals are to live the highest quality lives possible, we simply must teach students how to relate better to people from different ethnic, racial, cultural, language, and gender backgrounds" (p 21).

Another component of teaching cultural competency through any pedagogy involves the cultural sensitivity of the teacher, and perhaps even an imperative to "do what's right" in terms of not standing by as bullying occurs or as one particular group of children is singled out or behaviorally reprimanded within the school system. Teachers who utilize a child-centered approach and who listen closely to their students might be able to determine the ways that children see themselves and the ways that others may hurtfully label them. Even well-meaning teachers can accidentally perpetuate stereotypes if they are not listening carefully and communicating with sensitivity. Randall Allsup and Eric Shieh (2012) point out,

> There is never one way to be Asian, or gay, or Mormon. There is never one song that fits an ethnic label, never one musical practice that encompasses an entire culture . . . our humility toward our own perspective and our capacity to listen to the perspectives of others are key to the work of social justice.
>
> (p. 50)

As music teachers listen to children and model humility through demonstrating that all musical cultures have value, children can learn to appreciate varying perspectives in a music classroom. In addition to opening their ears and minds to the musical expressions of people from many different cultural groups, World Music Pedagogy might also help children learn that music can be a powerful expression of cultural identity, as well as a healthy way to express emotions, so that they can build effective strategies for dealing with challenging socioemotional situations that are an inevitable part of living in a multicultural society.

Ethnomusicological Considerations

Historically, the combined work of ethnomusicologists and music educators gave birth to World Music Pedagogy as an educational field with listening at the center and one that recognizes music as a way that groups of people make meaning in their lives. In elementary school music classes that incorporate WMP, issues such as authenticity, transmission, and transculturation come into play.

Authenticity

In elementary schools where teachers aim for children to build meaningful connections to a musical culture, in addition to including cultural context in each lesson, the key is to listen, listen, and then listen some more to the sonic qualities of the music. Of course, most elementary-aged children will not be able to duplicate a musical selection exactly as it was recorded, but they can certainly get close to the music through repeated Attentive and Engaged Listening!

As discussed in Chapter 1, authenticity is a term that can be interpreted in many ways. In the past, some music educators have expressed an expectation that a particular musical tradition should be taught or performed exactly as it was originally created or presented. This expectation could be problematic for well-meaning teachers who want to bring musical cultures of the world to life for their elementary-aged students but may feel so concerned about not teaching "authentically enough," that they avoid using World Music Pedagogy all together. The notion of authenticity as a hierarchy in which recreating the "original" is the highest goal is becoming less popular in current music education scholarship. Although elementary school teachers should learn as much as possible about the musical culture, examine issues of representation, and ask contextual questions related to bridging the gap between classroom culture and a more unfamiliar musical culture, it is important to remember that authenticity does not have to be confined to capturing a static ancient and traditional product. Music changes as it travels over time and between places and peoples. Sherry Johnson (2000) points out that, in fact, such an original product may not even exist! She notes,

> Even in Western European art music, with its emphasis on musical products, how do we choose what constitutes 'the original': the score, the first performance, or even the sounds in the composer's head before she or he captures them on paper? How do teachers begin to work towards reproducing the 'original cultural context' when in many cases 'the original' does not exist? Why must we be limited to the 'original' when music is often performed in a variety of contexts?
>
> (p. 281)

This contextual variety has been discussed by other contemporary music education scholars who point out that each time a musical tradition is taught, learned, or performed in a new setting or at a different time, it may have a unique context and purpose. One of the leading experts on global music education, Huib Schippers (2010), suggests that although music teachers might feel compelled to introduce world music traditions as "frozen in time," teachers should actually be "making choices of 'strategic inauthenticity'" (p. 52) in which the old (piece, transmission/performance practices from the "original" people/time/place) and the new (piece, transmission/performance practices as shared in a modern school setting) are viewed along a continuum from being completely identical, through overlapping to a certain extent, to being completely separate from each other. Of course, the ends of this continuum are extreme: it is impossible for the "old" and "new" to be completely identical if the music is being recreated in a new context, and if the "old" and "new" are completely separate from each other, that would not support the goals of most world music education programs.

So how do elementary school teachers deal with issues of authenticity through the lens of WMP? In her book, *Tunes and Grooves for Music Education*, Patricia Shehan Campbell (2008) writes that

> So long as the ears are open to the sounds of musicians at the source of a tradition, and those who wish to learn the music and musical style are listening with

> frequency to recordings of the music, then a credible musical performance can occur.
>
> (p. xvi)

For example, after attentively listening to several Zambian drum pieces and answering questions about how the sounds of the music relate to the cultural context, children learn to play part of one of the pieces on two classroom *tubano* drums and several large inverted plastic buckets instead of the *budima* drums on the recording, thus bringing the music to life, even without having access to the original instruments.

Music teachers can consider that there are many ways of looking at issues of authenticity and that there are multiple questions to consider when choosing musical material for World Music Pedagogy lessons. Sherry Johnson comments:

> For me as a music educator, the question is not 'is this song/instrument/recording authentic?' or even 'is it more or less authentic?' Rather, the questions raised by concerns for authenticity, when interacting with any musical processes and products, might be better phrased as: How was this music produced? For whom? By whom? In what context? For what purpose? With what influences?
>
> (pp. 284–285)

These questions can be asked by teachers who utilize World Music Pedagogy to learn as much as possible about the context of the musical material before deciding how to introduce the music to elementary-aged children. Teachers will also want to decide which of these questions are appropriate for children to ask, and determine when and how they will encourage children to ask these questions. The main point when dealing with issues of authenticity is that teachers should feel empowered to be resourceful in finding community connections and to use the resources provided in this book in order to make decisions based on their own students, available resources, and other contextual factors. Where there's a will, there's a way!

Transmission

Teachers who use World Music Pedagogy strive to learn about the ways that music is taught and learned by people who are most familiar with the musical culture. They must also consider whether children of a particular age group will be able to succeed in learning to perform the music of that culture in the context of a music classroom, and if so, whether the original mode of transmission would be practical in the particular educational setting.

Music can be taught through oral/aural transmission or visual transmission (reading some sort of visual notation). The difference between oral and aural transmission is that if a teacher plays or sings with the purpose of teaching the music to a student, the teacher is transmitting music *orally*. The child who listens to music (whether from a teacher, recording, or video) to learn it instead of reading it is learning music *aurally*.

Visual transmission (reading musical notation) is commonly used in most secondary music classrooms throughout the world where Western art music is the main repertoire to be shared. In many elementary music classrooms, although reading basic Western traditional notation is often taught to a certain extent, musical content (even that of Western art music traditions) is often transmitted orally/aurally because children are able to perform music that is much more complex than the music that most children can read using Western standard notation. Therefore, transmission practices of many elementary music classrooms, particularly those whose teachers utilize active music-making approaches, are compatible with transmission practices of many of the world's musical practices that are taught/learned through oral and aural transmission. The prevalence of this type of transmission is in contrast to that of many secondary music education programs, in which visual transmission through reading standard Western music notation is the main mode of transmission.

Although oral and aural transmission is one of the most popular ways of learning music of the world's traditions, visual transmission can be a useful memory aid or it can provide access (to some aspects of a musical tradition) to large populations across time and space. Music notation cannot capture the nuances that live or recorded music can, but Bonnie Wade (2004) points out that "notation is a kind of access to information. Whereas in an orally transmitted musical tradition the teacher controls whether or not a pupil may learn something, writing the music down makes it more accessible to greater numbers of people" (p. 23).

It is important for children to know that standardized Western notation is only one of many systems for notating music. Traditional Japanese music has a specific notation system for each instrument. Stringed instruments such as the guitar, ukulele, and Chinese *qin* have tablature-type notation systems that indicate fingerings on the strings rather than pitch. As children recreate music "by ear" or compose new music based on various musical cultures, they may be motivated to make some marks on paper, on a technological tablet, or on the board to help them remember what they are learning or recall the musical patterns that they are creating. This is a natural desire, particularly for children whose main learning modality is visual, and teachers can seize such an opportunity as a "teaching moment" to engage students in discussion about the multiple purposes of writing down music.

Transculturation, Fusion, and Musical Mixes

In an age of globalization, in which borderlines are often blurred, another issue that teachers of World Music Pedagogy have the opportunity to explore is the blending of musical sounds from various cultural traditions through space and over time. *Transculturation* occurs when new cultural elements are added and others are changed or left behind when two cultures interact, usually as a result of war, colonialism, diasporic movement of populations, or globalization. For example, William Tompkins (1981) writes about the transcultural nature of Afro-Peruvian music, which developed over several centuries. This particular musical culture was born with the attempted preservation of musical traditions of slaves who came from various parts of Africa to Peru with Spanish conquistadors starting in the 16th century, changed as blacks integrated into the wider Peruvian society during the 19th century, developed more through the Black Pride Movement in the 20th century, and continued to change as it was commercialized and performers travelled internationally into the 21st century.

> Afro-Peruvian music tradition consists of a quilt work of different combinations and permutations of elements from the Spanish, African, and to a lesser extent, indigenous Indian musical traditions, the proportions of which vary between

> genres and geographical areas, changing with social and economic developments throughout Peruvian history. Thus, in the final analysis the music of the blacks of coastal Peru is neither Spanish nor African, for like new wine put into old skins, it broke beyond the parent musical traditions that would contain it, and developed its own rich music culture.
>
> (Tompkins, 1981, p. 400)

There are many examples of musical genres that are fusions or mixes of musics of two or more "cultures," or groups of people who define themselves in terms of ethnicity, nationality, or diasporic community. World Music Pedagogy lessons that focus on such fusions provide an excellent opportunity for elementary school music teachers to work with other classroom teachers to develop integrated curricula that help children make connections between the ways that music can reflect cultural changes related to colonialism, diaspora and/or other historical, political or social events and movements.

Especially when considering lessons that include Creating World Music, it is important for teachers and children to consider the viewpoint of traditionalists or conservationists who feel strongly about preserving a particular musical piece or practice as a marker of identity or as a way to keep from losing a certain cultural heritage. Groups of marginalized people may feel threatened by anything other than recreating traditional music and preserving transmission practices, so sensitivity to such concerns is particularly important when working with musical cultures of native peoples who may have grieved the loss of their land, their way of life, their language, and other cultural values, so they are keen to hold tight to their musical traditions and identities.

Strategies for Successful Implementation

As with all curricular innovations, there are challenges that must be considered when working towards implementation. World Music Pedagogy is no exception.

Determining the Amount of Time for Each Dimension

When first presenting lessons of World Music Pedagogy, it can take time to ascertain the appropriate proportion of lessons to dedicate to the various dimensions of WMP. It may be that initial lessons devote too *much* time in the early phases to Attentive Listening and there is difficulty maintaining the students' interest. Alternatively, lessons may devote too *little* time to Attentive Listening so that the Engaged and Enactive experiences that follow do not lead to fruitful engagement or to a solid musical performance by the students because they have not heard the music enough. Each teaching context is idiosyncratic, and teachers must experiment with the pedagogy to determine what works best for their teaching situation. The sequences provided in the learning episodes in this volume suggest only one possibility, and teachers should plan to modify them based on the needs of their students.

The age of the students also influences the way that the pedagogy can be implemented; a lesson sequence that will lead to learning in a fifth or sixth grade class will likely not be successful for first graders. Once again, because of differing contexts, there are no steadfast rules that will surely lead to productive learning experiences. With students in early elementary, the children's previous musical experiences and skill levels can be particularly variable—if most students enter an elementary school having had preschool education, they will be more likely to be able to engage in the types of behaviors that will lead to effective experiences with the more sedentary dimensions of WMP, such as Attentive Listening and Integrating World Music. Further, with first graders in particular, the ability of the group to focus on tasks at hand can vary immensely from year to year, and a lesson that may work with one set of first graders may not be successful with another. Through experimentation, teachers can determine the most effective balance of the WMP dimensions to meet the students with lesson plans that will lead to student growth and interest.

Investing Time to Come to Know the Culture and Create Curriculum

Creating a lesson or series of lessons that incorporate World Music Pedagogy is not a 30-minute process. Teachers must find musical works, research the culture, and create the teaching sequences as laid out in Chapters 2, 3, 5, and 6. This takes time. However, there are a number of resources that provide help during this process. First, online lesson plan depositories such as Smithsonian Folkways Recordings and the Association for Cultural Equity provide lesson plans that teachers can consult. Typically, although they collectively offer a wide array of the world's musical expressions, they have not been created with WMP dimensions in mind. However, the authors have often done some of the initial legwork, identifying music that they believe will work for a specific age group and creating lessons that can provide suggestions for content that can serve as the musical or cultural focus. Teachers will almost always need to modify the lessons, but the lesson planning process can be much more rapid when using one of these sites. See Appendix 2 for additional resources in world music lesson planning.

Further, once the lessons have been created, they can be adjusted the following year to make improvements in lesson design, and then taught to a new group of students. This is particularly effective when the music teacher has created a unit to integrate with a classroom teacher on a particular culture. When PowerPoint presentations or other visual aids have been created, it can be immensely satisfying to know that they will be used for more than one year.

Many music teachers find that school vacations during the summer and other breaks during the year are a good time to work on units of World Music Pedagogy. They can explore a novel musical culture in unhurried fashion, immersing themselves in unfamiliar genres so that they understand them more fully. When there is not the stress of an impending lesson plan that needs to be created and implemented, it can be an enriching and joyful experience to leisurely consider another musical culture and think about the ways that it can be shared with young charges. Additionally, there are often professional development opportunities during the summer for teachers who wish to create WMP lesson plans with more guidance. Such professional development might include taking private vocal or instrumental lessons with a culture-bearer or attending a Smithsonian Folkways Certificate Course in World Music Pedagogy.

Eschewing Essentializing

When teaching about musical cultures that are unfamiliar to many students, educators run the risk of "essentializing" the experience of the culture. Essentializing refers to the idea that if children learn about the experiences of one music and musician from a particular culture, they may believe that all music and musicians from that country, state, or province are identical—when there can be marked differences within and across geopolitical boundaries. A musician from a specific rural area in northwestern China, for example, may be an expert on a musical tradition common only in that locale. As the largest nation in the world, China is an incredibly diverse country, with areas both densely urban and sparsely populated, and topography that varies from desert to mountains to flat plains. Musically, too, the range of genres is as vast as the plateaus found in the northern parts of the country. Unfortunately, there have been many more examples of "essentializing" when studying musical cultures over the years, with the most common being the entire continent of Africa, where over 1,500 languages are spoken! In addition to the vast variety of musical cultures on the African continent, there are also many musical traditions that are part of the African diaspora.

One way to address this particular concern is to create WMP units that incorporate more than one musical selection, with pieces chosen that reflect a varied range of musical genres from a region. At other times, the teacher may only have time to teach one song, or may decide to focus on a particular genre of a region. In these cases, the teacher can quickly play recordings of other genres and display images of people in other parts of the geopolitical area, calling attention to the fact that the experiences are varied. Another option is to raise the issue of the students' own experiences, noting the diversities that are present in their country, region, or even within their classroom. For example, a teacher in Toronto, Canada, might ask the children if they can think of a song that is representative of all Canadians, then discuss how even the national anthem can't represent all of the musical cultures of such a diverse country. The intent is to ensure that children understand that most countries and cultures consist of a range of peoples and experiences, and that the experiences that are highlighted in the unit represent only some of them.

Using Apps and Technologies

When Campbell offered her vision of World Music Pedagogy in *Teaching Music Globally* in 2004, internet-connected smartphones had yet to be marketed and sold to millions of people across the world. As the world hurtles towards the middle of the 21st century, WMP must incorporate the technological and social changes that keep society constantly pushing forward in new directions. In addition to logistical issues such as the availability of live-streaming sound and video, other changes in the nature of music-in-culture warrant attention. These include technological advances in the form of apps and other online resources.

Internet-connected whiteboards are found in many classrooms, and they can be used in WMP to project images of the musicians, the instruments, and specific aspects of their lives, such as housing or food, to name a few. In addition to interactive whiteboards and computers, some students have access during the school day to tablets such as iPads. A school may have two or three class sets that can be borrowed by a teacher, or intact classes may have a set in which each child is provided with a tablet for use while they are at school. In some fortunate cases, a set may be assigned to the music classroom, tablets that students in each class can use when they come to music class.

Applications (apps) that incorporate aspects of world music have proliferated in recent years, and they are increasingly utilized by performers of world music. The *tambura* or *shruti box* that provides a drone to accompany singing in Hindustani classical music is often supplanted by an amplified app in contemporary concerts of this North Indian musical culture. It is likely that such technological changes will multiply as we move towards the middle of the 21st century.

For music teachers incorporating World Music Pedagogy, apps can provide specific benefits. First, many apps of the world's musical cultures supply sounds that emulate instruments that are difficult or expensive to obtain. Balinese *gamelan* ensembles, Japanese *koto* stringed instruments, *Trinidadian steel pans*, and Indonesian *anklung* are just some of the instruments that are available through apps for phones and electronic tablets. To be sure, the technological version of a *gamelan* does not provide the same experience as an actual ensemble, but the sound provided by the apps on tablets can be surprisingly satisfying and allow children to participate in music making in a way that would not be possible at the turn of the last century. Also, such apps on tablets might make it possible for children with special needs to participate in answering listening questions if they are nonverbal, and participating in making and creating music if they have physical limitations that prevent them from singing or playing instruments.

To ensure that the musical experience continues to be grounded in the culture, it is all the more imperative when working with apps to consistently utilize recordings of culture-bearers creating the music on traditional instruments. While the objective of engaging in musically satisfying experiences is an essential aspect of WMP, it is also imperative that children participate in repeated listening to gain an understanding of the culture(s) from which the music originated or was produced. When relying on apps, it is possible for what might seem like "weird, cool instruments" to become divorced from their cultural context, making recordings and integrative material indispensable. Nonetheless, apps provide an effective means by which children can engage in "making" the music of unfamiliar musical cultures.

In addition to apps, other technological resources are available to children for engaging in world music activities both in school and at home. The interactive features of the website of Smithsonian Folkways Recordings are attractive, in that they include activities and games that encourage children to "play" online with "Holiday Music from Around the World" (click on a location on a global map and hear a recording of holiday music), "Música del Pueblo" (a Flash-based virtual exhibition of Latin American and Latino music), and "Meet the Mariachi: Explore Mexico's Musical Gift to the World" (maps, videos, and interactive instrument demonstrations).

Worthy Outcomes

During the age span of six through twelve years, children are at a perfect age for opening their ears and minds to sounds and knowledge of the richness that the millions of musical cultures of the world have to offer, including everything from singing games played by Shona children in Zimbabwe, to fusions of *flamenco* and hip hop piped through booming speakers in a bar in Barcelona, Spain, from *roda* circles of Brazilian *capoeira* to Balinese *kecak*, and from early Australian ballads to Persian classical court music.

In and out of school, children all over the world are being enculturated into popular and commercial music that surrounds them through media and musical toys and games in daily life, and they tend to value popular music increasingly as they grow older. If music teachers take advantage of these years to expose and involve children in listening to musics of the world and learning about the people who make meaning of that music, children may be more likely to develop and maintain acceptance and valuing for cultural differences and an appreciation for human similarities.

In a world of increased access to recordings and videos online, children have many opportunities to peek through the keyhole of a number of musical cultures, but World Music Pedagogy allows children to move from just peeking to actually opening the door and stepping into a foreign musical culture, and perhaps even building bridges between classroom music cultures and more unfamiliar music cultures.

Parents of children around the world want their children to succeed in school, and many value music education as contributing to that success. Many administrators in schools with diverse student populations encourage teachers and staff to create stronger connections between schools and families to increase parental involvement in children's success in school. World Music Pedagogy provides an excellent avenue to invite parents into the classroom by asking them to serve as culture-bearers to share their cultural heritage with children of different backgrounds.

There are many opportunities for music teachers to implement World Music Pedagogy with elementary-aged children. Other teachers at school may be excited to create integrative units of study on a particular cultural group, so that children are playing Javanese *gamelan* music on metallophones during music class, making puppets for *wayang kulit* (a theatrical performance that uses shadow screen) in visual art class, reading a story for the *wayang* performance during language arts, and examining Javanese geography, language, holidays, clothing, and living conditions in social studies. This integrated unit could culminate with a performance involving all of the teachers and children who studied this culture. Current events might also spark children's interest in a particular culture.

Putting It All Together

Each of the previous chapters has explored issues surrounding each of the five dimensions of WMP, as well as the practical implications and recommendations for performances that are so common in elementary schools. In these chapters, the episodes have highlighted activities limited to the phase(s) of the particular chapter. However, in the elementary setting, an effective lesson will almost always incorporate more than one dimension. When designing lessons, the teacher almost always creates a plan that incorporates multiple aspects of WMP to maximize student interest and boost the quality of their learning. Providing integrative content is vital to the success of a unit, but it is most effective when the content is spread throughout a series of lessons on the particular piece of music, rather than occurring all at once.

Like most aspects of teaching, the shifts between the dimensions of WMP within a lesson are an art form rather than a formula. Each teacher will develop his or her own route through the process, and determine the means that lead to the most growth of the children that populate his or her classroom. Some basic approaches to good teaching will apply in WMP contexts, to be sure, and teachers should keep in mind issues such as quick pacing, minimal teacher talk, and constant formative assessment to ensure that the students are meeting the objectives of a given lesson. But the specifics of a final lesson plan of WMP will always be dependent upon the teacher, the students, and the characteristics of the music.

Episode 7.1 provides one possible day-by-day sequence for *Maburu We*. The lessons are structured so that each lesson will last between 7 and 15 minutes. Other teachers may decide that in their context, the students will be best served by longer lessons that last a full class period of 30 or 45 or 60 minutes; other teachers may decide that even 7 minutes is too long, and that their students might benefit from WMP learning experiences that last 5 minutes each.

Episode 7.1: Botswana: "Maburu We" (Learning Pathway #1)

Specific Use: Upper Elementary General Music Class

Materials:

- "Maburu We" (Oh, a Shoe, a Shoe), young children of the Bakgaladi culture group (from *Traditional Music of Botswana, Africa: A Journey with Tape Recorder along Southern Botswana from Mochudi to Kang*), Smithsonian Folkways Recordings

Procedure (Class 1):

1. Identify the different sounds that occur on the recording.
   a. Play track (0:00–0:30), then field responses. Repeat to check answers.
2. "Listen again, and figure out where you think it might be from, and why." (A: Botswana; children may have different reasons.)
   a. Play track (0:00–0:29), then field answers. If answers are general (e.g. "Africa"), redirect towards specific region (Southern Africa) and country (Botswana).
3. Show map of Africa with Botswana highlighted, then a map of Botswana. Inform students that the song comes from the Bakgaladi culture group from the town of Letlhakeng, in the southern part of Botswana. Note that it abuts South Africa.
4. "Listen again, and think about how you would describe the affect of the singers. What does it sound to you like they might be doing or feeling?" (A: No correct answers; student opinion.)
   a. Play track (0:00–0:29), then field answers.

5. Provide historical context:
    a. "Black people have been in South Africa for a very long time. In the 1600s, Europeans began moving to South Africa. At first, they were Europeans who lived in South Africa, but over time they ceased to consider themselves Europeans and became white South Africans. They began to be known as the Boer people, eventually called the Afrikaners. The Afrikaners amassed power over the many black culture groups in South Africa, and instituted a political regime called *apartheid*. Under apartheid, black Africans in South Africa were subject to very strict restrictions on the types of jobs they could hold and where they could live. It was a harsh system for the black South Africans, and many resisters were sent to prison or killed."
    b. "Botswana, where this song is from, did not have the same political system, but there is often migration between countries next to each other. It is possible that some people from Botswana went to South Africa for jobs, such as those in diamond mines, and that some black South Africans moved to Botswana in search of a better life."
    c. Inform the students that this song was recorded in 1982, when apartheid was still in effect. Show them the translation of the text (see Chapter 2 for text and notation).
6. T: "Knowing this, does it make the singing sound any different to you?" (A: No correct answer; student opinion.)
    a. Play track (0:00–0:29), then field answers.

Procedure (Class 2):

1. Review the meaning of the words.
    a. Play track (0:00–0:29), then field answers.
2. Inform children how far Botswana is from their town or city, and how long it would take to fly there in an airplane. Display pictures (found online) of cultural aspects that he or she believes will be interesting to the students: images of the children, the food, or the typical housing of the Bakgaladi culture group, for example.
3. Listen to determine the pattern of the claps.
    a. Play track (0:00–0:29).
4. Clap along with the recording.
    a. Play track (0:00–0:29), observing responses. Repeat if necessary.
5. Show lyrics on board. Listen to the recording while looking at the words, trying to figure out how to pronounce them.
    a. Play track (0:00–0:29).
6. Sing with the recording.
    a. Play track (0:00–0:29), observing responses.

7. "Listen to the recording again, try to notice which words we should pronounce differently to sound more like the recording."
   a. Play track (0:00–0:29). Field two answers.
   b. Play track again (0:00–0:29), with the specific suggestions in mind. Discuss.
8. Sing with recording again, incorporating suggestions.
   a. Play track (0:00–0:29), observing responses.

Procedure (Class 3):

1. "Listen to the recording, and see if you remember how to sing the words. Sing in your head, not out loud."
   a. Play track (0:00–0:29).
2. Sing with recording.
   a. Play track (0:00–0:29), observing responses. Repeat if necessary.
3. "Listen to the recording again, try to notice which words we should pronounce differently to sound more like the recording."
   a. Play track (0:00–0:29). Field two answers.
   b. Play track again (0:00–0:29), with the specific suggestions in mind. Discuss.
4. Sing without the recording, trying to take the suggestions into consideration.
5. After singing: "How did we sound?" Field answers.
6. Repeat steps 2–6, above, for as long as time and interest allow.

Procedure (Class 4):

1. Sing with recording
   a. Play track (0:00–0:29), observing responses.
2. Sing without recording.
3. Report that this song probably has a dance or singing game to go with it, despite the text that suggests challenging life experiences. Brainstorm other singing games they know that describe negative life experiences, if they have learned any in class.
4. "I can't find the actual game or dance directions. From the liner notes, I only know that it is typical that Bakgaladi children use some sort of foot or leg movement to accompany their songs, or actually a dance pattern performed by a small group in front of the singers. Neither you nor I are from Botswana, but you fifth graders are kids and I'm an adult—so you probably know better than I do. See if you can make up a game or dance to go with this."
5. In small groups of 4–6 children, create a game to accompany the song. Share with class.

Diving In!

It is an exciting time to be a music teacher and to share musics of the myriad of cultures of the world with children who are anxious to listen, sing, dance, play, and make connections between their school, community, and home lives. Teachers and children can access sound recordings and videos from remote places at the touch of a tablet, and they can invite culture-bearers and visiting artists from local ethnic groups into the classroom to share cultural and musical knowledge and skills. World Music Pedagogy provides a tried and true model for organizing these resources into meaningful learning in music classrooms through Attentive, Engaged, and Enactive Listening, Creating, and Integrating World Music and culture. Children and teachers are invited to "dive in" to listen and explore the delightfully diverse world of musical meaning that is illuminated through World Music Pedagogy!

References

Allsup, R. E., & Shieh, E. (2012). Social justice and music education: The call for a public pedagogy. *Music Educators Journal, 98*, 47–51.

Campbell, P. S. (2008). *Tunes and grooves for music education.* Upper Saddle River, NJ: Pearson Education.

Gay, G. (2010). *Culturally responsive teaching: Theory, research, and practice* (2nd ed.). New York: Teacher's College Press.

Johnson, S. (2000). Authenticity: Who needs it? *British Journal of Music Education, 17*, 277–286.

Schippers, H. (2010). *Facing the music: Shaping music education from a global perspective.* Oxford: Oxford University Press.

Tompkins, W. (1981). *The musical traditions of the blacks of coastal Peru.* Ph.D. dissertation, UCLA, Los Angeles, CA.

Wade, B. C. (2004). *Thinking musically: Experiencing music, expressing culture.* New York: Oxford University Press.

Appendix 1
Learning Pathways

Three of the musical examples in this volume have returned in Chapters 2, 3, 5, and 6 as "Learning Pathways" episodes based upon the five dimensions of World Music Pedagogy. These progressive WMP episodes can be parceled out over many class sessions, repeated in part, varied and extended, so that students can orient themselves to the nuances of new musical expressions. They are not intended to be lessons that are taught one right after the other. The intent of each Learning Pathway is to map how teaching and learning of one piece of music might proceed over the course of time when using the dimensions of World Music Pedagogy, where listening, participatory musicking, performance, creating and integrating experiences open students to the many splendors of a musical culture.

Learning Pathway #1

"Maburu We"

Episode 2.1: Botswana: "Maburu We" (Learning Pathway #1)

Specific Use: Upper Elementary General Music Class

Materials:

- "Maburu We (Oh, a Shoe, a Shoe)," young children of the Bakgaladi culture group (from *Traditional Music of Botswana, Africa: A Journey with Tape Recorder along Southern Botswana from Mochudi to Kang*), Smithsonian Folkways Recordings
- Visual map of the melodic contour

Procedure:

(Attentive)

1. Invite children to listen to the recording, identifying the different sounds that occur in the performance. (Answer: Singers, clapping, a whistle.)
   a. Play track (0:00–0:30), then field responses. Repeat to check answers.
2. Listen to the recording again, attempting to determine whether the performers are men, women, or children. (A: The liner notes report that the performers are children, although their specific ages are not provided.)
   a. Play track (0:00–0:30), field responses. Repeat to check answers.
3. "Listen again, and think: How do you think that the children might be feeling as they are singing the song? Why do you think so?" (A: This can be interpreted in a variety of ways.)
   a. Play recording (0:00–0:30), then field responses.
4. Inform the children that the sung word "*ijoo*" means "ouch" to the Bakgaladi people. Listen to the recording to identify the number of times that the word is sung. (A: Four in first two lines.)
   a. Play track (0:00–0:30), then field responses. Repeat to check answers.
5. Show the pattern of the melody with a hand, while looking at a visual map of the melodic contour.
   a. Play track (0:00–0:30). Repeat if necessary.

6. Listen to the recording, trying to determine the rhythmic pattern of the clapping that accompanies the singing.

   a. Play track (0:00–0:30), field responses. Repeat to check answers.

Figure 2.2 "Maburu We (Oh, a Shoe, a Shoe)" from Botswana

x = hand claps

Traditional Music of Botswana, Africa *(FW album 4371), Collected by Elizabeth Nelbach Wood, 1963*

Episode 3.7: Botswana: "Maburu We" (Learning Pathway #1)

Specific Use: Upper Elementary General Music Class

Materials:

- "Maburu We (Oh, a Shoe, a Shoe)," young children of the Bakgaladi culture group (from *Traditional Music of Botswana, Africa: A Journey with Tape Recorder along Southern Botswana from Mochudi to Kang*), Smithsonian Folkways Recordings

Procedure:

1. While the recording sounds, softly imitate the clapping of the performers.

   a. Play track (0:00–0:48).

2. While the recording sounds, listen for pronunciation of the first two verses of the song text.

   a. Play track (0:00–0:30).

3. While the recording sounds, sing the first two verses.
   a. Play track (0:00–0:30).
4. With the recording turned off, sing the first two verses.
5. Listen to the first two verses again, considering what how they might sound more like the recording. (A: Answers will vary, but may include a discussion about whether the words "chang chang" at the end of the line are actually present on the recording; the slight vocal descending slide at the end of the words "we" and "*ijoo*"; the emphasis on the word "*ijoo*.")
   a. Play track (0:00–0:30), then field responses. After one or two answers, listen to the recording again to check if other students in the class agree.
6. Sing along with first two verses (0:00–0:30), trying to implement the suggestion from the Attentive Listening step above.
   a. Play track (0:00–0:30), observing response.
7. Sing the first two verses without the recording, implementing the suggestion from the Attentive Listening step.
8. Repeat steps 5–7, above, taking another suggestion from a student.

Episode 5.2: Botswana: "Maburu We" (Learning Pathway #1)

Specific Use: Upper Elementary General Music Class

Materials:

- "Maburu We" (Oh, a Shoe, a Shoe), young children of the Bakgaladi culture group (from *Traditional Music of Botswana, Africa: A Journey with Tape Recorder along Southern Botswana from Mochudi to Kang*), Smithsonian Folkways Recordings
- Open space to play

Procedure:

(Attentive, Engaged, and Enactive)

1. Children have participated in the Attentive, Engaged, and Enactive experiences in Chapters 2 and 3. They can sing the song without the recording.

2. To review, ask the children to sing the song with the recording.
   - Play track while children sing.
3. Sing again, without the recording. Check for accuracy of the children's performance.

(Integrating)

4. Inform the children that the singers are doing something while the performance is occurring. Ask them to listen to the recording again, attempting to determine what the performers are doing.
   a. Field answers. (A: Playing a singing game.)
   b. If answers are incorrect, remind them that the singers are children, and say, "They are doing something that you sometimes do in music class, when we sing songs." Lead the children to understand that it is a game song or a singing game.
5. Inform the children that directions for the game are not provided on the liner notes to the album. However, game songs of children from the Bakgaladi culture group usually involve some sort of leg or foot movement, or a dance pattern performed by a small group in front of the singers.

(Creating)

6. Lead the class through a process where they create movement for the singing game to accompany the song, one that involves leg or foot movement: i.e. (a) ask for volunteers to demonstrate movements that can be made by feet or legs, (b) decide on two to three movements that the entire class can do, (c) sing the song again, maybe replacing the claps with sounds made via the new movements with feet or legs, (d) decide how many times each movement should be done to make the singing game work with the song.
7. As an entire class, sing the song while playing the singing game that the class created.
8. If they are able to do this up to tempo, try it with the recording.
   - Play track.
9. If successful, divide the children into groups, asking them to work with their peers to repeat the activity.

Episode 6.4: Botswana: "Maburu We" (Learning Pathway #1)

Specific Use: Middle or Upper Elementary General Music Class

Materials:

- "Maburu We" (Oh, a Shoe, a Shoe), young children of the Bakgaladi culture group (from *Traditional Music of Botswana, Africa: A Journey with Tape Recorder along Southern Botswana from Mochudi to Kang*), Smithsonian Folkways Recordings
- PowerPoint slides of images from the internet (per the procedure below)

Procedure (Class 1):

(Attentive)

1. After the children have identified that the song is from Botswana, show images of Gaborone, the capital city of the country, then the town of Letlhakeng in the Kalahari Desert, where the song was recorded.
2. Note similarities and differences between the locations.
3. Provide historical context about South Africa, which is just over the border from Letlhakeng. Inform the children about the role of Europeans in Southern Africa and the nature of the apartheid political regime, then give the translation for the text:
    - *Maburu We*: the Boers (i.e. white South Africans)
    - *Ijoo*: (a sound indicating pain, somewhat like "ouch")
    - *Dichankananna*: prisons
    - *Setlhako we*: a shoe
    - *Komorago we*: from the back
4. Discuss the song's meaning, in light of the textual translation and the history of apartheid in the region.

Procedure (Class 2):

(Attentive and Engaged)

1. Inform the children that the song is from the Batswana people, one of the different culture groups within Botswana. Show images of the typical houses of the Batswana, often circular structures made of clay.
2. Compare the housing structures to those familiar to the students.

3. Show images of typical food in Botswana, such as *seswaa*, a thick meat stew and maize porridge that resembles polenta, and *morogo*, greens that are commonly served with *seswaa*.
4. Compare the food to that which is eaten in the students' cultures.

(Lesson continues with Engaged and Enactive Listening)

Learning Pathway #2

"El Carnaval de mi Tierra"

Episode 2.2: El Salvador: "El Carnaval de mi Tierra" (Learning Pathway #2)

Specific Use: Middle or Upper Elementary General Music Class

Materials:

- "El Carnaval de mi Tierra," Los Hermanos Lovo (from *¡Soy Salvadoreño! Chanchona Music from Eastern El Salvador*), Smithsonian Folkways Recordings

Procedure:

(Attentive)

1. Identify the different instruments on the recording. (A: Bass, two guitars, two violins, shaker, drum.)
   a. Play track (0:00–0:26), then field responses.
   b. Repeat to check answers.
2. View short videos of each of the instruments Attentive Listening (found online), then listen to the recording and pretend to play one of the instruments.
   a. Play track (0:00–0:26).
3. After imitating the teacher's clapping of the following pattern or reading notation, identify the instrument that is playing the rhythm. (A: A shaker or *guiro*; the term in this area of El Salvador is *media caña*.)
   a. Play track (0:00–0:26), then field responses.
   b. Repeat to check answers.

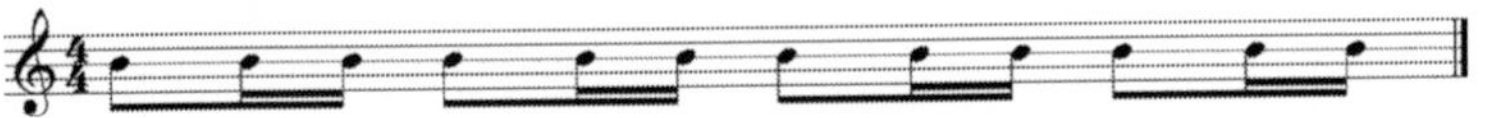

4. Identify the number of times the violins repeat the melody before changing the pattern. (A: Two.)
   a. Play track (0:00–0:26), then field responses.
   b. Repeat to check answers.

5. "Listen again, and raise your hand when you hear a sound that we haven't heard in this song yet." (A: Voice.)
   a. Play track (0:00–0:30, or until hands are raised), then field responses.
6. Starting the recording when the voice enters, identify the language that is being sung, and the number of singers. (A: Spanish; two.)
   a. Play track (0:26–1:03), then field responses.
7. Listen to the recording with the song text displayed on the board. Identify any Spanish words that are already known.
   a. Play track (0:26–1:03), then field responses.
8. Listen to the song from the beginning, raising a hand when the tune on the violins repeats later in the song. Provide the hint that the tune will be played on a different instrument. (A: The chorus.)
   a. Play track (0:00–1:03), observing student response.
   b. Repeat, if necessary.

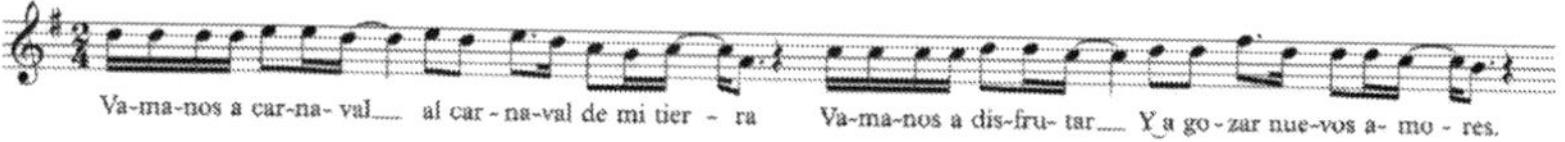
Va-ma-nos a car-na- val___ al car - na-val de mi tier - ra
Va-ma-nos a dis-fru- tar___ Y a go - zar nue-vos a- mo - res.

Figure 2.4 "El Carnaval de mi Tierra" from El Salvador

Episode 3.5: El Salvador: "El Carnaval de mi Tierra" (Learning Pathway #2)

Specific Use: Upper Elementary General Music Class

Materials:

- "El Carnaval de mi Tierra," by Los Hermanos Lovo (from *¡Soy Salvadoreño! Chanchona Music from Eastern El Salvador*), Smithsonian Folkways Recordings

Procedure:

(Engaged)

1. Pat the beat on different parts of the body, copying the teacher.
   a. Play track (0:00–1:01).

(Attentive)

2. Identify the instruments in the introduction. (A: Bass, two guitars, two violins, shaker, percussion.)
    a. Play track (0:00–0:26), field responses. Repeat to check answers.

(Engaged)

3. Lightly pat the beat on laps and identify which instrument is playing the beat during the introduction. (A: It sounds like a wooden instrument.)
    a. Play track (0:00–0:26), field responses.
4. Play the beat on the rhythm sticks, through the chorus.
    a. Play track (0:00–1:01).

(Attentive)

5. Listen to the teacher clap the following pattern, then identify the instrument playing it on the recording. (A: A *guiro*-like instrument called a *media caña*.)
    a. Play track (0:00–0:26).

(Engaged)

6. Echo the teacher, who models the modified rhythm of the *media caña* shaker on the consonants "ch":

7. Chant the ostinato of the *media caña* rhythm on "ch-ch-ch" with the recording.
    a. Play track (0:00–0:26), observing responses. Repeat if necessary.

(Engaged and Attentive)

8. Repeat step (7), but play the recording further. Raise hand when a new voice or instrument enters, and identify the sound. (A: Male voice enters at 0:26.)
    a. Play track (0:00–0:40), field responses.

(Attentive)

9. Listen to the voice, identifying the language in which the performers are singing, and the number of singers. (A: Spanish; two.)
   a. Play track (0:26–1:01), field responses.
10. Listen to the chorus, following along with words posted on the board. Identify any known words. (A: Students may recognize "*carnaval*" as "carnival.")
    a. Play track (0:43–1:01), field responses.

(Engaged and Enactive)

11. Learn words by rote, echoing the teacher.
12. Sing chorus with recording.
    a. Play track (0:43–1:01), observing responses. Repeat if necessary.

(Enactive)

13. 1/3 class sings chorus; 1/3 class keeps beat on sticks; 1/3 class chants rhythm on "ch."
14. Check performance against recording, identifying areas to improve.
    a. Play track (0:00–1:01), field responses.
15. Repeat (13): Perform all three parts without recording, with student suggestions in mind.

Episode 5.5: El Salvador: "El Carnaval de mi Tierra" (Learning Pathway #2)

Specific Use: Upper Elementary General Music Class

Materials:

- "El Carnaval de mi Tierra," Los Hermanos Lovo (from *¡Soy Salvadoreño! Chanchona Music from Eastern El Salvador*), Smithsonian Folkways Recordings
- Form of the chords written on the board using Roman numerals and/or letter names
- Visual aid with harmonic structure of chorus, verse, and bridge

- Visual aid showing the chord pitches of a G major chord and the chord pitches of a D major chord
- *Marimbas* or xylophones with F removed, replaced by F#

Procedure:

Students have participated in Attentive, Engaged, and Enactive activities in previous lessons.

(Creating)

1. Play track (00:00–01:01) to review singing the chord roots of the song.
2. Using a visual aid that shows the chord pitches of a G major chord (I) and the chord pitches of a D major chord (V), practice playing and singing the note names for each chord.
   - Play track (01:19–1:27) to listen to the harmonic structure of the bridge.
3. Practice playing the harmonic structure of the violin bridge using a visual that shows the chord structure of the bridge for each measure in the meter of 2/4 (G-B-D, D-F#-A; D-F#-A, G-B-D). Once this is mastered, practice repeating this 8-beat pattern.
4. While children sing and play the chord roots on the downbeat of each measure, the teacher models a melodic improvisation in which she plays and sings the chord root on the downbeat of each measure, then chooses which notes of the appropriate chord she will play and sing on the other beats in order to create a new 8-beat melody.
5. Half of the children play and sing chord roots ("one" and "five") on the first beat of each measure, while the other half of the class practices improvising new melodies for 8 beats as the teacher points to the visual aid. Encourage children to try to play and sing at once. Switch parts.
6. Children try to remember each 8-beat melody that they improvise so that they can play it twice in a row for a total of 16 beats. If it is not exactly the same, that's okay.
   - Play track (00:00-02:00) in order to review the form of the entire song, then asks for volunteers to perform solos during each violin bridge (slowly, without the recording). If necessary, practice just the solo improvisations before performing without the recording.
7. Perform the entire song with half of the children accompanying on small percussion or playing chord roots on *marimbas*/xylophones, while others sing along for the verse and chorus with volunteer soloists improvising sections played during the verse or chorus of the song.
8. Extension: Children could improvise a vocal descant or harmony part for the chorus section by reviewing the harmonic structure for the chorus using a similar procedure.

Episode 6.7: El Salvador: "El Carnaval de mi Tierra" (Learning Pathway #2)

Specific Use: Middle or Upper Elementary General Music Class

Materials:

- "El Carnaval de mi Tierra," Los Hermanos Lovo (from *¡Soy Salvadoreño! Chanchona Music from Eastern El Salvador*), Smithsonian Folkways Recordings
- PowerPoint slides, per the procedure below

Procedure (Class 1):

1. Display a slide with an image of the globe, and the heading "Where in the World?" Ask where they think the next song may be from, and why.
   a. Play track (0:00–0:26), then field responses. Lead discussion so that children discover it is from Central America.
2. Display a slide with an image of Central America, and the text "Name countries you know in Central America."
   a. Field responses, inform that the song is from El Salvador.
3. Display a slide with an image of Central America with El Salvador highlighted.
4. Note that this song is from the Morazán region of Eastern El Salvador. Display images of the region, asking students to describe the rural, hilly pictures they see.

(Move into Attentive Listening that focuses on instrumentation, and Engaged Listening in which the children pat the beat and then perform the rhythm of the shaker.)

Procedure (Class 2):

1. Play track (0:00–1:01). As recording sounds at low volume, pose review questions based on previous lesson.
2. Quickly display maps of Central America and El Salvador, from the previous lesson.
3. Display a slide on which the words "Civil War" are written, and ask the children to identify its meaning. Discuss.
4. After discussion, inform the children that El Salvador had a civil war in the 1980s, and that some people from El Salvador came to the United States in search of a better life. Most of the performers from *Los Hermanos Lovo*, the group on this recording, came to the United States during this time and

settled in the Washington DC area, along with many other immigrants from El Salvador. Like many immigrants, they wanted to retain some of their own culture in this new country, and this *chanchona* music was important to them. Read one of the group member's words from the liner notes of the album:

   a. "We come from sadness, from war, which doesn't make us want to dance or rejoice. Here in the United States, after seeing that all one has is work, we sort of came up with the idea of bringing music into an afternoon family get-together to play whatever we felt like playing. When you get into playing music, you forget your problems for a little while."

5. "What are the different things that you like to do to forget your problems?" Discuss.

(Move into Engaged and Enactive experiences, learning the words of the chorus and beginning to put the song, shaker rhythm, and beat together.)

Procedure (Class 3):

(Through Engaged and Enactive Listening, continue to work on performing the song, shaker, and beat together, sounding as much like the recording as possible.)

1. Pose review questions about the civil war in El Salvador, and the immigration of the members of *Los Hermanos Lovo*.

2. Ask the children how old they think the performers are. Field answers.

3. Observe a video of *Los Hermanos Lovo* discussing their music, available on Smithsonian Folkways website, noting the age of the performers. "How do you think the boy that is a member of the group learned the music?"

4. Lead a discussion about learning music through enculturation, asking students to make connections to their own experiences.

(Return to Enactive Listening).

Learning Pathway #3

"Suwa Onbashira Kiyari-Taiko"

Episode 2.3: Japan: "Suwa Onbashira Kiyari-Taiko" (Learning Pathway #3)

Specific Use: Upper Elementary General Music Class

Materials:

- Ensemble O-Suwa-Daiko, "Suwa Onbashira Kiyari-Taiko" (from *Japan: O-Suwa-Daiko Drums*), Smithsonian Folkways Recordings

Procedure:

(Attentive)

1. Identify the instruments that can be heard on the recording, and the country that they think it might be from. (Convergent; Answer: Drums, clicking instruments, jingling instruments; the song hails from Japan.)
   - **a.** Play track (3:15–4:10), then field responses.
   - **b.** Repeat to check answers.
2. "Listen again, and note the similarities and contrasts: What is staying the same? What is changing?" (Convergent; A: Similarities: instruments, rhythmic patterns; Differences: tempo is gradually getting faster.)
   - **a.** Play track (3:15–3:44), then field responses.
   - **b.** Repeat to check answers.
3. "Listen to a longer section this time and raise your hand when you hear something other than the tempo change. Also, how many 'sections' you think this listening selection has, and how would you describe the musical differences between the sections?" (Convergent)

   (**A:** 3:44 New syncopated rhythmic pattern begins.)

   (**A:** 4:02 Beat stops and individual instruments take turns shaking/ rolling.)

   (**A:** 4:12 New beat begins on clicking rim and drum head, and a new syncopated rhythmic "solo" begins, passed from high drum to the rim of drum, to the low drum.)

   - **a.** Play recording (3:15–4:49), then field responses.
   - **b.** Repeat to check answers.

4. "What is your favorite and least favorite part of this music and why?" (Divergent)
    a. Play track (3:15–4:49), then field responses.
5. Listen, identifying an activity that the musicians might be doing, beyond playing instruments. (Divergent)
    a. Play track (3:15–4:49), then field responses. Inform the children that *taiko* performers typically move around the drums with specific choreographed movements.

Episode 3.2: Japan: "Suwa Onbashira Kiyari-Taiko" (Learning Pathway #3)

Specific Use: Upper Elementary General Music Class

Materials:

- Ensemble O-Suwa Daiko, "Suwa Onbashira Kiyari-Taiko," (from *Japan: Onbashira Kiyari-Taiko*) Smithsonian Folkways Recordings
- Tambourines or jingle bells (optional)
- *Taiko* or other drums, with felt mallets or drumsticks (optional)

Procedure:

(Engaged)

1. Pat the beat.
    a. Play track (3:15–4:10), observing responses. Repeat if necessary.
2. Walk the beat.
    a. Play track (3:15–4:10), observing responses. Repeat if necessary.
3. Walk the beat, moving arms low for the low drum sound and high for the high drum sound.
    a. Play track (3:15–4:10), observing responses. Repeat if necessary.
4. Repeat (3), shake different body parts during the "roll" section.
    a. Play track (3:15–4:10), observing responses. Repeat if necessary.
5. Standing still, "clap a repeated rhythmic pattern that stands out to you" during the first part of the excerpt.
    a. Play track (3:15–3:45), observing responses. Repeat if necessary.
6. Standing still, play the high drum sounds on the chest and low drum sounds on the legs.
    a. Play track (3:15–3:45), observing responses. Repeat if necessary.

7. Repeat (5) and (6), with the second part of the excerpt.
   a. Play track (3:45-4:10), observing responses. Repeat if necessary.
8. Distribute drums. "How might you imitate the sounds of the drums on the recording with the instruments that we have?"
   a. Give 30–60 seconds to explore. Field responses from individuals.
9. "Listen to the recording: Which suggestion sounded the most like the Ensemble O-Suwa Daiko?"
   a. Play track (3:15–4:10), field responses. Coalesce around a decision.
10. Perform rhythm with recording. "Don't play too loudly, so that we can hear the music."
    a. Play track (3:15–4:10), observing responses. Repeat, if necessary.
11. (Optional): Add tambourines or sleigh bells on beat, "rolling" when that sound occurs.
    a. Play track (3:15–4:10), observing responses. Repeat, if necessary.

Episode 5.4: Japan: "Suwa Onbashira Kiyari-Taiko" (Learning Pathway #3)

Specific Use: Any Age General Music Class (Small Group Work for Middle or Upper Only)

Materials:

- Ensemble O-Suwa Daiko, "Suwa Onbashira Kiyari-Taiko" (from Japan: Onbashira Kiyari-Taiko). Smithsonian Folkways Recordings
- Tambourines or jingle bells
- *Taiko* or other drums that can be hit hard with felt mallets or drumsticks
- Visual Aid: 1. Form (repetition/contrast), 2. Instruments and Order, 3.Tempo, 4. Movement

Procedure:

1. Listen to the piece (3:15-4:11) and ask, "Where does repetition and contrast occur? Do you think there might be repetition and contrast in the performers' body movements, as well?"
   - Play track (3:15–4:11) and field answers. (A: There are repeated rhythmic patterns played by particular instruments, parts that speed up and slow down, and different instruments that enter at different times.) Answers will vary regarding body movements.

3. Divide the class into small groups with about 5–6 children per group (make sure each group has at least one instrument from each category: high drum, low drum, clicking on drum rims, and jingling).
4. Small groups are given time to explore and to decide (Use vidual aid to remember the tasks):
    a. on a form for the piece (how to begin, continue, and end; how to include repetition and contrast).
    b. which instruments should play in which order.
    c. when to increase or decrease the tempo.
    d. how players should move (safely) while performing.
5. Small groups are given time to practice for performance of their compositions (this may take several class periods).
6. Small groups perform for the class, and the listening children are asked to give verbal feedback about what made the piece sound like or unlike the *taiko* drumming they had been studying.
7. Play track as needed for comparison to children's group compositions.

Episode 6.1: Japan: "Suwa Onbashira Kiyari-Taiko" (Learning Pathway #3)

Specific Use: Any Age General Music Class

Materials:

- "Suwa Onbashira Kiyari-Taiko," Ensemble O-Suwa Daiko (from *Japan: Onbashira Kiyari-Taiko*), (3:15–4:11). Smithsonian Folkways Recordings
- *Taiko* or other drums that can be hit hard with felt mallets or drumsticks
- PowerPoint slides of images from the internet (per the procedure below)

Procedure:

(Attentive and Engaged Listening experiences have occurred in previous lessons)

1. "What holidays do you know?" Field answers.
2. As answers are provided, write answers in two columns (one set of holidays are religious in nature, the other is not). Ask students to determine the difference between the two columns. Field answers.

3. Once class arrives at the answer, explain that the *taiko* drum piece that they have been playing is part of the Shinto tradition in Japan called the "Festival of the Honorable Pillars, " or "Onbashira" in Japanese. This festival occurs every six or seven years.
4. Report that this festival takes place in the Lake Suwa area, where the *taiko* piece that they have been playing is from. During the festival, four huge trees are found and cut down in the Yatsugatake Mountains that flank Lake Suwa. Brainstorm other types of huge trees. Field answers. (Possible A: Redwood trees, sequoia trees.)
5. Display images of trees in the Yatsugatake Mountains (available online). Compare to the tree types suggested by the students.
6. Explain that the trees are brought down to the town of Suwa. The word "*Kiyari*" in the song's title means "woodcutter," and this piece is played while the trees are cut down. Ask the children if they know any songs that are sung during work time. Field answers.
7. Note that after the trees are felled, they are slid down the mountain. Some festival participants actually ride on top the trees as they make their way to the bottom, an endeavor that can be very dangerous. Ask the children to make comparisons to other similar rides that they might know about. (Possible A: Log flumes at amusement parks; downhill skiing; some students may have heard of "running with the bulls" in Spain.)
8. Show pictures (available online) of various points of the ceremony.

(Depending on the skill of the students, some students can move into Enactive Listening, playing the drum piece, while other students "act out" the process of riding down the mountain on a log.)

Appendix 2
References and Resources

These lists include references that have been cited throughout the volume, as well as some resources that the authors have found useful in teaching and learning world music cultures. Also included are readings that inform further study of issues in ethnomusicology and music education, as well as recordings, video recordings, and internet resources of information that support the use of World Music Pedagogy in elementary school music settings.

References

Abril, C. R. (2006). Music that represents culture: Selecting music with integrity. *Music Educators Journal*, *93*, 38–45.

Allsup, R. E., & Shieh, E. (2012). Social justice and music education: The call for a public pedagogy. *Music Educators Journal*, *98*, 47–51.

Anderson, W. M., & Campbell, P. S. (Eds.). (2010). *Multicultural perspectives in music education*, Volume 3 (3rd ed.). Lanham, MD: Rowman & Littlefield Education.

Banks, J. A. (2007). *Educating citizens in a multicultural society* (2nd ed.). New York: Teachers College Press.

Banks, J. A. (2013). Approaches to multicultural curriculum reform. In J. A. Banks & C. A. McGee Banks (Eds.), *Multicultural education: Issues and perspectives* (8th ed., pp. 181–199). Hoboken, NJ: Wiley.

Campbell, P. S. (2004). *Teaching music globally*. New York: Oxford University Press.

Campbell, P. S. (2008). *Tunes and grooves for music education*. Upper Saddle River, NJ: Pearson Education.

Campbell, P. S., & Scott-Kassner, C. (2014). The listening child. In P. S. Campbell & C. Scott-Kassner (Eds.), *Music in childhood* (4th ed., pp. 239–263). Boston, MA: Schirmer.

Gold, L. (2005). *Music in Bali: Experiencing music, expressing culture*. New York: Oxford University Press.

Guidelines of the Orff Institute. (2011). *Orff Schulwerk Informationen: Special Ediction: 50 Jahre Orff-Institut 1961–2011*, *85*, 273–276.

Johnson, S. (2000). Authenticity: Who needs it? *British Journal of Music Education*, *17*(3), 277–286.

Kwon, D. L. (2012). *Music in Korea: Experiencing music, expressing culture*. New York: Oxford University Press.

Matras, Y. (2015). *The Romani gypsies*. Cambridge, MA: Belknap Press.

McCullough-Brabson, E. (2001). *We'll be in your mountains, we'll be in your songs: A Navajo woman sings*. Albuquerque: UNM Press.

Midgley, R. (Ed.). (1976). *Musical instruments of the world: An illustrated encyclopedia*. New York: Facts on File Publications.

Palmer, A. (1992). World musics in music education: The matter of authenticity. *International Journal of Music Education*, *19*, 32–40.

Rice, T. (2004). *Music in Bulgaria: Experiencing music, expressing culture*. New York: Oxford University Press.

Ruckert, G. (2003). *Music in North India: Experiencing music, expressing culture*. New York: Oxford University Press.

Schippers, H. (2009). *Facing the music: Shaping music education from a global perspective*. New York: Oxford University Press.

Small, C. (1998). *Musicking*. Middletown, CT: Wesleyan University Press.

Tompkins, W. (1981). *The musical traditions of the blacks of coastal Peru*. Ph.D. dissertation, UCLA, Los Angeles, CA.

Turino, T. (2008). *Music in the Andes: Experiencing music, expressing culture*. New York: Oxford University Press.

Wade, B. C. (2004). *Thinking musically: Experiencing music, expressing culture*. New York: Oxford University Press.

Wade, B. C. (2005). *Music in Japan: Experiencing music, expressing culture*. New York: Oxford University Press.

Recommended Resources

Books (most with Accompanying Recordings and/or DVDs)

Adzinyah, A. K., Maraire, D., & Tucker, J. C. (1986). *Let your voice be heard! Songs from Ghana and Zimbabwe: Call-and-response, multipart, and game songs*. Danbury, CT: World Music Press.

Anderson, W. M., & Campbell, P. S. (Eds.). (2010). *Multicultural perspectives in music education*, Volume 3 (3rd ed.). Lanham, MD: Rowman & Littlefield Education.

Barned-Lewis, S. (2010). *Ukuti, Ukuti: A Swahili children's song book*. Dar es Salaam, Tanzania: Dhow Countries Music Academy.

Brumfield, S. (Ed.). (2006). *Hot peas and barley-o: Children's songs & games from Scotland.* New York: Hal Leonard.

Brumfield, S. (Ed.). (2010). *Over the garden wall: Children's songs and games from England.* Milwaukee, WI: Hal Leonard.

Burton, J. B. (1993). *Moving within the circle: Contemporary Native American music and dance.* Danbury, CT: World Music Press.

Campbell, P. S. (2004). *Teaching music globally.* New York: Oxford University Press.

Campbell, P. S., & Frega, A. L. (2001). *Songs of Latin America: From the field to the classroom.* Miami: Warner Bros. Publications.

Campbell, P. S., McCullough-Brabson, E., & Tucker, J. C. (1994). *Roots & branches: A legacy of multicultural music for children.* Danbury, CT: World Music Press.

Dilberto, R. (1999). *Welcome to Mussomeli: Children's songs from an Italian country town.* Danbury, CT: World Music Press.

Gault, B. (2016). *Listen up! Fostering musicianship through active listening.* New York: Oxford University Press.

Gold, L. (2005). *Music in Bali: Experiencing music, expressing culture.* New York: Oxford University Press.

Han, K. H., & Campbell, P. S. (1996). *The lion's roar: Chinese luogu percussion ensembles* (2nd ed.). Danbury, CT: World Music Press.

Kalani, & Camara, R. M. (2006). *West African drum & dance: A Yankadi-Macrou celebration.* Van Nuys, CA: Alfred Publishing Co., Inc.

Klinger, R. (2017). *One, two, three! Achat, shtayim, shalosh! Children's songs from Israel.* Los Angeles, CA: OAKE.

Kwon, D. L. (2012). *Music in Korea: Experiencing music, expressing culture.* New York: Oxford University Press.

Lew, J. C. (2006). *Games children sing: Malaysia.* Van Nuys, CA: Alfred Publishing Co, Inc.

Lomax, A., Elder, J. D., & Hawes, B. L. (Eds.). (1997). *Brown girl in the ring: An anthology of song games from the Eastern Caribbean.* New York: Pantheon Books.

Loong, C. (2016). *Ni Hao! Sing and chant your way to China!* Mentor, OH: Impel Training.

Lopez-Ibor, S. (2006). *Quien canta su mal espanta (Singing drives away sorrow).* New York: Schott Music Corporation.

Matras, Y. (2015). *The Romani gypsies.* Cambridge, MA: Belknap Press.

McCullough-Brabson, E. (2001). *We'll be in your mountains, we'll be in your songs: A Navajo woman sings.* Albuquerque, NM: University of New Mexico Press.

Montoya-Stier, G. (2008). *El patio de mi casa: 42 traditional rhymes, chants, and folk songs from Mexico.* Chicago, IL: GIA Publications.

Oxford global music series: Experiencing music, expressing culture (24 volumes focused on the musical cultures of 24 geographic locations). Retrieved from https://global.oup.com/academic/content/series/g/global-music-series-gms/?cc=us&lang=en&

Pascale, L. M. (2008). *Children's songs from Afghanistan.* Washington, DC: National Geographic Society.

Ruckert, G. (2003). *Music in North India: Experiencing music, expressing culture*. New York: Oxford University Press.

Serwadda, W. M. (1974/1987). *Songs and stories from Uganda*. Danbury, CT: World Music Press.

Stock, J. (1996). *World sound matters: An anthology of music from around the world.* London: Schott.

Talbot, B. (2017). *Gending rare: Children's songs and games from Bali*. Chicago, IL: GIA Publications.

Turino, T. (2008). *Music in the Andes: Experiencing music, expressing culture*. New York: Oxford University Press.

Wade, B. C. (2004). *Thinking musically: Experiencing music, expressing culture*. New York: Oxford University Press.

Wade, B. C. (2005). *Music in Japan: Experiencing music, expressing culture*. New York: Oxford University Press.

DVD

Kreutzer, N. (2003). Zimbabwe Children's Singing Games: 20 Singing Games and Dances in the Shona Language.

Online Resources

Alan Lomax Sound Recording Archives and the Association for Cultural Equity (ACE): www.culturalequity.org/rc/ce_rc_teaching.php

Kodály Center American Folk Song Collection (Holy Names University): http://kodaly.hnu.edu/collection.cfm

Smithsonian Folkways Recordings: www.folkways.si.edu

British Library Sound: sounds.bl.uk

Children's Book Suggestions for Learning Pathways

BOTSWANA (LEARNING PATHWAY #1)

Nelson, M., & San Artists of the Kuru Art Project. (2012). *Ostrich and lark*. Honesdale, PA: Boyds Mills Press.

Smith, A. M. (2012). *The great cake mystery*. New York: Anchor Books.

EL SALVADOR (LEARNING PATHWAY #2)

Argueta, J. (2001). *A movie in my pillow/Una Pelicula en mi almohada*. San Francisco, CA: Children's Book Press.

Argueta, J., & Ruano, A. (2016). *Somos como las nubes/We are like the clouds*. Toronto, Canada: Groundwood Books.

JAPAN (LEARNING PATHWAY #3)

Sakade, F., & Kurosaki, Y. (2005). *Japanese children's favorite stories*. Tokyo, Japan: Tuttle Publishing.

Sakurai, G. (1997). *Peach boy: A Japanese legend.* Mahwah, NJ: Troll Communications.

Yasuda, Y. (1956). *Old tales from Japan.* Tokyo: Tuttle Company.

Index